William Shakespeare

The Merchant of Venice

with annotations, analysis and commentary by
Patrick Murray

Edco

The Educational Company of Ireland

First published 2016

The Educational Company of Ireland
Ballymount Road
Walkinstown
Dublin 12

www.edco.ie

A member of the Smurfit Kappa Group plc

ISBN: 978–1–84536–654–4

The paper used in this book comes from Managed Forests in Northern Europe For every tree felled, at least one new tree is planted

Editor: Jennifer Armstrong

Design, layout and cover: Liz White Designs

Front cover photograph: *Merchant of Venice* (2004) Jeremy Irons © Moviestore Collection Ltd / Alamy Stock Photos

Back cover photograph: Ryan Imhoff (left) as Gratiano, Chelsea Steverson as Nerissa, Grant Goodman as Bassanio and Emily Trask as Portia in the Utah Shakespeare Festival's 2010 production of *The Merchant of Venice*. (Photo by Karl Hugh. © Utah Shakespeare Festival 2010)

Photo acknowledgements: Alamy Stock Photos, Atlanta Shakespeare Company, Cincinnati Shakespeare Company, Shakespeare's Globe Picture Library, Shutterstock, TopFoto, Utah Shakespeare Festival, Wikimedia

01J24

Preface

ALL MODERN STUDENTS of Shakespeare's plays struggle with the difference between his language, particularly his diction, and present-day English. Some of the words in *The Merchant of Venice* are no longer in common use, and some have different meanings from those they had when the play was written over four hundred years ago. The syntax, or ordering of words, can also be complex, even puzzling.

In response, this edition of the play seeks to enlighten the reader by providing useful explanatory notes in the margins of the text, summaries for each scene and detailed commentary on the play. These features will ensure that students have a good understanding of the text.

To appreciate *The Merchant of Venice*, we must think about what is happening to and within the characters, as revealed by their actions, dialogue with other characters, soliloquies and asides. Questions at the end of each scene and activities at the end of each Act should stimulate such thinking. They are designed to suit both Ordinary and Higher Level students. Detailed notes on characters, themes and genre are included at the back of the book. Ordinary Level students will find the list of key words on the opening pages and the summaries particularly useful, and Higher Level students can dip in and out of these sections, as required.

It is also important to be aware of the kind of world in which *The Merchant of Venice* was written (Elizabethan England). This edition therefore includes contextual information on the type of theatre and audience for which Shakespeare wrote.

Topics discussed include the kind of play *The Merchant of Venice* is, the main themes of the play, character change and development, and the relationships between characters.

Colour photographs from various theatre and film productions of *The Merchant of Venice* are displayed throughout the book. These images remind students that they are reading a play, and provide a chance to consider different casting and staging decisions.

To assist with revision and exam preparation, key moments in the play are identified and useful quotations are highlighted. A final section is devoted to typical exam questions, accompanied by some tips for the exam, revision suggestions and sample answers.

The approach taken to *The Merchant of Venice* in this edition will help students to:

- develop an appreciation of Shakespeare's use of language

- acquire a sound knowledge of the meaning of the text

- understand the workings of the plot

- recognise the play's comic and fairy-tale elements

- explore the play's main themes and use of imagery

- understand the characters, their motives and their interactions with each other

- remember that *The Merchant of Venice* was written for performance rather than reading

- learn about Shakespeare's theatre and audience

- consider how the play might be performed and produced today.

Teachers can access *The Merchant of Venice* e-book at **www.edcodigital.ie**.

Contents

Introduction

About William Shakespeare

THE MOST REMARKABLE THING about Shakespeare is how little we know of him. We know that he was the son of John Shakespeare, who made gloves and traded in wool in Stratford-upon-Avon, England, and that he was baptised there on 26 April 1564.

Royal Shakespeare Theatre in Stratford-upon-Avon

Records show that he was married in 1582 and his first child was baptised in 1583, followed by his twin children in 1585. We also know that in 1592 he was working in London as an actor and a playwright. Apart from these few facts, we have no certain knowledge of where Shakespeare was, or what he was doing, during the first twenty-eight years of his life.

It is very likely, though not certain, that Shakespeare was educated at the free grammar school in his home town. The standard of education at this kind of school was very high. Education was entirely in Latin, and students were not allowed to speak English. Students learned the rules of Latin grammar, read the works of famous Roman authors and studied Roman history and mythology, as well as rhetoric, which is the art of public speaking.

Why or how Shakespeare became a playwright is a mystery. If he chose this career with the aim of making his fortune, he was taking a gamble that luckily paid off. Many of his fellow playwrights died in poverty and none was prosperous. Shakespeare was the exception as he wrote extremely popular plays over a twenty-year period.

Shakespeare was also an actor, a poet and a shareholder, and he ended up a very wealthy man. He bought valuable properties in London and Stratford. He was

a shrewd businessman who avoided taxes and who always sued debtors – even those who owed him very small sums.

He retired to Stratford in 1611, and died there in 1616, aged fifty-two. His collected plays were first published seven years later, in 1623, in an edition known as the First Folio. This book was prepared for publication by two of his fellow actors.

We may not know much about Shakespeare but we can be certain that he did not expect his plays to be studied in classrooms around the world more than four hundred years after his death. When reading Shakespeare's plays, always remember that his words were written for performance on stage rather than to be read. He wrote plays to entertain the people of his day and dealt with issues that mattered to those audiences.

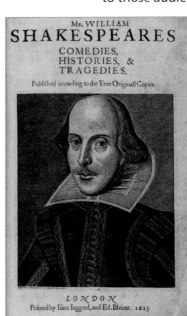

Title-page of the First Folio (1623)

Nevertheless, Shakespeare's reputation as the world's greatest playwright is secure. His plays are constantly performed throughout the world. Countless books have been written about him and his works and, despite the shortage of established facts, new biographies are still appearing. When studying *The Merchant of Venice*, you might like to consider why his work remains so popular four centuries after his death.

About Shakespeare's theatre

THE THEATRES FOR WHICH Shakespeare wrote his plays were public, open-air ones. Shakespeare owned a share in one of these theatres, the Globe, which opened in 1599 and was situated close to the River Thames in south London.

Modern-day Shakespeare's Globe theatre, London

Another famous London theatre at that time was the Swan. A Dutch visitor to London, Johannes de Witt, made a drawing of the Swan theatre around 1596. A copy of this drawing is shown opposite. It is the only surviving sketch of the kind of theatre in which Shakespeare's plays were first performed.

De Witt estimated that the Swan could hold 3,000 spectators – many more than Ireland's largest modern theatres such as the Belfast Waterfront (2,200), Bord Gáis Energy Theatre, Dublin (2,100) or Royal Theatre, Castlebar (2,000). The modern-day Globe in London has a capacity of around 1,600, and Cork's Everyman can seat 650 people.

The drawing, which De Witt labelled in Latin, shows a round, open-air playhouse. The main feature is the large stage (labelled *proscaenium*), with its overhead canopy known as 'the heavens'. The stage extends into an open yard, described as level ground without sand (*planities sine arena*).

For the price of a penny, spectators called 'groundlings' stood in the yard looking up at the actors. There were also three tiers of galleries where, for an extra penny or two, people could sit and enjoy some shelter under the projecting piece of roofing (*tectum*).

The wealthiest members of the audience wanted to have a clear view of the stage, and also wished to be seen by the rest of the audience. They would sit in a private gallery above the stage. The gallery was part of the tiring-house (*mimorum ades*) at the back of the stage. This housed a dressing area where actors changed their costumes or attire; hence the term 'tiring-house'. They also stored props there.

The tiring-house was topped by a storage loft and a flagpole. A flag with the symbol of the theatre (e.g. a globe or a swan) was hoisted to indicate that a play was about to be staged that afternoon. When members of the audience entered the theatre, they would be able to tell what kind of play to expect. For example, if *The Merchant of Venice* was to be performed, the tiring-house would be covered with a light cloth to indicate a comedy (a black cloth was used for a tragedy).

The man shown outside the loft in the drawing is sounding a trumpet. The trumpet would be played more and more loudly as the time for the performance drew near. Plays took place during daylight hours in the afternoon.

Actors entered and exited the stage through two sets of large doors in the front of the tiring-house. All actors were male, with most female parts being played by boys. These boy actors were chosen for their public-speaking skills and then trained by the adult actors to play female roles convincingly. In *The Merchant of Venice*, the female characters Portia and Nerissa dress up as a male lawyer and his clerk – this means that in Shakespeare's theatre the audience would have seen boys pretending to be women pretending to be men.

Sketch of the interior of the Swan Theatre, by Johannes de Witt, as copied by Aernout van Buchel, c. 1596

KEY

1 Playhouse flag	**5** Tiring-house	**9** Entrance to lower gallery
2 Storage loft	**6** Stage doors	**10** Stage
3 The heavens	**7** Upper gallery	**11** Hell (under stage)
4 Gallery over stage	**8** Middle gallery	**12** Yard

The audience could be very noisy. People would move about, talk, munch apples and crack nuts. If an actor was not doing a good job, the audience would be sure to let him know about it. If a play was boring, spectators would find other ways to amuse themselves, such as playing cards or dice games. Even when the play caught their interest, they would be more likely to make loud comments about it than to enjoy the action in silence.

There was no painted scenery to indicate where the action was taking place. Playwrights like Shakespeare were experts in using words to set the scene, and the audience accepted that the stage could be any place that the action required, from a courtroom to a garden, or a public street to a private home.

One problem Shakespeare had to solve for *The Merchant of Venice* was how to present night scenes when the actual performances took place in daylight. To overcome this problem, Shakespeare makes the actors suggest darkness through the words they speak. For example, Act 5, Scene 1 opens with the characters noting that the moon is bright and repeating the phrase 'in such a night'.

About *The Merchant of Venice*

THE MERCHANT OF VENICE was written in 1596/97 and published in 1600 under the title 'The most excellent history of the Merchant of Venice. With the extreme cruelty of Shylock the Jew towards the said Merchant, in cutting a just pound of his flesh, and the obtaining of Portia by the choice of three chests.' This description suggests that the original publishers considered the character of Shylock and the Portia–Bassanio relationship to be the main selling points of the play.

Shakespeare did not invent his plots. He borrowed these from works by other European writers. At the time it was not considered necessary to invent new stories. It was better to be creative with well-known stories and make them your own. Stories of a loan guaranteed by a bond of human flesh, and of a test to win the hand of a rich and beautiful heiress, had appeared in many ancient legends and fairy tales.

As far as Shakespeare was concerned, the most important source was a short story by Ser Giovanni in his collection of tales, *Il Pecorone*, which was written in Italian in the late fourteenth century. The story is based in Venice and Belmont and includes a similar trial scene to the one in *The Merchant of Venice*. Shakespeare added in extra elements to make his play.

The Merchant of Venice is one of Shakespeare's most popular plays and is frequently performed on stage and adapted for film. Well-known actors such as Dustin Hoffman, Patrick Stewart and Al Pacino have played the coveted role of Shylock.

Dustin Hoffman

Patrick Stewart

Al Pacino

The Merchant of Venice

Dramatis personae

DUKE OF VENICE

ANTONIO, a merchant of Venice

BASSANIO, his friend

GRATIANO, LORENZO, SALERIO, SOLANIO: friends to Antonio and Bassanio

LEONARDO, servant to Bassanio

SHYLOCK, a rich Jew

JESSICA, his daughter

TUBAL, friend to Shylock

LAUNCELOT GOBBO, a clown, servant to Shylock

OLD GOBBO, his father

PORTIA, a rich heiress of Belmont

NERISSA, her waiting-woman

PRINCE OF MOROCCO, PRINCE OF ARRAGON: suitors to Portia

BALTHAZAR, STEPHANO: servants to Portia

MAGNIFICOES OF VENICE, OFFICERS OF THE COURT
OF JUSTICE, GAOLER, SERVANTS AND OTHER ATTENDANTS

ACT 1 ✝ Scene 1

Plot summary

Antonio, a rich merchant, is talking to two friends. He is in a sad mood, but cannot explain why. His friends wonder if he is worried about the dangers his cargo ships face on the high seas. Antonio denies this and also rejects the idea that his sadness has anything to do with love. Bassanio, Antonio's closest friend, arrives with Gratiano and Lorenzo. Gratiano loves to talk and act the fool. He advises Antonio not to be sad, but does nothing to help him change.

Once they are left alone together, Bassanio tells Antonio about his problems. He has been living beyond his means and is now in debt. He wants to marry Portia, a wealthy heiress, but without money he does not think he can impress her properly. He would like Antonio to lend him the money he needs. If Portia agrees to marry him, Bassanio will be able to use her wealth to repay all his debts. Antonio's money is tied up in his business deals at the moment, but he agrees to guarantee any loan that Bassanio may be able to raise in Venice.

I owe you much, and, like a wilful youth,
That which I owe is lost

BASSANIO, Act 1, Scene 1, 146–7

Venice. A street.

Enter ANTONIO, SALERIO and SOLANIO.

ANTONIO

In sooth, I know not why I am so sad.

It wearies me, you say it wearies you;

But how I caught it, found it, or came by it,

What stuff 'tis made of, whereof it is born,

I am to learn;   5

And such a want-wit sadness makes of me

That I have much ado to know myself.

SALERIO

Your mind is tossing on the ocean;

There, where your argosies with portly sail

Like signiors and rich burghers on the flood,   10

Or as it were the pageants of the sea,

Do overpeer the petty traffickers

That curtsy to them, do them reverence,

As they fly by them with their woven wings.

SOLANIO

Believe me, sir, had I such venture forth,   15

The better part of my affections would

Be with my hopes abroad. I should be still

Plucking the grass to know where sits the wind,

Peering in maps for ports and piers and roads,

And every object that might make me fear   20

Misfortune to my ventures, out of doubt

Would make me sad.

SALERIO

                              My wind cooling my broth

Would blow me to an ague when I thought

What harm a wind too great might do at sea.

I should not see the sandy hour-glass run   25

But I should think of shallows and of flats,

And see my wealthy *Andrew* docked in sand,

Vailing her high-top lower than her ribs

To kiss her burial. Should I go to church

And see the holy edifice of stone   30

And not bethink me straight of dangerous rocks,

1	*In sooth:* to tell the truth
2	*It:* my depression
4	*'tis:* it is
	whereof: of what
5	*am to learn:* have no idea
6	*want-wit:* fool
7	*have … know:* do not know what to make of
9	*argosies:* large trading ships
	portly sail: swollen sails
10	*Like … burghers:* seem like gentlemen and wealthy citizens (i.e. Antonio's ships appear superior)
	flood: waves
11	*pageants:* decorated spectacles
12–14	*Do … wings:* look down on smaller boats, which bow respectfully to them as they pass by at speed
15	*venture forth:* risky investments out there (i.e. at sea)
16	*affections:* thoughts
17	*abroad:* in the world
	still: always
18	*where sits:* the force and direction of
19	*roads:* places where ships might anchor
21	*Misfortune … ventures:* bad luck for my investments
	out of: beyond
22	*wind:* breath
23	*blow … ague:* make me shiver
25	*hour-glass:* timer
26	*flats:* sandbanks
27	*Andrew:* a common name for a big ship
28–9	*Vailing … burial:* this is an image of a ship going over on her side, as the tip of the mast drops down to touch the sand that will bury her
30	*edifice:* building
31	*bethink me straight:* immediately think

Which, touching but my gentle vessel's side,

Would scatter all her spices on the stream,

Enrobe the roaring waters with my silks,

35 And, in a word, but even now worth this,

And now worth nothing? Shall I have the thought

To think on this, and shall I lack the thought

That such a thing bechanced would make me sad?

But tell not me; I know Antonio

40 Is sad to think upon his merchandise.

ANTONIO

Believe me, no: I thank my fortune for it,

My ventures are not in one bottom trusted,

Nor to one place; nor is my whole estate

Upon the fortune of this present year;

45 Therefore my merchandise makes me not sad.

SOLANIO

Why then you are in love.

ANTONIO

                              Fie, fie!

SOLANIO

Not in love neither? Then let us say you are sad

Because you are not merry; and 'twere as easy

For you to laugh and leap and say you are merry

50 Because you are not sad. Now, by two-headed Janus

Nature hath framed strange fellows in her time:

Some that will evermore peep through their eyes

And laugh like parrots at a bagpiper,

And other of such vinegar aspect

55 That they'll not show their teeth in way of smile

Though Nestor swear the jest be laughable.

Enter BASSANIO, LORENZO and GRATIANO.

Here comes Bassanio, your most noble kinsman,

Gratiano and Lorenzo. Fare ye well,

We leave you now with better company.

SALERIO

60 I would have stayed till I had made you merry,

If worthier friends had not prevented me.

33 *stream:* current

34 *Enrobe:* dress

35 *even now:* just now, at this moment

38 *bechanced:* if it happened

40 *merchandise:* goods that he has invested in

42–4 *My . . . year:* my goods are not all in one ship, and my ships are not all in one place; besides, everything I have does not depend on this year's trade

46 *Fie:* an expression of disgust or disapproval

48 *'twere:* it would be

50 *Janus:* a Roman god, often shown with one happy face and one sad face
51 *hath framed:* has created
52 *evermore . . . eyes:* always laugh with their eyes half-closed

54 *other . . . aspect:* others with sour faces

56 *Nestor:* a Greek hero who took life very seriously – a joke had to be really funny for Nestor to declare it laughable

57 *kinsman:* relative

ANTONIO

Your worth is very dear in my regard.

I take it your own business calls on you

And you embrace th'occasion to depart.

SALERIO

Good morrow, my good lords. 65

BASSANIO

Good signiors both, when shall we laugh? Say, when?

You grow exceeding strange: must it be so?

SALERIO

We'll make our leisures to attend on yours.

Exeunt SALERIO and SOLANIO.

LORENZO

My Lord Bassanio, since you have found Antonio

We two will leave you, but at dinner-time 70

I pray you have in mind where we must meet.

BASSANIO

I will not fail you.

GRATIANO

You look not well, Signior Antonio;

You have too much respect upon the world:

They lose it that do buy it with much care — 75

Believe me, you are marvellously changed.

ANTONIO

I hold the world but as the world, Gratiano;

A stage where every man must play a part,

And mine a sad one.

GRATIANO

                    Let me play the fool:

With mirth and laughter let old wrinkles come, 80

And let my liver rather heat with wine

Than my heart cool with mortifying groans.

Why should a man, whose blood is warm within,

Sit like his grandsire cut in alabaster?

Sleep when he wakes and creep into the jaundice 85

By being peevish? I tell thee what, Antonio —

I love thee, and 'tis my love that speaks —

There are a sort of men whose visages

Glossary

64 *embrace … depart:* take the opportunity to leave

65 *morrow:* morning

66 *laugh:* get together for some fun or entertainment

67 *You … so?* I do not see much of you these days: does it have to be like this?

68 *make … yours:* keep some time free to suit your arrangements
Exeunt: exit of more than one character

70 *We … you:* Lorenzo is giving Gratiano a hint that Antonio and Bassanio should be left to themselves. The hint is not taken up

71 *have in mind:* remember

74–5 *You … care:* you are too concerned with your business affairs: people who are too interested in their wealth often lose it

77 *hold:* observe, consider. Antonio is saying that he does not take his business affairs, or life itself, more seriously than he should

80 *With … come:* let happy laughter cause the wrinkles of old age to appear in my face

82 *mortifying groans:* groans that bring about an early death

84 *Sit … alabaster:* be as lifeless as the stone carving on his grandfather's tomb

85 *wakes:* is awake

85–6 *creep … peevish:* this refers to an old belief that being irritable caused jaundice

88 *visages:* faces

89 *cream and mantle:* thicken	Do cream and mantle like a standing pond,
90 *do . . . entertain:* remain deliberately silent	90 And do a wilful stillness entertain,
91–2 *With . . . of:* in order to make others think that they have	With purpose to be dressed in an opinion
92 *gravity:* seriousness, importance *profound conceit:* deep judgement	Of wisdom, gravity, profound conceit,
	As who should say, 'I am Sir Oracle,
94 *ope:* open	And when I ope my lips let no dog bark.'
	95 O my Antonio, I do know of these
96 *reputed:* thought to be	That therefore only are reputed wise
	For saying nothing, when I am very sure
	If they should speak, would almost damn those ears,
	Which, hearing them, would call their brothers fools.
	100 I'll tell thee more of this another time.
101–2 *fish . . . opinion:* do not use sadness to try to gain a reputation for wisdom *gudgeon:* small fish, foolish person	But fish not with this melancholy bait
	For this fool gudgeon, this opinion. —
	Come, good Lorenzo. — Fare ye well a while.
104 *exhortation:* inspirational speech, lecture	I'll end my exhortation after dinner.

LORENZO

105 Well, we will leave you then till dinner-time.

I must be one of these same dumb wise men,

For Gratiano never lets me speak.

106 dumb: wordless, silent

GRATIANO

Well, keep me company but two years more

Thou shalt not know the sound of thine own tongue.

109 thine: your

ANTONIO

110 Fare you well, I'll grow a talker for this gear.

110 grow . . . gear: become a chatterbox like you in return for this nonsense you have just been telling me

GRATIANO

Thanks, i' faith, for silence is only commendable

In a neat's tongue dried and a maid not vendible.

Exeunt GRATIANO and LORENZO.

111–12 only . . . vendible: to be praised only in an ox's tongue and in a woman no one will marry

ANTONIO

Is that anything now?

113 Is . . . now? What was he talking about?

BASSANIO

Gratiano speaks an infinite deal of nothing, more than any

115 man in all Venice. His reasons are as two grains of wheat

hid in two bushels of chaff: you shall seek all day ere you

find them, and when you have them, they are not worth

the search.

114 infinite: never-ending

115–16 His . . . chaff: the intelligent points Gratiano makes are as few as two grains of wheat hidden in two heaps of waste

116 ere: before

ANTONIO

Well, tell me now what lady is the same

To whom you swore a secret pilgrimage, 120

That you today promised to tell me of?

BASSANIO

'Tis not unknown to you, Antonio,

How much I have disabled mine estate,

By something showing a more swelling port

Than my faint means would grant continuance: 125

Nor do I now make moan to be abridged

From such a noble rate; but my chief care

Is to come fairly off from the great debts

Wherein my time, something too prodigal,

Hath left me gaged. To you, Antonio, 130

I owe the most in money and in love,

And from your love I have a warranty

To unburden all my plots and purposes

How to get clear of all the debts I owe.

ANTONIO

I pray you, good Bassanio, let me know it, 135

And if it stand, as you yourself still do,

Within the eye of honour, be assured

My purse, my person, my extremest means

Lie all unlocked to your occasions.

BASSANIO

In my schooldays, when I had lost one shaft, 140

I shot his fellow of the self-same flight

The self-same way, with more advisèd watch,

To find the other forth, and by adventuring both,

I oft found both. I urge this childhood proof

Because what follows is pure innocence. 145

I owe you much, and, like a wilful youth,

That which I owe is lost; but if you please

To shoot another arrow that self way

Which you did shoot the first, I do not doubt,

As I will watch the aim, or to find both 150

Or bring your latter hazard back again,

And thankfully rest debtor for the first.

119–20 *what … pilgrimage:* who is this woman whom you have promised to make a special trip to see. Antonio speaks as if she were a saint

122–5 *'Tis … continuance:* you already know how I wasted my wealth ('disabled mine estate') by living far beyond my small income

126–7 *make … rate:* complain that I am forced to cut back on my high spending

127 *chief care:* main concern

128–30 *come … gaged:* find a way to repay the high amount that I owe as a result of my wasteful overspending
gaged: bound, committed

132–4 *from … owe:* because you love me, you will permit me to explain my plans to rid myself of debt

136–7 *if … honour:* if your plans are as honourable as yourself

138 *my extremest means:* all that I have

139 *Lie … occasions:* is available for your needs

140 *shaft:* arrow

141 *his … flight:* its companion (i.e. another arrow) of exactly the same size and weight

142 *advisèd:* careful

143 *adventuring:* risking

144 *oft:* often
I … proof: I've brought up this experience from my youth (i.e. that I lost an arrow, but was able to recover it by shooting another after it)

146 *wilful:* stubborn, spoiled

148 *self:* same

150 *or:* either

151 *latter hazard:* latest risk (i.e. loan)

152 *rest:* remain. Bassanio is arguing that to recover the money he has already loaned him, Antonio should lend him more in the hope of getting both amounts back, or at least the second amount

153 *herein:* in your speech

154 *wind ... circumstance:* use a roundabout way of winning me over

156 *making ... uttermost:* doubting that I would be willing to do all I could for you

160 *prest unto it:* more than willing to do it

161 *richly left:* who has inherited great wealth

162 *fair:* beautiful
fairer ... word: better still

163 *wondrous virtues:* extraordinary qualities

165–6 *nothing ... Portia:* Portia is no less great than the other Portia, who was the daughter of Cato and wife of Brutus (and who was regarded as a model for all wives). Cato and Brutus were Roman statesmen

169 *Renownèd suitors:* famous men seeking to marry her
sunny locks: golden hair

171 *seat ... strand:* estate of Belmont like the Black Sea region of Colchis/Colchos. This is a reference to the Greek legend of Jason, who searched for and found the Golden Fleece at Colchis

172 *quest:* search, pursuit

173 *means:* resources, money

174 *hold ... place:* compete

175–6 *I ... fortunate:* I can predict such advantages ('thrift') for me that without doubt I will be successful

178 *commodity:* goods

179 *a present sum:* ready money

180 *Try:* find out

181 *racked:* stretched

182 *furnish thee to:* provide all you need to get to

183 *presently:* immediately

184–5 *no ... sake:* do not mind whether it is as a formal business loan or as a personal loan from a friend

ANTONIO

You know me well, and herein spend but time

To wind about my love with circumstance;

155 And out of doubt you do me now more wrong

In making question of my uttermost

Than if you had made waste of all I have.

Then do but say to me what I should do

That in your knowledge may by me be done,

160 And I am prest unto it. Therefore speak.

BASSANIO

In Belmont is a lady richly left,

And she is fair, and, fairer than that word,

Of wondrous virtues. Sometimes from her eyes

I did receive fair speechless messages.

165 Her name is Portia, nothing undervalued

To Cato's daughter, Brutus' Portia;

Nor is the wide world ignorant of her worth,

For the four winds blow in from every coast

Renownèd suitors, and her sunny locks

170 Hang on her temples like a golden fleece,

Which makes her seat of Belmont Colchos' strand,

And many Jasons come in quest of her.

O my Antonio, had I but the means

To hold a rival place with one of them,

175 I have a mind presages me such thrift

That I should questionless be fortunate.

ANTONIO

Thou know'st that all my fortunes are at sea;

Neither have I money nor commodity

To raise a present sum. Therefore go forth —

180 Try what my credit can in Venice do —

That shall be racked even to the uttermost,

To furnish thee to Belmont, to fair Portia.

Go presently inquire, and so will I,

Where money is, and I no question make

185 To have it of my trust or for my sake.

Exeunt.

Key points

This scene introduces us to two important characters: Antonio and Bassanio. Bassanio's request to borrow money from Antonio sets the main action of the play in motion.

- Antonio confesses that he is sad (melancholy or depressed), but seems unable to explain to his friends why he is like this. This sadness will remain with him throughout the play. It was a common belief in Shakespeare's time that some people are melancholy by nature. Antonio makes this point when he sees the world as a stage where everyone is given a part, and his part is 'a sad one' (line 79).

- Antonio's depression makes him stand out from his friends, who are generally light-hearted and fun-seeking.

- Possible reasons are offered for Antonio's sadness. He could be anxious about the fate of the ships he has at sea or he could be in love. Antonio dismisses these suggestions. A more likely explanation is that Bassanio, his best friend, is anxious to marry an extremely wealthy heiress, and if he succeeds it will take him away for good from Venice and from Antonio.

- The real action of the play begins when Bassanio arrives on stage. He admits that he has been living extravagantly and is now in serious debt. His solution to this situation involves trying to borrow more money from Antonio. Instead of coming straight to the point, he tells a childish story by way of a hint that he is in debt and needs more money. Eventually he gets to the point. He sees a big financial gain for himself if he can marry the wealthy Portia. First, however, Antonio will have to provide him with the money he needs to finance his campaign to win her and to give Portia the impression that he is worthy of her. When Bassanio marries Portia, he will be able to pay back Antonio's money.

- Bassanio puts Antonio in a difficult position, but Antonio is very willing to help him. As the greater part of his wealth is tied up in his ships at sea, Antonio does not have access to the money Bassanio needs. Antonio gives Bassanio permission to raise whatever money he can and he (Antonio) will guarantee to pay back the lenders.

- Note that some lines in the play are split between two characters (e.g. lines 22, 46 and 79). Actors should deliver these shared lines as though they are one line, without a pause in between.

Useful quotes

> In sooth, I know not why I am so sad.
>
> (Antonio, line 1)

> I hold the world but as the world, Gratiano;
> A stage where every man must play a part,
> And mine a sad one.
>
> (Antonio, lines 77–9)

> And from your love I have a warranty
> To unburden all my plots and purposes
> How to get clear of all the debts I owe.
>
> (Bassanio, lines 132–4)

> My purse, my person, my extremest means
> Lie all unlocked to your occasions.
>
> (Antonio, lines 138–9)

> In Belmont is a lady richly left,
> And she is fair, and fairer than that word,
> Of wondrous virtues.
>
> (Bassanio, lines 161–3)

> Go presently inquire, and so will I,
> Where money is, and I no question make
> To have it of my trust or for my sake.
>
> (Antonio, lines 183–5)

? Questions

1 Describe Antonio's state of mind. What might improve it?

2 What worries would Solanio and Salerio expect to have if they invested their money in trading ships?

3 Comment on the way in which Bassanio goes about asking Antonio for a loan. What does this tell us about Bassanio?

4 Does Antonio think that Bassanio deserves financial help from him? What does this tell us about Antonio?

5 On the evidence of this scene, do you think Bassanio deserves a loan? Give reasons for your answer.

6 On the evidence of this scene, do you think Antonio is wise to offer Bassanio the chance to raise a loan, or is he acting against his own interests? Give reasons for your answer.

7 What does this scene tell us about the connection between love and money?

8 In your opinion, which does Bassanio love more: (a) himself; (b) Portia; (c) Portia's money? Give a reason for your answer.

9 'your argosies with portly sail like signiors and rich burghers' (lines 9–10). In this **simile** Antonio's ships are compared to high-ranking and wealthy citizens. Find another simile, i.e. a comparison using the words 'like' or 'as', in this scene.

10 Did this opening scene make you want to read more of this play? Give reasons for your answer.

Talking point

This scene deals with borrowing and lending. These practices remain a common feature of life today. Why do people borrow and lend? Is borrowing always a good idea? What are the advantages and disadvantages of lending? Can you think of any modern examples like the one in this scene? What problems might arise when one friend wants to borrow from another friend?

Portia tells her troubles to Nerissa. Her main problem is that she is not free to choose a husband. Anyone who wants to marry her must come to her home in Belmont and take part in a lottery. This arrangement was decided on by her father before he died. The lottery involves three caskets, one of gold, one of silver and one of lead. Only the suitor who chooses the casket containing Portia's portrait can marry Portia.

Men of noble birth from various parts of Europe have come to Belmont hoping to win Portia. She does not like any of them and is glad when they decide not to try their luck in the casket lottery. She would prefer Bassanio, a Venetian who once visited her father, to any of the suitors she has so far met. However, another candidate, the Prince of Morocco, is expected shortly.

I am glad this parcel of wooers are so reasonable, for there is not one among them but I dote on his very absence, and I pray God grant them a fair departure.

PORTIA, Act 1, Scene 2, 95–8

Belmont. A room in Portia's house.

Enter PORTIA with her waiting-woman, NERISSA.

PORTIA

By my troth, Nerissa, my little body is aweary of this great world.

NERISSA

You would be, sweet madam, if your miseries were in the same abundance as your good fortunes are; and yet, for aught I see, they are as sick that surfeit with too much as they that starve with nothing. It is no mean happiness therefore to be seated in the mean: superfluity comes sooner by white hairs, but competency lives longer.

PORTIA

Good sentences, and well pronounced.

NERISSA

They would be better if well followed.

PORTIA

If to do were as easy as to know what were good to do, chapels had been churches and poor men's cottages princes' palaces. It is a good divine that follows his own instructions — I can easier teach twenty what were good to be done than be one of the twenty to follow mine own teaching. The brain may devise laws for the blood, but a hot temper leaps o'er a cold decree. Such a hare is madness the youth, to skip o'er the meshes of good counsel the cripple. But this reasoning is not in the fashion to choose me a husband. O me, the word 'choose'! I may neither choose who I would nor refuse who I dislike; so is the will of a living daughter curbed by the will of a dead father. Is it not hard, Nerissa, that I cannot choose one nor refuse none?

NERISSA

Your father was ever virtuous, and holy men at their death have good inspirations; therefore the lottery that he hath devised in these three chests of gold, silver and lead, whereof who chooses his meaning chooses you, will no doubt never be chosen by any rightly but one who shall rightly love. But what warmth is there in your affection towards any of these princely suitors that are already come?

Glossary

1   *troth:* faith
    aweary: tired

3   *miseries:* troubles

5   *aught:* anything

5–6   *they ... nothing:* those who have too much are just as badly off as those who have too little

6–8   *It ... longer:* it is better to have a moderate share: those who have too much ('superfluity') age more quickly than those who have just enough ('competency')

9   *sentences:* words of wisdom

11–13   *If ... palaces:* it is easier to know what is the right thing to do than to actually do it

13   *divine:* priest, clergyman

16–17   *The ... decree:* our reason (head) tells us what we should do, but is often overruled by our feelings (heart)

17–19   *Such ... cripple:* wisdom and good advice are not able to control the excitement of youth

19–20   *But ... husband:* but all our wise talk will do nothing to help me choose a husband

21   *would:* wish, want to

22   *curbed:* limited

25   *was ever virtuous:* always had fine qualities, was a good man

26   *lottery:* test, game of chance

28   *whereof ... you:* in which the suitor who correctly interprets your father's intentions will select the casket containing you (i.e. Portia's picture will be inside it)

29–30   *any ... love:* anyone correctly except for the one who will truly love you

PORTIA

I pray thee overname them, and as thou namest them I will describe them, and according to my description, level at my affection.   35

NERISSA

First, there is the Neapolitan prince.

PORTIA

Ay, that's a colt indeed, for he doth nothing but talk of his horse, and he makes it a great appropriation to his own good parts that he can shoe him himself. I am much afeard my lady his mother played false with a smith.   40

NERISSA

Then, there is the County Palatine.

PORTIA

He doth nothing but frown, as who should say, 'An you will not have me, choose.' He hears merry tales and smiles not: I fear he will prove the weeping philosopher when he grows old, being so full of unmannerly sadness in his   45 youth. I had rather be married to a death's-head with a bone in his mouth than to either of these. God defend me from these two!

NERISSA

How say you by the French lord, Monsieur Le Bon?

PORTIA

God made him, and therefore let him pass for a man. In   50 truth, I know it is a sin to be a mocker, but he — why, he hath a horse better than the Neapolitan's, a better bad habit of frowning than the Count Palatine! He is every man in no man. If a throstle sing, he falls straight a-cap'ring. He will fence with his own shadow. If I should marry him, I   55 should marry twenty husbands. If he would despise me, I would forgive him, for if he love me to madness, I shall never requite him.

NERISSA

What say you then to Falconbridge, the young baron of England?   60

33	*I pray thee:* please
	overname them: list their names
34–5	*level ... affection:* you will be able to guess how much I like them
36	*Neapolitan prince:* prince from Naples
37	*colt:* foolish young man
38–9	*great ... parts:* big point in his own favour
40	*afeard ... smith:* afraid that his mother cheated with a blacksmith (i.e. his real father is a blacksmith)
41	*County Palatine:* count from the Rhine area of Germany
42	*who should:* if to
42–3	*An ... choose:* if you do not want me, just pick someone else
44	*the weeping philosopher:* a reference to the Greek philosopher Heraclitus, who could not help crying at the stupidity of human beings
45	*unmannerly:* inappropriate
46	*death's-head:* skull
49	*How ... by:* what do you think of
54	*throstle:* thrush
	falls straight a-cap'ring: immediately starts dancing
57	*to madness:* with a passion
58	*requite him:* return his love

63–4 *come . . . English:* back me up when I say that my English is very poor indeed

64–5 *He . . . dumb-show?* He looks handsome enough, but how can we have a proper conversation?

66 *suited:* dressed
doublet: jacket

67 *round hose:* baggy trousers
bonnet: hat, cap

70 *neighbourly charity:* generous attitude. Portia is making an ironic reference to the strong dislike between England and Scotland

70–72 *borrowed . . . able:* when the Englishman hit him on the head he said he would return the favour later

73 *surety:* backer. The French were allies of the Scots in Shakespeare's time
sealed . . . another: guaranteed to give the Englishman a slap in return

76–7 *Very . . . drunk:* he behaves very badly at the start of the day, when he is sober, and even worse later, when he is drunk

79 *the worst . . . fell:* no matter how bad things may be for me

80 *make shift:* manage

85 *Rhenish wine:* strong white wine
contrary: wrong

86 *without:* outside

87 *ere:* before

88 *sponge:* drunkard

89 *the having:* at having to marry

89–90 *They . . . determinations:* they have told me of their decision

PORTIA

You know I say nothing to him, for he understands not me, nor I him: he hath neither Latin, French, nor Italian, and you will come into the court and swear that I have a poor pennyworth in the English. He is a proper man's picture, but, alas, who can converse with a dumb-show? How oddly he is suited! I think he bought his doublet in Italy, his round hose in France, his bonnet in Germany and his behaviour everywhere.

65

NERISSA

What think you of the Scottish lord, his neighbour?

PORTIA

70 That he hath a neighbourly charity in him, for he borrowed a box of the ear of the Englishman and swore he would pay him again when he was able. I think the Frenchman became his surety, and sealed under for another.

NERISSA

How like you the young German, the Duke of Saxony's
75 nephew?

PORTIA

Very vilely in the morning when he is sober, and most vilely in the afternoon when he is drunk: when he is best, he is a little worse than a man, and when he is worst, he is little better than a beast — and the worst fall that ever fell,
80 I hope I shall make shift to go without him.

NERISSA

If he should offer to choose, and choose the right casket, you should refuse to perform your father's will if you should refuse to accept him.

PORTIA

Therefore, for fear of the worst, I pray thee set a deep glass
85 of Rhenish wine on the contrary casket; for if the devil be within, and that temptation without, I know he will choose it. I will do anything, Nerissa, ere I will be married to a sponge.

NERISSA

You need not fear, lady, the having any of these lords. They
90 have acquainted me with their determinations, which is indeed to return to their home, and to trouble you with

no more suit unless you may be won by some other sort than your father's imposition depending on the caskets.

PORTIA

If I live to be as old as Sibylla, I will die as chaste as Diana unless I be obtained by the manner of my father's will. I am glad this parcel of wooers are so reasonable, for there is not one among them but I dote on his very absence, and I pray God grant them a fair departure.

NERISSA

Do you not remember, lady, in your father's time, a Venetian, a scholar and a soldier, that came hither in company of the Marquis of Montferrat?

PORTIA

Yes, yes, it was Bassanio; as I think so was he called.

NERISSA

True, madam; he, of all the men that ever my foolish eyes looked upon, was the best deserving a fair lady.

PORTIA

I remember him well, and I remember him worthy of thy praise.

Enter a SERVINGMAN.

How now, what news?

SERVINGMAN

The four strangers seek for you, madam, to take their leave; and there is a forerunner come from a fifth, the Prince of Morocco, who brings word the prince his master will be here tonight.

PORTIA

If I could bid the fifth welcome with so good a heart as I can bid the other four farewell, I should be glad of his approach. If he have the condition of a saint and the complexion of a devil, I had rather he should shrive me than wive me. Come, Nerissa. [*to SERVINGMAN*] Sirrah, go before.

Whiles we shut the gates upon one wooer,
Another knocks at the door.

Exeunt.

95

100

105

110

115

92–3 *unless ... caskets:* unless there is some other way of winning you than the conditions of the casket lottery set out in your father's will

94 *Sibylla:* a reference to the Greek legend of Sibyl, a priestess who lived to a great age. She was promised as many years as the number of grains of sand she held in her hand
Diana: a Roman goddess and symbol of virginity

95 *manner of:* conditions set out in

96 *parcel of wooers:* group of suitors, admirers

99 *in ... time:* when your father was alive

100 *hither:* here

101 *company of:* a party that travelled with

108 *four strangers:* Shakespeare seems to have forgotten that there were six visiting suitors

108–9 *take their leave:* say goodbye

109 *a forerunner:* an advance messenger

114 *condition:* character

115 *complexion of a devil:* devils were imagined as having black skin

115–16 *had ... wive me:* would prefer him to hear my confession than to marry me

116 *Sirrah:* a form of address used by a master/mistress to his/her servant

117 *before:* ahead

Key points

In this scene we meet Portia, the rich young woman Bassanio wants to marry.

- This scene gives us some idea of the kind of woman Portia is, and explains why she lacks freedom of choice in selecting a husband.

- Portia's father has stated in his will that his daughter's husband will be the one who succeeds in a casket lottery he has invented. The man who chooses the right casket will become Portia's husband.

- Nerissa points out that Portia's father was a good man who would never do anything to make his daughter unhappy. She believes that his scheme will find a good husband for Portia.

- Much of this scene is taken up with descriptions of six of Portia's suitors. Each suitor has a peculiarity that is supposed to be typical of his nation. The prince from Naples is so devoted to horses that he is like a horse himself; the County Palatine, a German, lacks a sense of humour; the French lord shows off and tries to outdo everyone else; the English baron is poorly educated; the Scottish lord plans to fight the Englishman with French help; and a second German is a drunkard.

- Portia is not impressed by any of these suitors; she is happy to discover that they have decided to leave for home: 'there is not one among them but I dote on his very absence' (lines 96–7).

- Portia's comments on her suitors suggest a dislike of outsiders. It is often the case that natives of any nation tend to find foreigners comical, or even ridiculous. However, her response to the expected arrival of the Prince of Morocco, the first non-European and non-white suitor, indicates a stronger dislike of difference. It seems that Portia would prefer a husband who is racially and culturally similar to herself, such as Bassanio.

- When Nerissa mentions Bassanio's name, it at first appears as though Portia hardly remembers him (line 102), but this is followed by a brief suggestion that she would consider him a suitable husband (lines 105–6).

- Bassanio is described as 'a scholar and a soldier' (line 100), two qualities that were considered ideal for a courtier in Shakespeare's day.

Useful quotes

> By my troth, Nerissa, my little body is aweary of this great world.
>
> (Portia, lines 1–2)

> O me, the word 'choose'! I may neither choose who I would nor refuse who I dislike; so is the will of a living daughter curbed by the will of a dead father.
>
> (Portia, lines 20–23)

Questions ?

1 Why should Portia be 'aweary of this great world' (lines 1–2)? Are there any clues in this scene?

2 There is a similarity between Portia's comment at the beginning of this scene and Antonio's comment at the beginning of the previous one. What else do these two characters have in common?

3 Does Nerissa take Portia's statement seriously (lines 3–8)? Explain your answer.

4 Portia's late father has left her with a problem. What is this problem?

5 Do you think Portia's father has been fair to her? Explain your answer.

6 What do Portia's comments on her suitors tell you about her?

7 Portia expresses a high opinion of Bassanio. How did she come to form this opinion? On the evidence of the first scene, does he deserve it?

8 Nerissa tells Portia that wealth does not bring happiness. How would Bassanio respond to that point of view?

9 Assess Portia's comments on the Prince of Morocco (lines 112–16). Do you think she is being fair?

10 Is Nerissa of any help to Portia in this scene? Explain your answer.

Talking point

Portia has no say in her choice of husband. Instead, she must marry the man who wins a casket lottery by choosing the casket containing her picture. Do you think this is a sensible arrangement? Would you like to be involved in an arrangement like this?

ACT 1 ✝ Scene 3

Plot summary

Bassanio tries to borrow 3,000 ducats, a huge sum of money, from Shylock, a Jewish moneylender. Shylock admits that Antonio, who will guarantee the loan, is very rich, but points out that much of Antonio's wealth is at the mercy of the seas. He refuses to dine with Bassanio or Antonio because this would offend his religious beliefs. Shylock tells the audience why he hates Antonio: he is a Christian, he lends without charging interest and thus damages Shylock's business, he hates Jews and he insults Shylock in public. Shylock would like to punish Antonio for calling him names and for kicking and spitting at him.

Shylock decides to lend the money to Bassanio free of interest, but only if Antonio agrees to a strange bargain. If the money is not repaid within three months, Shylock will be entitled to a pound of flesh from any part of Antonio's body he chooses. Antonio believes he will have the money within two months, and so agrees to Shylock's conditions.

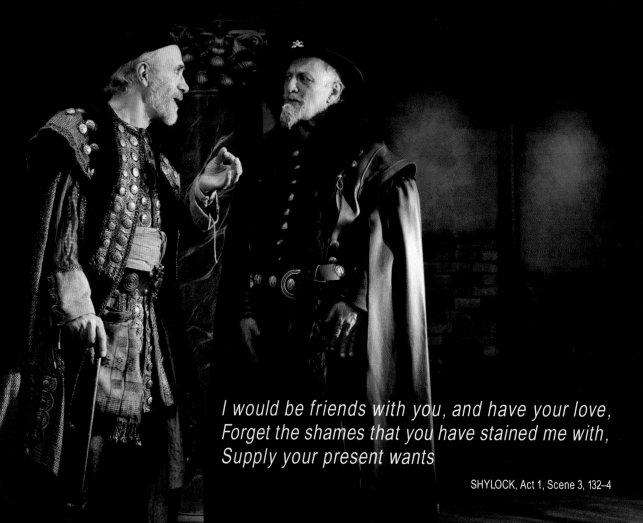

I would be friends with you, and have your love,
Forget the shames that you have stained me with,
Supply your present wants

SHYLOCK, Act 1, Scene 3, 132–4

Venice. A public place.

Enter BASSANIO with SHYLOCK the Jew.

SHYLOCK

Three thousand ducats, well.

BASSANIO

Ay, sir, for three months.

SHYLOCK

For three months, well.

BASSANIO

For the which, as I told you, Antonio shall be bound.

SHYLOCK

Antonio shall become bound, well.   5

BASSANIO

May you stead me? Will you pleasure me? Shall I know your answer?

SHYLOCK

Three thousand ducats for three months, and Antonio bound.

BASSANIO

Your answer to that.   10

SHYLOCK

Antonio is a good man.

BASSANIO

Have you heard any imputation to the contrary?

SHYLOCK

Ho no, no, no, no: my meaning in saying he is a good man is to have you understand me that he is sufficient. Yet his means are in supposition: he hath an argosy bound   15 to Tripolis, another to the Indies; I understand moreover, upon the Rialto, he hath a third at Mexico, a fourth for England, and other ventures he hath squandered abroad. But ships are but boards, sailors but men: there be land-rats and water-rats, water-thieves and land-thieves — I   20 mean pirates — and then there is the peril of waters, winds and rocks. The man is, notwithstanding, sufficient. Three thousand ducats; I think I may take his bond.

1 *ducats:* gold pieces. 3,000 ducats would be worth well over €100,000 today
well: I see

4 *shall be bound:* will act as guarantor (i.e. Antonio will give a bond to Shylock to guarantee repayment of the loan)

6 *stead me:* supply me with the money
pleasure: please

12 *imputation:* suggestion, accusation

13–14 *my … sufficient:* when I say he is good, I mean that he is rich enough to guarantee the loan

15 *his … supposition:* I wonder how sound his finances really are
an argosy bound: a large trading ship on its way

17 *upon the Rialto:* from the stock exchange in Venice (a place where merchants meet and do business)

18 *other … abroad:* he has, perhaps foolishly, scattered his other business risks all over the world

19 *boards:* pieces of wood

22 *notwithstanding:* in spite of all that
sufficient: rich enough

25–6 *I will be . . . me:* I am going to make quite certain that Antonio's bond is sound and shall have to think of ways of making sure

28–9 *Yes . . . into:* oh yes (Shylock is being sarcastic), I'd love to eat in the home ('habitation') of Christians, particularly if pork is on the menu, which Christ ('the Nazarite') drove evil spirits into (pork is forbidden to Jews)

31 *so following:* so on

33 *Who . . . here?* Shylock, by way of insult, pretends not to recognise Antonio

aside: a speech to the audience (not heard by the other characters on stage)

35 *fawning publican:* grovelling tax-gatherer, also a hypocrite

37 *simplicity:* honest dealing (which Shylock considers 'low' or base)

38 *gratis:* without charging interest

39 *usance:* interest

40 *upon the hip:* at a disadvantage

41 *ancient:* longstanding (i.e. based on centuries of hatred and resentment between Christians and Jews)

42 *our sacred nation:* people of the Jewish faith
rails: speaks words of abuse

44 *well-won thrift:* profit made through hard work and good business sense

47 *debating . . . store:* working out my current supply of money

49 *gross:* full amount

BASSANIO

Be assured you may.

SHYLOCK

25 I will be assured I may; and, that I may be assured, I will bethink me. May I speak with Antonio?

BASSANIO

If it please you to dine with us.

SHYLOCK

Yes, to smell pork, to eat of the habitation which your prophet the Nazarite conjured the devil into! I will buy
30 with you, sell with you, talk with you, walk with you, and so following, but I will not eat with you, drink with you, nor pray with you. What news on the Rialto?

Enter ANTONIO.

Who is he comes here?

BASSANIO

This is Signior Antonio.

SHYLOCK [*aside*]

35 How like a fawning publican he looks.
I hate him for he is a Christian;
But more, for that in low simplicity
He lends out money gratis and brings down
The rate of usance here with us in Venice.
40 If I can catch him once upon the hip,
I will feed fat the ancient grudge I bear him.
He hates our sacred nation, and he rails,
Even there where merchants most do congregate,
On me, my bargains and my well-won thrift,
45 Which he calls interest. Cursèd be my tribe
If I forgive him!

BASSANIO

Shylock, do you hear?

SHYLOCK

I am debating of my present store,
And, by the near guess of my memory,
I cannot instantly raise up the gross
50 Of full three thousand ducats. What of that?
Tubal, a wealthy Hebrew of my tribe,

Will furnish me. But soft! How many months
Do you desire? [to ANTONIO] Rest you fair, good signior,
Your worship was the last man in our mouths.

ANTONIO
Shylock, albeit I neither lend nor borrow   55
By taking nor by giving of excess,
Yet, to supply the ripe wants of my friend,
I'll break a custom. [to BASSANIO] Is he yet possessed
How much ye would?

SHYLOCK
                    Ay, ay, three thousand ducats.

ANTONIO
And for three months.   60

SHYLOCK
I had forgot — three months — [to BASSANIO] you told
  me so.
Well then, your bond; and let me see — but hear you,
Methought you said you neither lend nor borrow
Upon advantage.

ANTONIO
                    I do never use it.

SHYLOCK
When Jacob grazed his uncle Laban's sheep —   65
This Jacob from our holy Abram was
(As his wise mother wrought in his behalf)
The third possessor; ay, he was the third—

ANTONIO
And what of him? Did he take interest?

SHYLOCK
No, not take interest, not, as you would say,   70
Directly int'rest. Mark what Jacob did:
When Laban and himself were compromised
That all the eanlings which were streaked and pied
Should fall as Jacob's hire, the ewes, being rank,
In the end of autumn turnèd to the rams,   75
And, when the work of generation was
Between these woolly breeders in the act,
The skilful shepherd peeled me certain wands,

52 *furnish:* supply
soft: wait

54 *Your worship:* Shylock is being sarcastic here
in our mouths: we spoke of

55 *albeit:* although

56 *excess:* interest

57 *supply … wants:* meet the urgent needs

58 *custom:* habit

58–9 *Is … would?* Have you already told him how much you want?

63 *Methought:* it seemed to me

64 *Upon advantage:* at interest

64 *I … it:* I do not charge interest

65 *Jacob:* an Old Testament figure, the son of Isaac and grandson of Abraham

66–8 *This … possessor:* Jacob's elder brother Esau should have been the heir to their father Isaac, and so the third owner of the property after Abraham and Isaac, but Jacob's mother helped him to cheat Esau out of his rights

71 *Mark:* listen to

72 *compromised:* agreed

73 *eanlings:* new-born lambs
pied: multi-coloured

74 *fall … hire:* count as Jacob's wages
rank: in heat, in season

76 *generation:* reproduction, creation

78 *The … wands:* Jacob prepared some spotted sticks

And in the doing of the deed of kind

80   He stuck them up before the fulsome ewes,

Who, then conceiving, did in eaning time

Fall parti-coloured lambs, and those were Jacob's.

This was a way to thrive, and he was blest:

And thrift is blessing, if men steal it not.

ANTONIO

85   This was a venture, sir, that Jacob served for —

A thing not in his power to bring to pass,

But swayed and fashioned by the hand of heaven.

Was this inserted to make interest good?

Or is your gold and silver ewes and rams?

SHYLOCK

90   I cannot tell, I make it breed as fast.

But note me, signior—

ANTONIO

                Mark you this, Bassanio,

The devil can cite Scripture for his purpose.

An evil soul producing holy witness

Is like a villain with a smiling cheek,

95   A goodly apple rotten at the heart.

O what a goodly outside falsehood hath!

SHYLOCK

Three thousand ducats. 'Tis a good round sum.

Three months from twelve; then let me see, the rate.

ANTONIO

Well, Shylock, shall we be beholding to you?

SHYLOCK

100   Signior Antonio, many a time and oft

In the Rialto you have rated me

About my moneys and my usances.

Still have I borne it with a patient shrug,

For suff'rance is the badge of all our tribe.

105   You call me misbeliever, cut-throat dog,

And spit upon my Jewish gaberdine,

And all for use of that which is mine own.

Well then, it now appears you need my help.

Go to then. You come to me, and you say,

Glossary

80 *before:* in front of
     fulsome: mating

81 *eaning:* lambing

82 *Fall parti-coloured:* give birth to spotted or streaked

83–4 *This . . . not:* Jacob's way of making profit was blessed by God and the profit made by charging interest is also blessed, as long as it is not made by stealing

85–7 *This . . . heaven:* Jacob took risks to make his profit, and his gains came about because God allowed them

88 *Was . . . good?* Did you tell this story to justify the charging of interest?

91 *note:* pay attention to

92 *The . . . purpose:* even the devil can quote the Bible to suit himself

93 *witness:* evidence

94–5 *a villain . . . heart:* two examples of hypocrisy

96 *what . . . hath:* lies can look like truths

99 *beholding to:* bound to, depending on

100 *oft:* often

101 *rated:* scolded, criticised

102 *usances:* rates of interest

104 *suff'rance:* patience, endurance

105 *misbeliever:* heathen
     cut-throat: killer

106 *gaberdine:* a long, loose robe

109 *Go to:* an expression of anger and impatience

O what a goodly outside falsehood hath!

ANTONIO, Act 1, Scene 3, 96

'Shylock, we would have moneys.' You say so;   110

You, that did void your rheum upon my beard,

And foot me as you spurn a stranger cur

Over your threshold; moneys is your suit.

What should I say to you? Should I not say,

'Hath a dog money? Is it possible   115

A cur can lend three thousand ducats?' Or

Shall I bend low and in a bondman's key,

With bated breath and whisp'ring humbleness,

Say this:

'Fair sir, you spat on me on Wednesday last;   120

You spurned me such a day; another time

You called me dog; and for these courtesies

I'll lend you thus much moneys'?

111 *void your rheum:* spit

112 *foot . . . cur:* kick me as you might kick a strange dog ('cur')

113 *suit:* request, goal

117 *bend . . . key:* bow humbly to you and in a slave's voice

118 *bated:* reduced, quieter

121 *spurned:* kicked, struck

124 *like:* likely

127–8 *when … friend:* whoever heard of friends taking interest on loans they make to each other. Gold is sterile (a 'barren metal') and does not produce more ('breed') of its own kind (i.e. by way of interest)

130 *break:* fails to meet his debts

130–31 *thou … penalty:* you won't be embarrassed when making him pay the penalty

134 *doit:* tiny sum

136 *This … offer:* I am making a generous, kind-hearted offer

137 *This were kindness:* coming from you, this would be a really kind offer

138 *notary:* a clerk who draws up legal contracts
seal: confirm to

139 *single bond:* agreement made with one person (i.e. Shylock)
a merry sport: an amusing game of forfeits

142 *Expressed … condition:* set out in the terms of the contract

143 *Be … pound:* be named as an accurately weighed pound

146 *Content … bond:* I'm happy to accept these terms

149 *dwell … necessity:* remain in search of the money

ANTONIO

I am as like to call thee so again,

125 To spit on thee again, to spurn thee too.

If thou wilt lend this money, lend it not

As to thy friends; for when did friendship take

A breed for barren metal of his friend?

But lend it rather to thine enemy,

130 Who, if he break, thou mayst with better face

Exact the penalty.

SHYLOCK

                Why look you, how you storm!

I would be friends with you, and have your love,

Forget the shames that you have stained me with,

Supply your present wants, and take no doit

135 Of usance for my moneys; and you'll not hear me —

This is kind I offer.

BASSANIO

This were kindness.

SHYLOCK

                This kindness will I show.

Go with me to a notary, seal me there

Your single bond; and, in a merry sport,

140 If you repay me not on such a day,

In such a place, such sum or sums as are

Expressed in the condition, let the forfeit

Be nominated for an equal pound

Of your fair flesh, to be cut off and taken

145 In what part of your body pleaseth me.

ANTONIO

Content, in faith, I'll seal to such a bond,

And say there is much kindness in the Jew.

BASSANIO

You shall not seal to such a bond for me!

I'll rather dwell in my necessity.

ANTONIO

150 Why fear not, man, I will not forfeit it —

Within these two months, that's a month before

This bond expires, I do expect return

Of thrice three times the value of this bond.

SHYLOCK

O father Abram, what these Christians are,

Whose own hard dealings teaches them suspect   155

The thoughts of others! Pray you tell me this:

If he should break his day, what should I gain

By the exaction of the forfeiture?

A pound of man's flesh taken from a man

Is not so estimable, profitable neither,   160

As flesh of muttons, beefs, or goats. I say,

To buy his favour, I extend this friendship —

If he will take it, so — if not, adieu,

And, for my love I pray you wrong me not.

ANTONIO

Yes, Shylock, I will seal unto this bond.   165

SHYLOCK

Then meet me forthwith at the notary's,

Give him direction for this merry bond,

And I will go and purse the ducats straight,

See to my house — left in the fearful guard

Of an unthrifty knave — and presently   170

I will be with you.

ANTONIO

                Hie thee, gentle Jew.

Exit SHYLOCK.

The Hebrew will turn Christian: he grows kind.

BASSANIO

I like not fair terms and a villain's mind.

ANTONIO

Come on, in this there can be no dismay,

My ships come home a month before the day.   175

Exeunt.

---

153 *thrice:* three times. He expects to get 18,000 (3 x 3 = 9; 9 x 3,000 = 18,000) ducats before he has to pay back the 3,000 he will owe Shylock

154 *Abram:* Abraham, who is regarded as the father of the Jewish people

155–6 *hard . . . others:* severe behaviour makes them believe that other people are likely to be as severe and pitiless as themselves

157 *break his day:* fail to pay by the due date

158 *exaction . . . forfeiture:* taking of the pound of flesh

160 *estimable:* worth admiring

163 *adieu:* goodbye

164 *for my love:* if you please

166 *forthwith:* without delay

167 *direction:* instructions

168 *purse:* obtain
     straight: immediately

169–70 *left . . . knave:* being minded by a servant whom I cannot trust

170 *presently:* very soon

171 *Hie thee:* off with you

Key points

The play comes fully to life with the arrival of Shylock. The deal struck in this scene is the basis for the main plot of the play.

- When Bassanio tells Shylock that 'Antonio shall be bound' (line 4), he means that Antonio, rather than Bassanio, will have to repay the loan. Shylock shows his satisfaction at this idea. He would like Antonio to be in his debt, and perhaps also at his mercy.

- Lines 35–46 are marked as an **aside**, which means that Shylock speaks directly to the audience, and Bassanio and Antonio do not hear what he is saying. An aside may be directed at the audience and/or another character. Here, it is a way of telling the audience how Shylock really feels about Antonio. Through it, we learn three important things about Shylock: (a) his deep hatred of Christians, especially Antonio; (b) his greed for money; and (c) his cunning.

- One reason for Shylock's hatred of Antonio is the fact that Antonio lends money free of charge and therefore does damage to Shylock's moneylending business. Note that Shylock would prefer to describe the profit he makes as 'thrift', which sounds better than 'interest' (lines 44–5).

- Shylock defends the charging of interest by quoting from the Old Testament (lines 65–84). Jacob was entitled to all sheep born with spotted fleeces. It was believed that the unborn could be affected by what the mother saw during conception, so during the breeding season Jacob let the ewes see sticks streaked with white so that their lambs would then also be streaked and spotted. In this way Jacob added to his stock. Shylock likens this to the way a moneylender adds to his money by charging interest. Jacob did not steal; neither does Shylock. Money, for Shylock, breeds more money.

- Shylock suggests that Antonio is a hypocrite. Antonio likes to boast that he never borrows from those who charge interest, but now he wants to borrow from Shylock, who always charges interest. Shylock feels morally superior to Antonio. He also makes Antonio feel ill at ease.

- Shylock presents himself as a victim of Antonio's behaviour in the past. He shows his bitter resentment of this in one of the key speeches of the play (lines 100–23). Up to this moment, he has not allowed Antonio to see how much he hates him. This speech tells us that Shylock has a motive for hating Antonio, who has criticised and mocked his religion, insulted him publicly, spat upon him and kicked him aside as he might kick a strange dog out of his house.

- It is important to note that Antonio does not deny the truth of Shylock's accusations. Instead, he admits that he is likely to spit on Shylock again and push him aside if he can. He does not want Shylock to lend him money as if he were his friend, but to lend it to him as an enemy.

- Before Shylock proposes his 'merry sport' (line 139), he becomes more playful. He acts as a man prepared to forgive and forget Antonio's past insults. Not only that, he will give Antonio the money without charging interest and instead will play an amusing game of forfeits for fun, which sounds harmless.

- Antonio is impressed – 'there is much kindness in the Jew' (line 147) – and is ready to sign Shylock's bond. His farewell to Shylock is significant: 'Hie thee, gentle Jew. The Hebrew will turn Christian: he grows kind' (lines 171–2).

I like not fair terms and a villain's mind.

BASSANIO, Act 1, Scene 3, 173

Useful quotes

> You call me misbeliever, cut-throat dog,
> And spit upon my Jewish gaberdine
>
> (Shylock, lines 105–6)

> I hate him for he is a Christian;
> But more, for that in low simplicity
> He lends out money gratis and brings down
> The rate of usance here with us in Venice.
>
> (Shylock, lines 36–9)

> I am as like to call thee so again,
> To spit on thee again, to spurn thee too.
>
> (Antonio, lines 124–5)

> He hates our sacred nation, and he rails,
> Even there where merchants most do congregate,
> On me, my bargains and my well-won thrift,
> Which he calls interest. Cursèd be my tribe
> If I forgive him!
>
> (Shylock, lines 42–6)

> If you repay me not on such a day,
> In such a place, such sum or sums as are
> Expressed in the condition, let the forfeit
> Be nominated for an equal pound
> Of your fair flesh, to be cut off and taken
> In what part of your body pleaseth me.
>
> (Shylock, 140–45)

Questions ?

1 Why is Bassanio meeting with Shylock?

2 Why does Shylock decline Bassanio's invitation to dine with him and Antonio?

3 Shakespeare uses an aside in this scene (lines 35–46). What function does this aside have? Is there any reason to disbelieve what Shylock says about Antonio?

4 Why does Shylock hate Antonio so much?

5 What, do you think, are Antonio and Bassanio doing while Shylock is speaking to the audience? Are they whispering to each other? What might they be saying if they are?

6 What does this scene tell you about the views of Antonio and of Shylock on the charging of interest on loans? Is this difference important?

7 Shylock agrees to lend the money Bassanio needs. What are the terms of the loan?

8 'Hie thee, gentle Jew. The Hebrew will turn Christian: he grows kind' (lines 171–2). What do these lines tell us about Antonio at this point? What has changed his attitude since he promised a few moments earlier to spit on Shylock again?

9 Which character do you find more impressive: Shylock or Antonio? Give reasons for your answer.

10 Imagine you are Antonio. Write an account of what happens between you and Shylock in this scene. State whether your attitude towards Shylock has been affected by these recent events.

Talking point

Antonio hates Shylock because he is a Jew and Shylock hates Antonio because he is a Christian. This conflict is described as an 'ancient grudge' (line 41), a feud that has been going on for centuries. Does this feud make any sense to you? Can you think of any religious or other groups who hate or dislike each other today?

ACT 1 ⚕ Key moments

Scene 1

- Antonio is depressed, but does not know why. His friends cannot cheer him up.

- Bassanio asks Antonio for a huge loan to help him pay his debts and because he wants to impress a wealthy heiress called Portia.

- Antonio cannot provide Bassanio with the money he needs. Instead, he offers to go guarantor for whatever loan Bassanio may be able to raise.

Scene 2

- Portia's suitors must come to her home in Belmont and take part in a lottery, an arrangement laid down by her father in his will. The person who chooses the casket (gold, silver or lead) that contains Portia's portrait may marry Portia.

- Six suitors, none of whom Portia likes, have arrived in Belmont. They decide not to take part in the lottery, much to the relief of Portia.

Scene 3

- Bassanio tries to borrow 3,000 ducats from Shylock, a wealthy Jewish moneylender, and tells him that Antonio will be his guarantor.

- Shylock, glad to think that his enemy Antonio will be in his debt, agrees to give the money to Bassanio. He will not charge interest, but if the money is not repaid within three months, Shylock will be entitled to cut a pound of flesh from Antonio's body.

ACT 1 ⚕ Speaking and listening

1 Select a student to play the part of Shylock. Members of the class interview him, based on what he says and does in Act 1. Shylock might be asked, for example, to talk about his hatred of Christians, and of Antonio in particular; or, given his hatred of Antonio, why he agrees to give him a loan; or why he comes up with the idea of taking a pound of Antonio's flesh if the loan is not paid back on time.

2 In groups of three, discuss how you would enact the events of Act 1, Scene 3. Consider where the actors might take up their positions on the stage, how they should move, the gestures they might make, what facial expression they should adopt, how they should speak their lines and whether they pause before speaking. Act out the scene (reading the lines) to see how your ideas work in practice.

Revision quiz: plot summary

Q

Use the words listed in the panel to fill in the blanks in this summary of Act 1:

alcoholic
Belmont
confident
ducats
English
flesh
guarantee
heiress
horses
husband
interest
Jews
lottery
merchant
money
moneylender
Nerissa
Portia
portrait
sad
ships
silver
suitor
Venice
will

Antonio, a rich _____ in the Italian city-state of Venice, does not know why he feels so _____. It is not because he is worried about the fate of his large trading _____ or because he is in love.

Antonio's closest friend, Bassanio, is in debt and needs _____. He wants to marry a rich _____ called _____, but thinks he has to appear wealthy to compete with her other suitors. Antonio loves Bassanio and wants to help him; however, his money is tied up in investments. The best he can do is _____ a loan that Bassanio finds elsewhere.

Portia is not free to choose a _____. Those who wish to marry her must come to _____, where she lives, and take part in a lottery, as set out in her father's _____. Suitors must select one of three caskets made of gold, _____ or lead. Whoever chooses the casket containing Portia's _____ may marry her.

Six suitors have come to Belmont: a Neapolitan prince who is obsessed with _____; a Palatine count with no sense of humour; a French lord who tries to outdo everyone else; a badly dressed _____ baron with no language skills; a Scottish lord who is always involved in fights; and an _____ German. Fortunately for Portia, they have decided not to take part in the _____.

Portia and _____ recall an eligible young scholar and soldier called Bassanio who once visited from _____. They think he would be a suitable husband for Portia. The Prince of Morocco, another _____, arrives.

Back in Venice, Bassanio wants to borrow the money he needs – 3,000 _____ for three months to be guaranteed by Antonio – from Shylock, a Jewish _____. Shylock hates Antonio because Antonio is a Christian who hates _____. He also lends money without charging _____, which affects Shylock's business. Antonio has spat on, kicked and shouted abuse at Shylock in the past and says he would do so again.

Shylock offers to lend money to Bassanio if Antonio agrees to a strange arrangement: if the money is not repaid on time, Shylock may cut a pound of _____ from any part of Antonio's body. Bassanio is uneasy with these terms, but Antonio is _____ that he can repay the loan before the deadline.

ACT 2 ✝ Scene 1

Plot summary

The Prince of Morocco prepares to try his luck with the three caskets. He points out that Portia should not dislike him for his colour, which he would not want to change unless the change helped him to win Portia. She tells him that he has as good a chance as any other suitor of winning her love. He considers himself a brave man, but realises that he is embarking on a game of chance. Portia reminds him that, under the terms of the lottery, a suitor must swear that if he chooses the wrong casket, he will never again seek to marry. He decides to go ahead.

Mislike me not for my complexion,
The shadowed livery of the burnished sun,
To whom I am a neighbour and near bred.

MOROCCO, Act 2, Scene 1, 1–3

Belmont. A room in Portia's house.

Flourish of cornets. Enter the PRINCE OF MOROCCO (a tawny Moor all in white) and three or four FOLLOWERS, with PORTIA, NERISSA, and their TRAIN.

MOROCCO

Mislike me not for my complexion,

The shadowed livery of the burnished sun,

To whom I am a neighbour and near bred.

Bring me the fairest creature northward born,

Where Phoebus' fire scarce thaws the icicles,   5

And let us make incision for your love,

To prove whose blood is reddest, his or mine.

I tell thee, lady, this aspect of mine

Hath feared the valiant — by my love I swear

The best-regarded virgins of our clime   10

Have loved it too. I would not change this hue,

Except to steal your thoughts, my gentle queen.

PORTIA

In terms of choice I am not solely led

By nice direction of a maiden's eyes.

Besides, the lott'ry of my destiny   15

Bars me the right of voluntary choosing.

But if my father had not scanted me,

And hedged me by his wit to yield myself

His wife who wins me by that means I told you,

Yourself, renownèd prince, then stood as fair   20

As any comer I have looked on yet

For my affection.

MOROCCO

               Even for that I thank you.

Therefore I pray you lead me to the caskets

To try my fortune. By this scimitar

That slew the Sophy and a Persian prince   25

That won three fields of Sultan Solyman,

I would o'erstare the sternest eyes that look,

Outbrave the heart most daring on the earth,

Pluck the young sucking cubs from the she-bear,

Yea, mock the lion when a roars for prey,   30

To win thee, lady. But alas the while,

Flourish of cornets: fanfare played by cornets (a horn-like wind instrument)

tawny . . . white: brown-skinned person of north African descent, who is dressed in white

Train: entourage, group of followers

1–3 *Mislike . . . bred:* do not hold my colour against me: my skin is like a uniform darkened by the blazing sun as I have been brought up in a sunny land

4 *fairest . . . born:* most white-skinned European

5 *Phoebus' fire:* the heat of the sun
scarce: barely

6 *make incision:* cut ourselves

8–9 *this . . . valiant:* my face has made brave men afraid

10 *best-regarded . . . clime:* most admired single women in my country

11 *hue:* colour

12 *steal your thoughts:* attract your interest

13–14 *In . . . eyes:* in looking for a husband, I am not guided only by what I see

16 *Bars . . . choosing:* does not permit me to make my own choice

17 *scanted:* restricted

18 *hedged . . . wit:* limited my choice in his own wise way

18–19 *yield . . . you:* give myself in marriage to the person who chooses the correct casket

20–22 *stood . . . affection:* would stand as good a chance as any of the other suitors I have so far seen

22 *that:* your compliment

24 *scimitar:* curved sword

25 *Sophy:* Emperor of Persia

26 *That . . . Solyman:* who won three battles against the Sultan of Turkey

27 *o'erstare:* outstare

28 *Outbrave . . . earth:* be braver than the bravest person alive

30 *a:* he, it

31 *alas the while:* unfortunately, we have to remember that

32–4	*If … hand:* if the great hero Hercules plays a game of dice with his servant Lichas, a lucky throw may favour the weaker man
35	*Alcides:* another name for Hercules *page:* servant boy
36–8	*And … grieving:* I, too, if it is my destiny, may be beaten by an inferior who may choose the right casket, and then I'll die of a broken heart
40–42	*if … marriage:* never to propose marriage to any woman if you choose the wrong casket
42	*advised:* warned
43	*Nor will not:* if I do not win you, I will never ask anyone else to be my wife
44	*forward:* go (to swear your oath in the temple)
45	*hazard:* gamble

If Hercules and Lichas play at dice

Which is the better man, the greater throw

May turn by fortune from the weaker hand:

35 So is Alcides beaten by his page,

And so may I, blind Fortune leading me,

Miss that which one unworthier may attain,

And die with grieving.

PORTIA

                     You must take your chance,

And either not attempt to choose at all,

40 Or swear before you choose, if you choose wrong

Never to speak to lady afterward

In way of marriage — therefore be advised.

MOROCCO

Nor will not. Come, bring me unto my chance.

PORTIA

First, forward to the temple. After dinner,

Your hazard shall be made.

MOROCCO

45   Good fortune then,

To make me blest or cursèd'st among men!

Cornets. Exeunt.

Key points

This scene introduces Morocco and provides more details on the conditions of the casket lottery.

- The theme of appearance versus reality is emphasised by Morocco in this scene. The key phrase here is his plea to Portia: 'Mislike me not for my complexion' (line 1). In other words, his tawny Moorish appearance should not deceive Portia into thinking that he is any less qualified as a suitor than his fair-skinned rivals. He is proud of his colour and does not want to change it. He is more concerned to stress his heroic qualities.

- Dark skin was associated with the devil in Shakespeare's day. Here, Morocco points out that colour is only skin deep and that his blood is as red as that of any fair-skinned person.

- We also learn the likely reason why the suitors mentioned in Act 1 decided not to take part in the lottery to marry Portia. Candidates must first swear an oath that if they choose the incorrect casket, they will remain unmarried for life. This condition does not deter Morocco.

Useful quotes

> *I would not change this hue,*
> *Except to steal your thoughts, my gentle queen.*
>
> (Morocco, lines 11–12)

> *In terms of choice I am not solely led*
> *By nice direction of a maiden's eyes.*
>
> (Portia, lines 13–14)

Questions ?

1 The racial theme is introduced in the opening stage direction ('a tawny moor all in white'). It is then raised by Morocco. What does he say about it?

2 How does Portia respond to Morocco's statement about his skin colour?

3 What brave deeds does Morocco say he would perform to win Portia?

4 In the theatre, our opinion of Morocco can depend on how the actor playing him delivers his speeches. The actor can make Morocco a dignified, noble, serious character, or a comic, self-centred individual who likes to hear himself talk. How would you play Morocco? Give reasons for your answer.

5 The scene exposes a problem facing Portia as she deals with suitors like Morocco. What is this problem and how does she deal with it?

6 Suitors must swear that if they choose the wrong casket they will never marry. Suggest why Portia's father included this condition.

7 In the photograph below the Prince of Morocco is played by a white actor. What affect, do you think, might this casting decision have on an audience's response to his comments on skin colour?

8 Imagine you are either Portia or Morocco and write an account of the events of this scene. What are your first impressions of Morocco/Portia? What are your hopes for the outcome of the casket lottery?

Talking point

Morocco states that a person's skin colour should not make a difference because everyone is the same inside. Is skin colour an issue for Portia? In your experience, is it an issue nowadays? Is it significant that this topic was raised in the play by a black character rather than a white character?

ACT 2 † Scene 2

Plot summary

Launcelot Gobbo tries to decide whether or not to stop working for Shylock. His half-blind father, Old Gobbo, arrives, looking for him. Launcelot plays a series of jokes on his father: he gives him confusing directions and then suggests he must be looking for 'Master Launcelot', a gentleman rather than a servant, who is dead. In the end Launcelot has to convince his father that he is in fact his son.

Launcelot decides to leave Shylock's service because he finds him mean and unpleasant. He offers to work for Bassanio, who accepts him, saying that Shylock had already arranged for the transfer.

Bassanio has been busy buying uniforms and other supplies for his trip to Belmont and arranging a farewell dinner for that evening. Gratiano wants to accompany Bassanio to Belmont, and promises to behave properly if he is allowed to go. Bassanio gives him permission, but wants to be sure that his friend will not cause Portia to think less of him.

I am a Jew if I serve the Jew any longer.

LAUNCELOT, Act 2, Scene 2, 100–1

Venice. A street.

Enter LAUNCELOT GOBBO the clown.

LAUNCELOT

Certainly my conscience will serve me to run from this
Jew my master. The fiend is at mine elbow and tempts me,
saying to me, 'Gobbo, Launcelot Gobbo, good Launcelot'
or 'good Gobbo' or 'good Launcelot Gobbo — use your
legs, take the start, run away.' My conscience says, 'No,   5
take heed, honest Launcelot; take heed, honest Gobbo'
or, as aforesaid, 'honest Launcelot Gobbo — do not run,
scorn running with thy heels.' Well, the most courageous
fiend bids me pack, 'Fia!' says the fiend. 'Away!' says the
fiend. 'For the heavens, rouse up a brave mind,' says the   10
fiend, 'and run.' Well, my conscience, hanging about the
neck of my heart, says very wisely to me, 'My honest friend
Launcelot' — being an honest man's son, or rather an
honest woman's son, for indeed my father did something
smack, something grow to, he had a kind of taste — well,   15
my conscience says, 'Launcelot, budge not!' 'Budge!' says
the fiend. 'Budge not!' says my conscience. 'Conscience,'
say I, 'you counsel well.' 'Fiend,' say I, 'you counsel well.' To
be ruled by my conscience, I should stay with the Jew my
master, who, God bless the mark, is a kind of devil; and to   20
run away from the Jew, I should be ruled by the fiend, who,
saving your reverence, is the devil himself. Certainly the
Jew is the very devil incarnation; and in my conscience,
my conscience is but a kind of hard conscience to offer
to counsel me to stay with the Jew. The fiend gives the   25
more friendly counsel. I will run, fiend; my heels are at
your command; I will run.

Enter Old GOBBO with a basket.

GOBBO

Master young man, you, I pray you which is the way to
Master Jew's?

LAUNCELOT [*aside*]

O heavens! This is my true-begotten father, who, being   30
more than sand-blind, high-gravel-blind, knows me not
— I will try confusions with him.

GOBBO

Master young gentleman, I pray you which is the way to
Master Jew's?

---

clown: a low comic character in a play

1   *serve:* allow
1–2   *this ... master:* Shylock
2   *fiend:* devil

6   *take heed:* pay attention

7   *aforesaid:* said before

8   *with thy heels:* completely

9   *pack:* pack up and leave
   Fia: go on, hurry up

10   *the heavens:* by the heavens (an oath)
   rouse up: awaken

14–15   *honest woman's ... taste:* Gobbo is saying that his
mother was a good woman, but that his father's
behaviour left a bad taste. To 'smack' means 'to
have a flavour'; the phrase 'grow to' refers to milk
burnt to the bottom of a saucepan and having an
unpleasant taste

18   *counsel:* advise

20   *God ... mark:* excuse my language

22   *saving your reverence:* begging your pardon. Gobbo
is apologising to the audience for talking so much
about the devil

23   *devil incarnation:* he means the 'devil incarnate' or
the devil in human form
   in my conscience: to tell the truth

31   *sand-blind:* half-blind
   high-gravel-blind: almost totally (or stone-) blind

32   *try confusions with:* see how I may confuse

LAUNCELOT

35 Turn up on your right hand at the next turning, but, at the next turning of all, on your left; marry, at the very next turning, turn of no hand, but turn down indirectly to the Jew's house.

GOBBO

By God's sonties 'twill be a hard way to hit. Can you tell me
40 whether one Launcelot that dwells with him, dwell with him or no?

LAUNCELOT

Talk you of young Master Launcelot? — [*aside*] Mark me now; now will I raise the waters. — Talk you of young Master Launcelot?

GOBBO

45 No 'master', sir, but a poor man's son: his father, though I say't, is an honest exceeding poor man and, God be thanked, well to live.

LAUNCELOT

Well, let his father be what a will, we talk of young Master Launcelot.

GOBBO

50 Your worship's friend and Launcelot, sir.

LAUNCELOT

But I pray you, ergo old man, ergo I beseech you, talk you of young Master Launcelot?

GOBBO

Of Launcelot, an't please your mastership.

LAUNCELOT

Ergo Master Launcelot. Talk not of Master Launcelot,
55 father, for the young gentleman, according to fates and destinies and such odd sayings, the Sisters Three, and such branches of learning, is indeed deceased, or as you would say in plain terms, gone to heaven.

GOBBO

Marry, God forbid! The boy was the very staff of my age,
60 my very prop.

LAUNCELOT

[*aside*] Do I look like a cudgel or a hovel-post, a staff or a prop? [*to GOBBO*] Do you know me, father?

---

36 *marry:* by the Virgin Mary (an oath)

39 *sonties:* saints
'twill . . . hit: it will be a difficult place to find

42 *Master:* a respectful form of address, not usually applied to a servant
43 *raise the waters:* make Old Gobbo cry

46 *exceeding:* exceptionally

47 *well to live:* this normally means 'prosperous' but Old Gobbo probably means 'in good health'

48 *a:* he

50 *Your worship:* a term of respect

51 *ergo:* therefore (in Latin). As Old Gobbo has mistaken his son for a gentleman, Launcelot tries to speak like one
beseech: politely request

53 *an't:* if it

55 *father:* old man
56 *the Sisters Three:* the three Fates of Greek mythology. When they cut the threads of a person's life, he or she died

59–60 *staff . . . prop:* one who would support me in my old age

61 *cudgel:* club, weapon
hovel-post: timber beam holding up a hovel or shack

GOBBO

Alack the day, I know you not, young gentleman, but I pray you tell me, is my boy, God rest his soul, alive or dead?

LAUNCELOT

Do you not know me, father?   65

GOBBO

Alack, sir, I am sand-blind; I know you not.

LAUNCELOT

Nay, indeed if you had your eyes you might fail of the knowing me: it is a wise father that knows his own child. Well, old man, I will tell you news of your son — [*kneels*] give me your blessing — truth will come to light, murder cannot   70 be hid long, a man's son may, but in the end truth will out.

GOBBO

Pray you, sir, stand up: I am sure you are not Launcelot, my boy.

LAUNCELOT

Pray you let's have no more fooling about it, but give me your blessing: I am Launcelot, your boy that was, your son   75 that is, your child that shall be.

GOBBO

I cannot think you are my son.

LAUNCELOT

I know not what I shall think of that: but I am Launcelot, the Jew's man, and I am sure Margery, your wife, is my mother.   80

GOBBO

Her name is Margery indeed: I'll be sworn, if thou be Launcelot thou art mine own flesh and blood. Lord worshipped might he be, what a beard hast thou got! Thou hast got more hair on thy chin than Dobbin my fill-horse has on his tail.   85

LAUNCELOT

It should seem then that Dobbin's tail grows backward. I am sure he had more hair of his tail than I have of my face when I last saw him.

63   *Alack:* an expression of regret or sorrow

67–8   *fail … knowing:* still not recognise

68   *it … child:* the original proverb was 'it is a wise child that knows his own father'

71   *may:* may hide

83   *what a beard:* Old Gobbo feels the back of his son's head and mistakes his long hair for a beard

84–5   *fill-horse:* draught-horse

GOBBO

Lord, how art thou changed! How dost thou and thy master agree? I have brought him a present. How 'gree you now?

LAUNCELOT

Well, well, but, for mine own part, as I have set up my rest to run away, so I will not rest till I have run some ground. My master's a very Jew — give him a present? Give him a halter! — I am famished in his service; you may tell every finger I have with my ribs. Father, I am glad you are come: give me your present to one Master Bassanio, who indeed gives rare new liveries — if I serve not him, I will run as far as God has any ground.

Enter BASSANIO with LEONARDO and FOLLOWERS.

O rare fortune! Here comes the man: to him, father; for I am a Jew if I serve the Jew any longer.

BASSANIO

You may do so, but let it be so hasted that supper be ready at the farthest by five of the clock. See these letters delivered, put the liveries to making, and desire Gratiano to come anon to my lodging.

Exit one FOLLOWER.

LAUNCELOT

To him, father.

GOBBO

God bless your worship.

BASSANIO

Gramercy. Wouldst thou aught with me?

GOBBO

Here's my son, sir, a poor boy—

LAUNCELOT

Not a poor boy, sir, but the rich Jew's man that would, sir, as my father shall specify.

GOBBO

He hath a great infection, sir, as one would say, to serve—

90

95

100

105

110

90 *agree:* get on

90–91 *How ... now?* How are you?

92 *set up my rest:* decided

93 *run some ground:* covered some distance

94 *a very Jew:* a true Jew; here, a mean person

95 *halter:* rope to hang himself with
famished: starved

95–6 *tell ... ribs:* count all my fingers if I place them in the hollows between my ribs

97 *give me your:* give your

98 *rare new liveries:* splendid new servants' uniforms

100 *to:* give it (i.e. the present) to

101 *am:* will become

102 *You:* Bassanio is speaking to one of his attendants
hasted: rushed, hurried

103 *at ... clock:* by five o'clock at the latest

104 *put ... making:* get the uniforms made
desire: request, invite

105 *anon:* soon
lodging: living quarters

106 *To him:* speak to him

108 *Gramercy ... me?* Thanks. What do you want with me?

111 *specify:* explain in more detail

112 *infection:* he means 'affection' or desire

LAUNCELOT

Indeed the short and the long is I serve the Jew, and have a desire as my father shall specify.

GOBBO

His master and he, saving your worship's reverence, are scarce cater-cousins—

LAUNCELOT

To be brief, the very truth is that the Jew, having done me wrong, doth cause me, as my father, being, I hope, an old man, shall frutify unto you.

GOBBO

I have here a dish of doves that I would bestow upon your worship, and my suit is—

LAUNCELOT

In very brief, the suit is impertinent to myself, as your worship shall know by this honest old man, and though I say it, though old man, yet poor man, my father.

BASSANIO

One speak for both. What would you?

LAUNCELOT

Serve you, sir.

GOBBO

That is the very defect of the matter, sir.

BASSANIO

I know thee well; thou hast obtained thy suit.
Shylock thy master spoke with me this day,
And hath preferred thee, if it be preferment
To leave a rich Jew's service to become
The follower of so poor a gentleman.

LAUNCELOT

The old proverb is very well parted between my master Shylock and you, sir: you have the grace of God, sir, and he hath enough.

BASSANIO

Thou speak'st it well. Go, father, with thy son.

---

113 *the short ... is:* to cut a long story short

115

116 *scarce cater-cousins:* hardly good friends

119 *frutify:* he means 'notify' or tell

120

120 *bestow upon:* give as a present to

121 *my suit:* the favour I want

122 *impertinent:* he means 'pertinent' or connected

125

125 *What would you?* What do you want?

126 *Serve:* to work for

127 *defect:* he means 'effect', and wants to say 'point'

128 *thou ... suit:* your request has been approved

130

130–32 *hath ... gentleman:* has recommended you for a better job as my servant, that is if it is promotion to leave a rich Jew and join a poor gentleman

133–5 *The ... enough:* the proverb is 'The grace of God is near enough'. Launcelot has divided ('parted') it between Shylock and Bassanio: Bassanio will have the grace of God and Shylock will have enough

135

137–8 *inquire . . . out:* find out where I live

139 *More . . . fellows':* with more ornamental braid on it than there is on the uniforms of the other servants

140–41 *I cannot . . . head:* Launcelot is mocking his father, who thought he would never get a decent job or speak up for himself

141 *table:* part of the palm of the hand. Launcelot is going to tell his own future

145 *simple coming-in:* small income. Launcelot, like Bassanio, thinks of marriage as a means of making money

146 *scape drowning thrice:* avoid drowning three times

147–8 *simple scapes:* harmless scrapes

148 *wench:* woman

149 *gear:* business (either what he has read in his palm or his change of employer)

150 *twinkling:* winking of an eye (i.e. very quickly)

152 *orderly bestowed:* put carefully on board the ship that is to take them to Belmont

153–4 *do . . . acquaintance:* will treat someone I greatly respect to a fine dinner tonight

155 *My . . . herein:* I'll do my best

156 *Yonder:* over there

158 *suit to:* favour to ask of

158 *have obtained it:* may have anything you ask

Take leave of thy old master and inquire
My lodging out. [*to a* FOLLOWER] Give him a livery
More guarded than his fellows'. See it done.

LAUNCELOT

140 Father, in. I cannot get a service, no! I have ne'er a tongue in my head. Well, if any man in Italy have a fairer table which doth offer to swear upon a book, I shall have good fortune. Go to, here's a simple line of life, here's a small trifle of wives — alas, fifteen wives is nothing! Eleven

145 widows and nine maids is a simple coming-in for one man, and then to scape drowning thrice, and to be in peril of my life with the edge of a feather-bed; here are simple scapes. Well, if Fortune be a woman, she's a good wench for this gear. Father, come; I'll take my leave of the Jew in

150 the twinkling.

Exeunt LAUNCELOT and OLD GOBBO.

BASSANIO

I pray thee, good Leonardo, think on this:
These things being bought and orderly bestowed,
Return in haste, for I do feast tonight
My best-esteemed acquaintance: hie thee, go.

LEONARDO

155 My best endeavours shall be done herein.

Enter GRATIANO.

GRATIANO

Where is your master?

LEONARDO

Yonder, sir, he walks.

Exit.

GRATIANO

Signior Bassanio.

BASSANIO

Gratiano.

GRATIANO

I have a suit to you.

BASSANIO

You have obtained it.

GRATIANO

You must not deny me: I must go with you to Belmont.

BASSANIO

Why then you must. But hear thee, Gratiano,   160

Thou art too wild, too rude and bold of voice;

Parts that become thee happily enough,

And in such eyes as ours appear not faults;

But where thou art not known — why there they show

Something too liberal. Pray thee take pain   165

To allay with some cold drops of modesty

Thy skipping spirit, lest through thy wild behaviour

I be misconst'red in the place I go to,

And lose my hopes.

GRATIANO

            Signior Bassanio, hear me:

If I do not put on a sober habit,   170

Talk with respect, and swear but now and then,

Wear prayer-books in my pocket, look demurely,

Nay more, while grace is saying hood mine eyes

Thus with my hat, and sigh and say 'amen',

Use all the observance of civility,   175

Like one well studied in a sad ostent

To please his grandam, never trust me more.

BASSANIO

Well, we shall see your bearing.

GRATIANO

Nay, but I bar tonight: you shall not gauge me

By what we do tonight.

BASSANIO

              No, that were pity,   180

I would entreat you rather to put on

Your boldest suit of mirth, for we have friends

That purpose merriment. But fare you well,

I have some business.

GRATIANO

And I must to Lorenzo and the rest,   185

But we will visit you at supper-time.

Exeunt.

---

161 *too wild … voice:* too undisciplined, too coarse, too loud-mouthed

162 *Parts … enough:* qualities that suit you reasonably well

164–5 *why … liberal:* people who do not know you will find them unrestrained and offensive

165–9 *Pray … hopes:* please make an effort to show more decency and self-control, otherwise your uncivilised conduct may be misunderstood ('misconst'red') and cause Portia to reject me

170 *sober habit:* sedate appearance

172 *Wear:* have, carry
    demurely: modestly, solemnly

173–4 *while … hat:* cover my eyes like this with my hat while grace before meals is being said

175–7 *Use … grandam:* have the good manners expected of polite people, as though I have practised appearing to be serious to impress my grandmother

178 *bearing:* behaviour

179 *bar:* exclude
    gauge: judge

180 *were pity:* would be a shame (to be serious tonight)

181–3 *I … merriment:* instead I wish you would make everybody laugh as much as possible because we all intend to have fun

185 *must:* must go
    rest: others

Key points

This comic scene introduces Launcelot Gobbo, who is Shylock's servant but is about to become Bassanio's servant instead.

- This scene offers a contrast to the previous one. We move from the noble verse of Morocco to the clownish prose of Launcelot Gobbo. Elizabethan plays were usually written in verse, but Shakespeare often included passages of prose. He tended to use prose to create a conversational tone between characters (e.g. Portia and Nerissa in Act 1, Scene 2) or to indicate an uneducated or comic character such as Launcelot.

- Here we have low comedy combined with **farce**, a kind of entertainment based on crude horseplay, practical jokes and mistaken identities. It is introduced by the arrival of Old Gobbo, Launcelot's half-blind father, who does not recognise his son.

- Much of the humour in this scene is derived from the misuse and abuse of language. Both Launcelot and Old Gobbo use words in ways the other characters do not. The result is that their dialogue sounds comically absurd. For example, Launcelot talks of his conscience as 'hanging about the neck of my heart' (lines 11–12), and Old Gobbo refers to Launcelot's 'great infection … to serve' (line 112) when he means 'affection' or desire.

- Launcelot's opening speech (lines 1–27) is a **soliloquy**. A soliloquy is a speech in which a character who is alone on stage expresses his or her thoughts and feelings aloud. The character speaks the truth as he or she sees it (i.e. soliloquies are not used to deceive the audience). Soliloquies provide the audience with information about a character's state of mind, deepest feelings, motives, intentions and outlook.

- Launcelot's soliloquy is used mainly for comic effect. He is unhappy working for Shylock and is considering running away. He acts out a little play involving his conscience, the devil and himself. His conscience tells him that it would be wrong to leave Shylock, but the devil encourages him to go. He decides that his conscience is being too strict and that he should follow the devil because Shylock himself 'is a kind of devil' (line 20).

- Launcelot refuses to refer to Shylock by name: he is always 'the Jew' or some kind of devil. When he says, 'I am a Jew if I serve the Jew any longer' (lines 100–1), he means to imply that Shylock lacks human feelings.

- The scene ends with two fortune-hunters, Bassanio and Gratiano, preparing to go to Belmont, where they hope to improve their situations. Bassanio is in a hurry to get there now that he has the money he needs, but decides to throw a final party before he leaves.

- Bassanio enjoys Gratiano's 'wild behaviour' (line 167), but worries that he is too loud-mouthed and coarse for the civilised society of Belmont. He fears that Gratiano may embarrass him and has to warn him to behave properly.

Useful quotes

> … my conscience is but a kind of hard conscience, to offer to counsel me to stay with the Jew. The fiend gives the more friendly counsel. I will run, fiend; my heels are at your command; I will run.
>
> (Launcelot, lines 24–7)

> I know thee well; thou hast obtained thy suit.
> Shylock thy master spoke with me this day,
> And hath preferred thee, if it be preferment
> To leave a rich Jew's service to become
> The follower of so poor a gentleman.
>
> (Bassanio, lines 128–32)

Questions ?

1 What is Launcelot's soliloquy (lines 1–27) about?

2 What tricks does Launcelot play on his father?

3 Is Launcelot's behaviour towards Old Gobbo humorous or cruel, or both? Give reasons for your answer.

4 'I pray you tell me, is my boy, God rest his soul, alive or dead?' (lines 63–4). Do you find the verbal exchanges between Launcelot and his father funny? Give reasons for your answer.

5 Why is Old Gobbo carrying a basket?

6 How does Shakespeare establish Launcelot and Old Gobbo as 'low' characters? How does their manner of speaking differ from that of Bassanio in this scene?

7 Do you think Launcelot is pleased to be leaving Shylock's employment? Give reasons for your answer.

8 Is Bassanio wise to employ Launcelot Gobbo? Give reasons for your answer.

9 What promises does Gratiano make about how he intends to behave in Belmont? Why does Bassanio ask him to make these promises?

10 How does Bassanio plan to spend his final night in Venice? What does this tell us about Bassanio?

Talking point

Bassanio realises that Gratiano may embarrass him in Belmont. What is embarrassing about Gratiano? Mention some things you would find embarrassing in other people, and say why. Is it important to have good manners? Should people adjust their behaviour to suit certain situations? What might happen if they didn't?

ACT 2 † Scene 3

Plot summary

Shylock's only child, Jessica, is saying goodbye to Launcelot, whose jokes and pranks have helped her to put up with her miserable life in her father's house. Jessica asks him to deliver a letter to Lorenzo and to do it secretly. Left alone, she tells us that she has nothing in common with Shylock. She does not share her father's outlook and does not approve of his character. She is prepared to become a Christian in order to marry Lorenzo.

O Lorenzo,
If thou keep promise, I shall end this strife,
Become a Christian and thy loving wife.
JESSICA, Act 2, Scene 3, 18–20

Venice. A room in Shylock's house.

Enter JESSICA and LAUNCELOT.

JESSICA

I am sorry thou wilt leave my father so,

Our house is hell, and thou, a merry devil,

Didst rob it of some taste of tediousness.

But fare thee well. There is a ducat for thee.

And, Launcelot, soon at supper shalt thou see   5

Lorenzo, who is thy new master's guest:

Give him this letter — do it secretly.

And so farewell: I would not have my father

See me in talk with thee.

LAUNCELOT

Adieu. Tears exhibit my tongue, most beautiful pagan,   10

most sweet Jew! If a Christian do not play the knave and

get thee, I am much deceived. But, adieu, these foolish

drops do something drown my manly spirit, adieu.

JESSICA

Farewell, good Launcelot.

Exit LAUNCELOT.

Alack, what heinous sin is it in me   15

To be ashamed to be my father's child!

But though I am a daughter to his blood,

I am not to his manners. O Lorenzo,

If thou keep promise, I shall end this strife,

Become a Christian and thy loving wife.   20

Exit.

3 *tediousness:* boredom

10 *Adieu:* goodbye
   exhibit: he means 'inhibit' or prevent
   pagan: person of no faith

11–12 *play ... thee:* make you his wife through trickery

13 *drops:* tears

15 *Alack:* an expression of regret or sorrow
   heinous: hateful

18 *to his manners:* like him in character

19 *strife:* struggle, conflict

Key points

This scene introduces Jessica, Shylock's daughter, who wants to leave her father's house to become a Christian and to marry Lorenzo.

- Jessica claims to live a tedious existence, with only Launcelot to relieve her of her boredom. Launcelot is a 'merry devil' (line 2) in a hell presided over by Shylock. Notice that Jessica demonises Shylock by describing their home as hell, and thus echoes the Christian view expressed many times in the play that he is a devil.

- Jessica's soliloquy (lines 15–20) reveals that she has been dealing with a conflict – 'this strife' (line 19) – between her duty to her father and her love for Lorenzo. Her shame at being her father's child troubles her conscience.

- It is worth noting that Launcelot dealt with a similar kind of conflict over leaving Shylock in the previous scene. Shylock, having lost his servant Launcelot, is now about to lose his only child as well. Both Launcelot and Jessica leave Shylock for friends of Antonio (Bassanio and Lorenzo).

- Launcelot shows his ignorance of Jessica's religion when he refers to her as 'most beautiful pagan, most sweet Jew' (lines 10–11). As Jewish people practise Judaism, one of the world's major religions, they cannot be described as pagans.

Useful quotes

> I am sorry thou wilt leave my father so,
> Our house is hell, and thou, a merry devil
>
> (Jessica, lines 1–2)

> Alack, what heinous sin is it in me
> To be ashamed to be my father's child!
>
> (Jessica, lines 15–16)

> O Lorenzo,
> If thou keep promise, I shall end this strife,
> Become a Christian and thy loving wife.
>
> (Jessica, lines 18–20)

? Questions

1 Why is Jessica sorry that Launcelot is leaving?

2 What does Launcelot hope will happen to Jessica?

3 Why does Jessica give Launcelot a letter?

4 Do you think Jessica would be right to give up her religion and desert her father?

5 Does this scene reflect badly on (a) Shylock; (b) Jessica; (c) Lorenzo? Explain your answers.

6 Imagine you are Jessica. Write a short letter to Agnes, the agony aunt at *Venice Today* magazine, setting out your issues with your father and your feelings for Lorenzo, and asking for her advice on what you should do.

Talking point

Jessica is ashamed of her father and does not like living under his roof. How, do you think, would Shylock react if he knew she felt that way? How should a father react to the news that his child is ashamed of him? What qualities should a good parent and a good son or daughter have?

Plot summary

Lorenzo and his friends are arranging a surprise event (a masque) to follow Bassanio's farewell dinner. Launcelot delivers Jessica's letter to Lorenzo and then goes off to invite Shylock to dine with Bassanio. Lorenzo reveals that Jessica has asked him to elope with her and that she will leave her father's house disguised as a page (a young male attendant) and will bring with her some of Shylock's gold and jewels.

Go gentlemen,
Will you prepare you for this masque tonight?
I am provided of a torch-bearer.

LORENZO, Act 2, Scene 4, 21–3

Venice. A street.

Enter GRATIANO, LORENZO, SALERIO and SOLANIO.

LORENZO
Nay, we will slink away in supper-time,
Disguise us at my lodging, and return
All in an hour.

GRATIANO
We have not made good preparation.

SALERIO
5   We have not spoke us yet of torch-bearers.

SOLANIO
'Tis vile, unless it may be quaintly ordered,
And better in my mind not undertook.

LORENZO
'Tis now but four o'clock, we have two hours
To furnish us.

Enter LAUNCELOT with a letter.

           Friend Launcelot, what's the news?

LAUNCELOT
10   An it shall please you to break up this, it shall seem to signify.

LORENZO
I know the hand, in faith 'tis a fair hand,
And whiter than the paper it writ on
Is the fair hand that writ.

GRATIANO
           Love-news, in faith.

LAUNCELOT
15   By your leave, sir.

LORENZO
Whither goest thou?

LAUNCELOT
Marry, sir, to bid my old master the Jew to sup tonight
with my new master the Christian.

LORENZO
Hold, here, take this. Tell gentle Jessica
20   I will not fail her — speak it privately.

Exit LAUNCELOT.

---

1   *slink:* slip, creep

2   *Disguise us:* put on our costumes/masks

5   *spoke . . . torch-bearers:* made arrangements to get people to carry torches (lights)

6–7   *'Tis . . . undertook:* unless it is arranged with good taste, it is going to be degrading or worthless ('vile'), and had better not take place at all

9   *furnish us:* get everything we need

10–11   *An . . . signify:* if ('An') you break open the seal on this letter, you will learn the news you want to know

12   *hand:* handwriting

15   *By your leave:* excuse me

16   *Whither goest thou?* Where are you going?

17   *bid:* ask
     sup: have supper

19   *Hold:* wait, hold on
     this: he may give him money for his troubles, or perhaps a token to pass on to Jessica
     gentle: noble, ladylike

Go gentlemen,

Will you prepare you for this masque tonight?

I am provided of a torch-bearer.

SALERIO

Ay, marry, I'll be gone about it straight.

SOLANIO

And so will I.

LORENZO

             Meet me and Gratiano   25

At Gratiano's lodging some hour hence.

SALERIO

'Tis good we do so.

Exeunt SALERIO and SOLANIO.

GRATIANO

Was not that letter from fair Jessica?

LORENZO

I must needs tell thee all. She hath directed

How I shall take her from her father's house,   30

What gold and jewels she is furnished with,

What page's suit she hath in readiness.

If e'er the Jew her father come to heaven,

It will be for his gentle daughter's sake.

And never dare misfortune cross her foot,   35

Unless she do it under this excuse:

That she is issue to a faithless Jew.

Come, go with me; peruse this as thou goest:

Fair Jessica shall be my torch-bearer.

Exeunt.

---

22 *masque:* show, entertainment

23 *I . . . torch-bearer:* I have found my torch-bearer (i.e. Jessica)

24 *straight:* immediately

26 *some hour hence:* in an hour from now

31 *furnished:* provided

32 *page's suit:* servant boy's uniform

33 *e'er:* ever

35–7 *never . . . Jew:* bad luck will never dare to cross her path unless it does so because she is the child of ('issue to') a Jew who lacks Christian faith

38 *peruse . . . goest:* read Jessica's letter as you go

Key points

Jessica's plan to elope with Lorenzo is developed in this scene.

- The only significant business in this scene is Lorenzo's disclosure to Gratiano of the contents of Jessica's letter. It seems that Jessica is at least as anxious to win Lorenzo as he is to win her. She has taken great care in making the arrangements for them to elope, including a plan to steal gold and jewels from her father's house.

- We know that Bassanio has borrowed Shylock's money to pursue a rich heiress, and now we learn that Lorenzo may also be about to gain a wealthy wife at Shylock's expense. Marriage is once again shown as a way of improving a person's financial situation.

- The surprise event that the men are planning at the start of the scene is a masque. Such forms of entertainment were very popular among the aristocracy in Shakespeare's day. They involved dance, mime and acting, and could last all night. Masques often led to wild and unruly behaviour; hence Shylock's later concern for his daughter and home. Those taking part wore costumes and masks, and were accompanied by musicians and people carrying torches. Lorenzo realises that this will give excellent cover for an eloping couple, as Jessica will blend in if she is dressed as a page and carries a torch.

Useful quotes

*I must needs tell thee all. She hath directed
How I shall take her from her father's house,
What gold and jewels she is furnished with,
What page's suit she hath in readiness.*

(Lorenzo, lines 29–32)

*If e'er the Jew her father come to heaven,
It will be for his gentle daughter's sake.*

(Lorenzo, lines 33–4)

Fair Jessica shall be my torch-bearer.

(Lorenzo, line 39)

? Questions

1. What arrangements are the four men making at the start of the scene?

2. What does Launcelot give to Lorenzo?

3. Why, do you think, is Launcelot going to invite Shylock to Bassanio's farewell dinner?

4. What information is contained in Jessica's letter?

5. Do you think Lorenzo is in love with Jessica, or is he influenced by the wealth she can bring him? Give reasons for your answer.

6. Comment on the idea that Jessica is to Lorenzo as Portia is to Bassanio. What do these relationships have in common?

Talking point

Jessica and Lorenzo intend to steal money and valuables from Shylock. Can you think of anything that might excuse this conduct? Can stealing ever be justified? How would you feel if someone stole something from you?

Launcelot is taking his leave of his old master, Shylock, and giving him an invitation to Bassanio's farewell dinner. Shylock accepts the invitation out of spite, although he is reluctant to go out and worries about leaving Jessica and his valuables alone in the house. He urges Jessica to keep the house secure and to stay away from the windows, particularly when he realises that there may be a masque procession in the streets outside. Meanwhile, Launcelot tells Jessica to look out for Lorenzo. When Shylock leaves, Jessica accepts that they will not see each other again.

Do as I bid you, shut doors after you,
Fast bind, fast find —
A proverb never stale in thrifty mind.

SHYLOCK, Act 2, Scene 5, 51–3

Venice. Before Shylock's house.

Enter SHYLOCK and LAUNCELOT.

Before: in front of

SHYLOCK
Well, thou shalt see, thy eyes shall be thy judge,
The difference of old Shylock and Bassanio. —

2 *of:* between

3 *What, Jessica!* Shylock interrupts his comment to Launcelot to call Jessica
gormandize: over-eat

What, Jessica! — Thou shalt not gormandize,
As thou hast done with me. — What, Jessica! —

5 *rend apparel out:* wear your clothes threadbare

5 And sleep, and snore, and rend apparel out. —
Why, Jessica, I say!

LAUNCELOT
                    Why, Jessica!

SHYLOCK
Who bids thee call? I do not bid thee call.

LAUNCELOT

8–9 *Your ... bidding:* you often complained that I could do nothing without being told (and now I am showing a little initiative)

Your worship was wont to tell me that I could do nothing without bidding.

Enter JESSICA.

JESSICA

10 *will:* wish (i.e. What are you calling me for?)

10 Call you? What is your will?

SHYLOCK

11 *bid forth:* invited out

I am bid forth to supper, Jessica;

12 *wherefore:* why

There are my keys. But wherefore should I go?

13 *bid for love:* invited because they love me

I am not bid for love; they flatter me:
But yet I'll go in hate, to feed upon

15 *prodigal:* wasteful

15 The prodigal Christian. Jessica, my girl,

16 *Look to:* keep an eye on
right loath: very unwilling

Look to my house. I am right loath to go,
There is some ill a-brewing towards my rest,

17 *ill ... rest:* evil threatening my peace/security

For I did dream of money-bags tonight.

LAUNCELOT

19 *beseech:* politely request

I beseech you, sir, go; my young master doth expect your

20 *reproach:* he means 'approach'

20 reproach.

SHYLOCK

21 *So ... his:* I also expect his reproach (or criticism). Shylock has taken Launcelot literally

So do I his.

LAUNCELOT

22 *conspired:* made plans

And they have conspired together — I will not say you shall see a masque, but if you do, then it was not for

24–6 *my ... afternoon:* Launcelot is mocking Shylock's habit of taking omens and superstitions seriously: what he says is nonsensical

nothing that my nose fell a-bleeding on Black Monday

25 last at six o'clock i' th' morning, falling out that year on Ash Wednesday was four year in th'afternoon.

SHYLOCK

What, are there masques? Hear you me, Jessica,

Lock up my doors, and when you hear the drum

And the vile squealing of the wry-necked fife,

Clamber not you up to the casements then 30

Nor thrust your head into the public street

To gaze on Christian fools with varnished faces,

But stop my house's ears, I mean my casements,

Let not the sound of shallow fopp'ry enter

My sober house. By Jacob's staff I swear 35

I have no mind of feasting forth tonight:

But I will go. [*to LAUNCELOT*] Go you before me, sirrah;

Say I will come.

LAUNCELOT

            I will go before, sir.

[*aside to JESSICA*] Mistress, look out at window for all this,

    There will come a Christian by, 40

    Will be worth a Jewës eye.

Exit.

SHYLOCK

What says that fool of Hagar's offspring, ha?

JESSICA

His words were 'Farewell mistress'; nothing else.

SHYLOCK

The patch is kind enough, but a huge feeder,

Snail-slow in profit, and he sleeps by day 45

More than the wild-cat. Drones hive not with me,

Therefore I part with him, and part with him

To one that I would have him help to waste

His borrowed purse. Well, Jessica, go in —

Perhaps I will return immediately — 50

Do as I bid you, shut doors after you,

Fast bind, fast find —

A proverb never stale in thrifty mind.

Exit.

JESSICA

Farewell — and if my fortune be not crost,

I have a father, you a daughter, lost. 55

Exit.

29 *wry-necked fife:* the fife, a small pipe, is played with the head turned to one side, or 'awry'

30 *Clamber . . . casements:* do not climb up to look out the windows ('casements')

32 *varnished faces:* masks

33 *stop:* block, close up

34 *shallow fopp'ry:* empty foolery

35 *sober:* serious
By Jacob's staff: a sacred oath

36 *mind . . . forth:* interest in going out to dinner

38 *before:* ahead of you

42 *Hagar's offspring:* Hagar, the Egyptian maid to Abraham's wife, bore Abraham a son named Ishmael, whom he disowned. Shylock, by comparing Launcelot to Ishmael, suggests that he has disowned his servant

44 *patch:* fool
feeder: eater

46 *Drones . . . me:* I refuse to support anyone who won't work

49 *His borrowed purse:* a sarcastic reference to the fact that Bassanio has borrowed all he has

52 *Fast bind, fast find:* if you keep a tight grip on what you have, you will quickly prosper

54 *if . . . crost:* as long as my plans work out for me

Key points

This scene sees the final steps put in place for the elopement: Shylock is invited to leave his home and Jessica is told to be ready for Lorenzo's arrival.

- We meet Shylock in a new setting, his own household, and learn something about his domestic life. He is a frugal, careful householder. He does not approve of waste or high living. He does not want Launcelot to overeat at his expense or wear out his clothes or sleep when he should be working.

- Shylock's conversation or **dialogue** with Jessica shows how vulnerable and anxious he is. His insecurity is emphasised by his unwillingness to leave his home because of a bad dream he had. He senses that some evil thing lies in wait to threaten his peace of mind.

- Shylock is further troubled to hear that a masque has been planned for a period during which he will be absent from his home. As a precaution, he warns Jessica to keep the windows closed to protect his 'sober house' (line 35) from the excitement outside. We already know that Jessica finds his house too 'sober' or serious.

- Although Shylock is somewhat fearful of going out, and realises that he is not being invited to dine with Bassanio out of respect, he still gets some satisfaction from the idea of eating at the wasteful Bassanio's expense.

- There is a transition in this scene from Shylock's hatred of Bassanio to his more loving attitude to Jessica. He speaks to her kindly: 'Jessica, my girl, look to my house' (lines 15–16). He shows genuine concern for her welfare and is worried in case she sees and is corrupted by the 'Christian fools with varnished faces' (line 32) taking part in the masque. He wants to protect her (too much for her liking).

- There is a sad aspect to this scene, at least with regard to Shylock's situation. He does not know what the audience knows: that the only significant person in his life, and perhaps the only one he loves, is about to rob him, escape from the home they share, convert to Christianity and marry Lorenzo, a friend of Shylock's enemy Antonio.

- Shylock clearly has a need for Jessica's affection and for her presence in his home, but does not know that all she has for him is contempt.

Useful quotes

> *I am bid forth to supper, Jessica;*
> *There are my keys. But wherefore should I go?*
> *I am not bid for love; they flatter me:*
> *But yet I'll go in hate, to feed upon*
> *The prodigal Christian.*
>
> (Shylock, lines 11–15)

> *Mistress, look out at window for all this,*
> *There will come a Christian by,*
> *Will be worth a Jewës eye.*
>
> (Launcelot, lines 39–41)

> *I am right loath to go,*
> *There is some ill a-brewing towards my rest,*
> *For I did dream of money-bags tonight.*
>
> (Shylock, lines 16–18)

> *Farewell — and if my fortune be not crost,*
> *I have a father, you a daughter, lost.*
>
> (Jessica, lines 54–5)

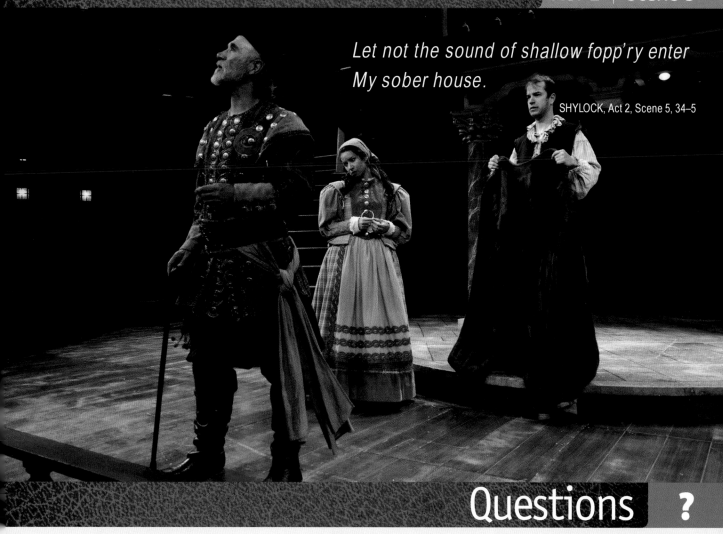

Let not the sound of shallow fopp'ry enter
My sober house.

SHYLOCK, Act 2, Scene 5, 34–5

Questions ?

1 What issues did Shylock have with the behaviour of his former servant Launcelot?

2 Shylock gives reasons why he should not accept Bassanio's invitation. What are these?

3 Why does he decide to accept this invitation, having declined another invite in Act 1, Scene 3?

4 Why does Shylock instruct Jessica to lock the doors and stay away from the windows?

5 Comment on the behaviour of Launcelot and Jessica in this scene.

6 Do you feel pity for Shylock at this point in the play? Explain.

7 There is **dramatic irony** when a character has less knowledge than the audience has and therefore does not recognise the full implications of what he or she is saying. Identify an example of dramatic irony in this scene.

8 Write an account of this scene from Shylock's point of view.

Talking point

There is a good deal of mockery in this scene. In your opinion, is this kind of mockery appropriate? In everyday life, can mockery ever be appropriate (for example, when students mock each other)? Why would someone decide to mock another person? How does it feel to be mocked?

ACT 2 † Scene 6

Plot summary

Lorenzo is late for his elopement and his friends wonder if he has changed his mind. He arrives and calls Jessica. Jessica, dressed as a boy, throws him a valuable casket and takes money with her from Shylock's stores. With Jessica carrying the torch, they head towards Bassanio's party. Antonio tells Gratiano that the masque has been cancelled. The weather has changed and Bassanio must sail for Belmont immediately.

And it is marvel he out-dwells his hour,
For lovers ever run before the clock.

GRATIANO, Act 2, Scene 6, 3–4

Venice. Before Shylock's house.

Enter the masquers, GRATIANO and SALERIO.

masquers: people dressed for the masque

GRATIANO

This is the penthouse under which Lorenzo

Desired us to make stand.

1 *penthouse:* the porch of Shylock's house

2 *make stand:* position ourselves

SALERIO

His hour is almost past.

2 *hour:* appointed time of meeting

GRATIANO

And it is marvel he out-dwells his hour,

For lovers ever run before the clock.

3 *marvel … hour:* surprising that he is late

4 *ever … clock:* are always early for their meetings

SALERIO

O ten times faster Venus' pigeons fly

To seal love's bonds new-made than they are wont

To keep obligèd faith unforfeited!

5

5 *Venus:* Roman goddess of love

6–7 *To … unforfeited:* to unite new lovers than to help married couples to keep their vows

GRATIANO

That ever holds: who riseth from a feast

With that keen appetite that he sits down?

Where is the horse that doth untread again

His tedious measures with the unbated fire

That he did pace them first? All things that are,

Are with more spirit chasèd than enjoyed.

How like a younger or a prodigal

The scarfèd bark puts from her native bay,

Hugged and embracèd by the strumpet wind!

How like the prodigal doth she return

With over-weathered ribs and raggèd sails,

Lean, rent and beggared by the strumpet wind!

Enter LORENZO.

10

15

8 *ever holds:* is always the case

8–9 *who … down?* Who gets up from dinner as hungry as he was when he first sat down?

10–12 *Where … first?* What horse enjoys repeating his training exercises again and again?

12–13 *All … enjoyed:* seeking something is more enjoyable than having it

14–19 *How … wind:* the adventurous young ship sets out from its harbour in hope, but returns wasted and worn. Gratiano has in mind the Prodigal Son, who left his father's house prosperous, but returned like a sick beggar. The lines are meant to remind us of Antonio's ships at sea and of the younger and wasteful ('prodigal') Bassanio

SALERIO

Here comes Lorenzo; more of this hereafter.

20

20 *hereafter:* later

LORENZO

Sweet friends, your patience for my long abode,

Not I, but my affairs, have made you wait:

When you shall please to play the thieves for wives,

I'll watch as long for you then. Approach;

Here dwells my father Jew. — How! Who's within?

Enter JESSICA above, dressed in boys' clothes.

25

21 *abode:* delay

22 *affairs:* business

23 *please … wives:* choose to act in a stealthy manner to gain a wife

25 *father:* future father-in-law

above: in the gallery over the stage (representing the window of her home; see p. 3)

JESSICA

Who are you? Tell me for more certainty,

Albeit I'll swear that I do know your tongue.

LORENZO

Lorenzo and thy love.

JESSICA

Lorenzo, certain, and my love indeed,

30 For who love I so much? And now who knows

But you, Lorenzo, whether I am yours?

LORENZO

Heaven and thy thoughts are witness that thou art.

JESSICA

Here, catch this casket; it is worth the pains.

I am glad 'tis night, you do not look on me,

35 For I am much ashamed of my exchange:

But love is blind and lovers cannot see

The pretty follies that themselves commit;

For if they could, Cupid himself would blush

To see me thus transformèd to a boy.

LORENZO

40 Descend, for you must be my torch-bearer.

JESSICA

What, must I hold a candle to my shames?

They in themselves, good sooth, are too too light.

Why 'tis an office of discovery, love,

And I should be obscured.

LORENZO

                         So are you, sweet,

45 Even in the lovely garnish of a boy.

But come at once,

For the close night doth play the runaway,

And we are stayed for at Bassanio's feast.

JESSICA

I will make fast the doors, and gild myself

50 With some more ducats, and be with you straight.

Exit above.

---

27 *Albeit:* although
   tongue: voice

29 *certain:* for sure

33 *pains:* trouble

34 *do . . . on:* cannot see

35 *exchange:* change of clothes

37 *pretty follies:* silly little things

38 *Cupid:* Roman love-god

41 *hold . . . shames:* Jessica expected to be a page, not a torch-bearer. Now she will be clearly lit and people will see her embarrassing disguise

42 *good sooth:* in truth
   light: easily seen

43–4 *'tis . . . obscured:* the job of a torch-bearer is to throw light on things, whereas I should be hidden

44–5 *So . . . boy:* you are indeed hidden in boys' clothes

47 *close . . . runaway:* darkness that keeps our secret is slipping away fast

48 *stayed for:* waited for, expected

49 *make fast:* secure
   gild: enrich

GRATIANO

Now, by my hood a gentle, and no Jew.

LORENZO

Beshrew me but I love her heartily;

For she is wise, if I can judge of her;

And fair she is, if that mine eyes be true;

And true she is, as she hath proved herself: 55

And therefore, like herself, wise, fair and true,

Shall she be placèd in my constant soul.

Enter JESSICA below.

What, art thou come? On, gentlemen; away!

Our masquing mates by this time for us stay.

Exeunt LORENZO, JESSICA and SALERIO. Enter ANTONIO.

ANTONIO

Who's there?   60

GRATIANO

Signior Antonio?

ANTONIO

Fie, fie, Gratiano! Where are all the rest?

'Tis nine o'clock: our friends all stay for you.

No masque tonight: the wind is come about;

Bassanio presently will go aboard.   65

I have sent twenty out to seek for you.

GRATIANO

I am glad on't; I desire no more delight

Than to be under sail and gone tonight.

Exeunt.

51 *by my hood:* an oath
  gentle: noble woman and also a pun on gentile or non-Jew

52 *Beshrew me:* an oath

55 *true:* faithful

57 *constant:* faithful

64 *is come about:* has changed direction

65 *aboard:* on board the ship that will take him towards Belmont

66 *twenty:* twenty people

67 *on't:* of it, to hear it

Key points

This is the elopement scene and it raises important questions for the audience.

- This scene is one of betrayal. Shylock has been invited to Bassanio's farewell dinner. The purpose of the invitation is to keep Shylock away from his home long enough to allow Jessica and Lorenzo to rob him of his valuable possessions, and for Jessica to leave him for good.

- Notice that, as an extra piece of cruel fun at Shylock's expense, Lorenzo and his friends plan to bring Jessica, disguised as a torch-bearer, to the party at which her father is a guest. They are prevented from going ahead with this 'joke' only because the wind changes and the planned masque has to be abandoned.

- Jessica's indifference to her father and his happiness, as well as to his property rights, is revealed as she throws a casket of his jewels down to Lorenzo. When she tells Lorenzo that she is 'much ashamed' of her 'exchange' (line 35), she is not talking about this transfer of money, or even about her change of religion, but about her change of clothes.

- Even this shame is merely a pretence. Jessica is happy to be wearing boys' clothes because they have plenty of pockets that she can stuff with gold pieces from her father's stock. As she says, she will 'gild' herself 'with some more ducats' (lines 49–50).

- *The Merchant of Venice* has always been included among Shakespeare's comedies. The characters in this scene speak and act as if they were taking part in a comedy and appear to find amusement in robbing Shylock's house. Despite what she does, Lorenzo describes Jessica as 'wise, fair and true' (line 56). Is the audience expected to find this scene amusing, and to be happy that the foundations of Shylock's life and happiness are being destroyed? Are we to see Shylock as a comic villain, whose sufferings are to be mocked and laughed at?

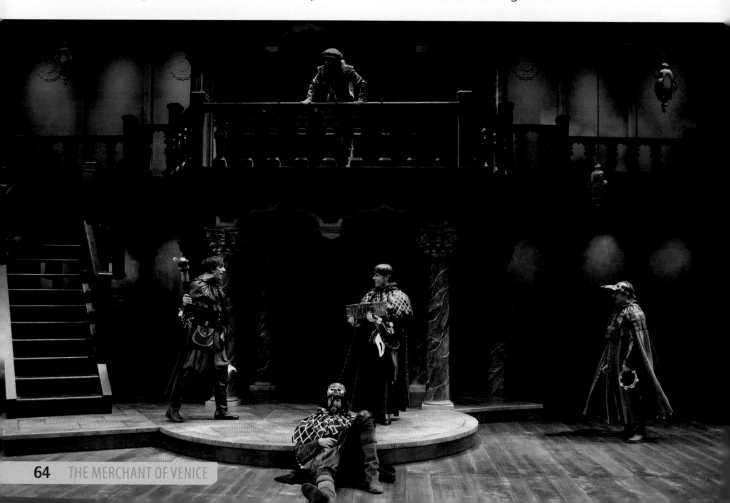

Useful quotes

> *Here, catch this casket; it is worth the pains.*
>
> (Jessica, line 33)

> *I will make fast the doors, and gild myself*
> *With some more ducats, and be with you straight.*
>
> (Jessica, lines 49–50)

Questions ?

1 Lorenzo is late, and Gratiano and Salerio speculate as to why he is not there. What theory do they put forward?

2 Do you think that Jessica is genuinely embarrassed by her disguise as a page (lines 34–9)? Give reasons for your answer.

3 'Beshrew me but I love her heartily' (line 52). What reasons does Lorenzo give for loving Jessica? Do you believe him?

4 What is your opinion of the behaviour of (a) Jessica and (b) Lorenzo in this scene?

5 What news does Antonio bring?

6 Why is Gratiano glad to hear it?

7 Imagine that Jessica's conscience troubles her, and she decides to leave a letter for Shylock explaining what she has done. Compose a version of that letter.

8 Imagine that you are the costume designer for a stage version of the play. Describe and sketch the costumes, masks and torches you will need for your presentation of this scene.

Masquer

Talking point

Jessica claims to feel 'much ashamed' about the boys' clothes she is wearing. Is it healthy to feel ashamed about how others see you? Does what other people think of you matter? Can you recall anything you have done or said that made you feel ashamed? How did you deal with this?

ACT 2 † Scene 7

Plot summary

Morocco has to make his choice among the caskets. He considers the inscriptions on each casket very carefully. He decides that Portia's portrait must be in the most beautiful and valuable setting and so he chooses the gold casket. Inside he finds a skull and a scroll telling him he has made the wrong choice. He accepts his failure with patience and without complaint. Portia admires his response to so great a loss, although she is glad he has not won her.

> *O hell! What have we here?*
> *A carrion Death, within whose empty eye*
> *There is a written scroll!*

MOROCCO, Act 2, Scene 7, 62–4

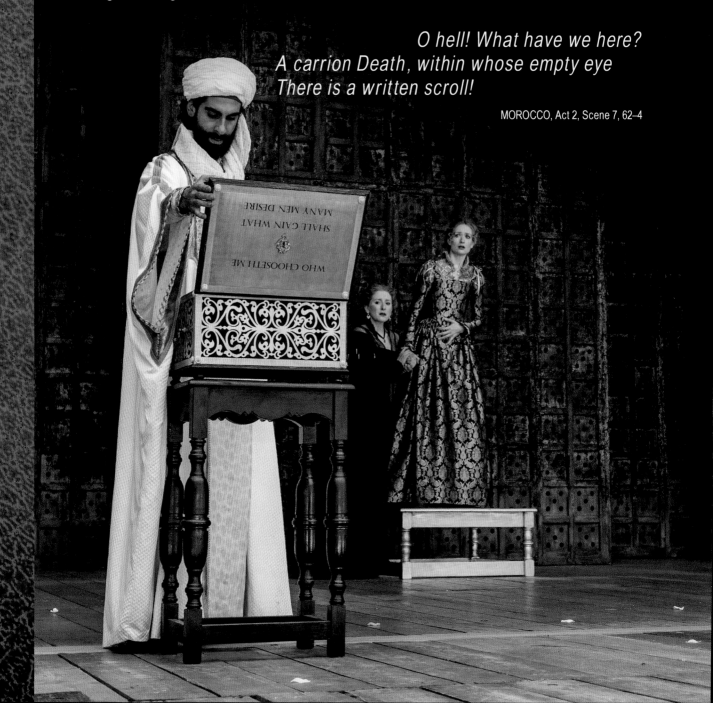

Belmont. A room in Portia's house.

Flourish of cornets. Enter PORTIA, with the PRINCE OF MOROCCO, and both their TRAINS.

PORTIA

Go, draw aside the curtains and discover

The several caskets to this noble prince.

[*to MOROCCO*] Now make your choice.

MOROCCO

The first, of gold, who this inscription bears,

'Who chooseth me, shall gain what many men desire.'   5

The second, silver, which this promise carries,

'Who chooseth me, shall get as much as he deserves.'

This third, dull lead, with warning all as blunt,

'Who chooseth me, must give and hazard all he hath.'

How shall I know if I do choose the right?   10

PORTIA

The one of them contains my picture, prince:

If you choose that, then I am yours withal.

MOROCCO

Some god direct my judgement! Let me see,

I will survey th'inscriptions back again.

What says this leaden casket?   15

'Who chooseth me, must give and hazard all he hath.'

Must give: for what? For lead? Hazard for lead!

This casket threatens. Men that hazard all

Do it in hope of fair advantages:

A golden mind stoops not to shows of dross;   20

I'll then nor give nor hazard aught for lead.

What says the silver with her virgin hue?

'Who chooseth me, shall get as much as he deserves.'

As much as he deserves — pause there, Morocco,

And weigh thy value with an even hand: 25

If thou be'st rated by thy estimation

Thou dost deserve enough, and yet enough

May not extend so far as to the lady:

And yet to be afeard of my deserving

Were but a weak disabling of myself.   30

As much as I deserve — why that's the lady.

I do in birth deserve her, and in fortunes,

---

1 *discover:* reveal

2 *several:* separate

9 *hazard:* risk

10 *the right:* correctly

12 *withal:* at the same time, along with the picture

14 *back again:* in reverse order

19 *fair advantages:* a good gain

20 *A ... dross:* a high, noble mind (like mine) does not occupy itself with mean, shoddy things (like lead)

21 *nor give ... aught:* neither give nor risk anything

22 *virgin hue:* white colour, symbolising innocence

25 *weigh ... hand:* consider your value in a balanced way

26 *If ... estimation:* if you were to judge yourself according to your own opinion

29–30 *And ... myself:* however, to be afraid that I do not deserve Portia shows weakness, and I am not a weak man

33 *graces:* virtue, good qualities	In graces, and in qualities of breeding;
	But more than these, in love I do deserve.
35 *strayed no further:* ignored the other caskets	**35** What if I strayed no further, but chose here?
36 *graved:* engraved	Let's see once more this saying graved in gold:
	'Who chooseth me, shall gain what many men desire.'
	Why that's the lady, all the world desires her.
39 *four ... earth:* north, south, east and west	From the four corners of the earth they come
40 *shrine:* image of a saint	**40** To kiss this shrine, this mortal breathing saint.
41 *Hyrcanian deserts:* wild, remote places south of the Caspian Sea	The Hyrcanian deserts and the vasty wilds
vasty wilds: huge deserts	Of wide Arabia are as throughfares now
42 *throughfares:* highways, main roads	For princes to come view fair Portia.
44–5 *watery ... heaven:* sea, which sends spray ('spets') skywards	The watery kingdom, whose ambitious head
45 *bar:* barrier, obstacle	**45** Spets in the face of heaven, is no bar
46 *spirits:* suitors	To stop the foreign spirits, but they come
47 *As ... brook:* as if crossing a small stream	As o'er a brook to see fair Portia.
	One of these three contains her heavenly picture.
49 *like:* likely	Is't like that lead contains her? 'Twere damnation
49–50 *'Twere ... thought:* such a low ('base') thought would be damnable	**50** To think so base a thought, it were too gross
50–51 *it ... grave:* Morocco imagines that Portia's picture in a casket is like her shrouded body in a grave, and thinks lead would be too crude a metal to house Portia's corpse	To rib her cerecloth in the obscure grave.
	Or shall I think in silver she's immured,
52 *immured:* closed up	Being ten times undervalued to tried gold?
53 *undervalued ... gold:* less valuable than gold	O sinful thought! Never so rich a gem
	55 Was set in worse than gold. They have in England
	A coin that bears the figure of an angel
57 *insculped upon:* engraved on the coin's surface	Stamped in gold, but that's insculped upon:
	But here an angel in a golden bed
59 *Lies all within:* is found inside	Lies all within. Deliver me the key.
60 *thrive ... may:* may I be successful	**60** Here do I choose, and thrive I as I may.
	PORTIA
61 *form lie there:* portrait is inside	There, take it, prince; and if my form lie there,
	Then I am yours.
	He unlocks the golden casket.
	MOROCCO
	O hell! What have we here?
63 *carrion Death:* skull	A carrion Death, within whose empty eye
	There is a written scroll! I'll read the writing:
65 *glisters:* sparkles, gleams	**65** 'All that glisters is not gold;
	Often have you heard that told.
	Many a man his life hath sold
67–8 *Many ... behold:* many men have lost their lives for the sight of gold	But my outside to behold.

Gilded tombs do worms infold.

Had you been as wise as bold,   70

Young in limbs, in judgement old,

Your answer had not been inscrolled:

Fare you well; your suit is cold.'

Cold indeed and labour lost,

Then farewell heat, and welcome frost.   75

Portia, adieu! I have too grieved a heart

To take a tedious leave: thus, losers part.

Exeunt MOROCCO and his TRAIN. Flourish of cornets.

PORTIA

A gentle riddance. Draw the curtains, go.

Let all of his complexion choose me so.

Exeunt.

69 *Gilded … infold:* tombs overlaid with gold still contain worms feeding on the corpses inside

70 *as bold:* as you are brave

72 *Your … inscrolled:* you would not have received this answer

73 *suit is cold:* hopes are dashed

74 *labour lost:* wasted effort

77 *tedious:* painstaking

78 *A gentle riddance:* farewell to a gentleman

79 *Let … so:* I hope all suitors like him will also fail to choose the correct casket

Key points

The first of three casket scenes sees the suitor incorrectly select the gold casket.

- The key words in this scene are inscribed on the caskets. The words are 'desire' (on the gold casket), 'deserves' (silver casket) and 'give and hazard all he hath' (lead casket). These words are spoken by Morocco as he reads the three inscriptions.

- Morocco's choice of the gold casket is determined by his extremely high opinion of Portia's worth. He will not choose the lead casket because it is too basic a metal to contain Portia's portrait. He cannot imagine that a woman as splendid as Portia could be represented by even a silver casket, since silver is much less valuable than gold.

- He concludes that Portia's portrait must be in the gold casket: 'Never so rich a gem was set in worse than gold' (lines 54–5). This line is a **metaphor** in which Morocco compares Portia's portrait (and Portia herself) to a precious jewel, a 'gem'.

- Morocco also has a high opinion of his own worth. He does not believe that 'a golden mind' (line 20) such as his should stoop to choose a lead casket. He feels that he is Portia's equal in terms of birth, upbringing, wealth, talents and love. He dismisses his doubt about whether he is 'enough' (line 27) to deserve Portia as a momentary weakness.

- Morocco previously stressed the importance of not being deceived by appearances (Act 2, Scene 1, line 1). Here he falls into that very trap, and must be reminded that 'all that glisters is not gold' (line 65), i.e. an attractive exterior does not always conceal an attractive interior.

- Morocco arrived at Belmont with great show and ceremony, but leaves sadly, quietly and with great dignity. Once again, Portia is happy to see a potential husband leave.

Useful quotes

> A golden mind stoops not to shows of dross;
> I'll then nor give nor hazard aught for lead.
>
> (Morocco, lines 20–21)

> All that glisters is not gold;
> Often have you heard that told.
> Many a man his life hath sold
> But my outside to behold.
> Gilded tombs do worms infold.
>
> (Morocco, lines 65–9)

> Never so rich a gem
> Was set in worse than gold.
>
> (Morocco, lines 54–5)

> A gentle riddance. Draw the curtains, go.
> Let all of his complexion choose me so.
>
> (Portia, lines 78–9)

? Questions

1 Morocco speaks all but eight of the lines in this scene. Does this suggest anything about him, or about Portia?

2 What kind of husband might Morocco have been for Portia? Which of his qualities might she like or dislike?

3 'Who chooseth me, shall gain what many men desire' (line 5). Does this inscription prove to be true for Morocco?

4 Was it wise for Portia's father to make sure that a suitor who would choose the gold casket should not marry Portia? Give reasons for your answer.

5 Is Portia happy at the end of this scene? Give reasons for your answer.

6 Imagine that Morocco decides to write a letter home about his experience at Belmont. Compose this letter for him.

Talking point

Morocco has a very high opinion of himself. Do you believe it is a good idea to behave like this? Can you think of real people who behave and think as Morocco does? Give an example. Some people have a very low opinion of themselves. What problems can result from this?

Plot summary

Shylock is distressed and angry because Jessica has eloped with Lorenzo. Solanio and Salerio discuss and make fun of Shylock's loss. Then they worry that Antonio may pay for it. Salerio has learned that a Venetian ship with a rich cargo has been lost in the English Channel. Antonio will have to be told gently and tactfully. Antonio is described as a kind man who has been completely unselfish in his friendship with Bassanio. He lives for Bassanio and is distressed by his absence. Solanio and Salerio decide to cheer him up.

Let good Antonio look he keep his day
Or he shall pay for this.

SOLANIO, Act 2, Scene 8, 25–6

Venice. A street.

Enter SALERIO and SOLANIO.

SALERIO

Why, man, I saw Bassanio under sail,
With him is Gratiano gone along;
And in their ship I am sure Lorenzo is not.

SOLANIO

The villain Jew with outcries raised the duke,
5   Who went with him to search Bassanio's ship.

SALERIO

He came too late, the ship was under sail,
But there the duke was given to understand
That in a gondola were seen together
Lorenzo and his amorous Jessica.
10   Besides, Antonio certified the duke
They were not with Bassanio in his ship.

SOLANIO

I never heard a passion so confused,
So strange, outrageous, and so variable
As the dog Jew did utter in the streets:
15   'My daughter! O my ducats! O my daughter!
Fled with a Christian! O my Christian ducats!
Justice, the law, my ducats, and my daughter!
A sealèd bag, two sealèd bags of ducats,
Of double ducats, stol'n from me by my daughter!
20   And jewels, two stones, two rich and precious stones,
Stol'n by my daughter! Justice! Find the girl,
She hath the stones upon her, and the ducats!'

SALERIO

Why all the boys in Venice follow him,
Crying his stones, his daughter and his ducats.

SOLANIO

25   Let good Antonio look he keep his day
Or he shall pay for this.

SALERIO

                Marry, well remembered.
I reasoned with a Frenchman yesterday,

1 *under sail:* sail away

4 *The . . . duke:* Shylock has called on the Duke of Venice (the chief legal officer of the city) to report his losses

8 *gondola:* long, narrow boat

9 *amorous:* loving

10 *certified:* assured, guaranteed to

12 *passion:* display of emotion

13 *so variable:* expressing various kinds of anger

24 *Crying:* as he cries about

25 *look . . . day:* make sure he pays his bond on time

27 *reasoned:* spoke

Who told me in the narrow seas that part

The French and English there miscarrièd

A vessel of our country richly fraught.   30

I thought upon Antonio when he told me,

And wished in silence that it were not his.

SOLANIO

You were best to tell Antonio what you hear;

Yet do not suddenly, for it may grieve him.

SALERIO

A kinder gentleman treads not the earth.   35

I saw Bassanio and Antonio part,

Bassanio told him he would make some speed

Of his return. He answered, 'Do not so,

Slubber not business for my sake, Bassanio,

But stay the very riping of the time;   40

And for the Jew's bond which he hath of me,

Let it not enter in your mind of love:

Be merry, and employ your chiefest thoughts

To courtship and such fair ostents of love

As shall conveniently become you there.'   45

And even there, his eye being big with tears,

Turning his face, he put his hand behind him

And, with affection wondrous sensible,

He wrung Bassanio's hand, and so they parted.

SOLANIO

I think he only loves the world for him.   50

I pray thee let us go and find him out,

And quicken his embracèd heaviness

With some delight or other.

SALERIO

                Do we so.

Exeunt.

28–9 *narrow . . . English:* English Channel

29 *miscarrièd:* perished

30 *richly fraught:* laden with valuable cargo

34 *do . . . him:* be sure to break it to him gently because it may distress him

37–8 *make . . . return:* hurry back (to Venice)

39 *Slubber not:* do not be too careless with

40 *stay . . . time:* wait for the best time to bring your business to its conclusion

41–2 *And . . . love:* do not let thoughts of the bond with Shylock remove thoughts of love from your mind

43 *chiefest:* main, foremost

44 *ostents:* expressions

45 *As . . . there:* as will do you credit while you are there

48 *affection wondrous sensible:* amazingly strong emotion

49 *wrung:* shook

50 *he . . . him:* Antonio's life is centred on Bassanio

51 *find him out:* search for him

52–3 *quicken . . . other:* rid him of the sadness he makes himself feel by cheering him up

Key points

We learn, through second-hand reports, about Shylock's response to his loss of Jessica and some of his wealth, and hear that Antonio may also have suffered a loss of fortune.

- Shylock's enemies are given another opportunity to demonise him. Annoyed that Shylock has reported the theft of his property to the duke, they call him 'the villain Jew' (line 4), as if he should have put up with the outrage without complaint.

- Solanio finds Shylock's response to his enormous losses amusing, as well as 'strange' and 'outrageous' (line 13). His report on Shylock's angry behaviour in the streets of Venice portrays Shylock as a figure of fun for the local boys to laugh at. He gossips with Salerio about Shylock's distress.

- This scene provides the first indication that all may not be well with Antonio's ships at sea. Unlike their response to Shylock, Salerio and Solanio react with sympathy and concern to the news of Antonio's potential loss.

- There is also a suggestion that Antonio is in real danger as Shylock, having been betrayed by Jessica and Lorenzo, will now be more likely to take his pound of flesh if Antonio fails to repay the loan on time.

- His friends take pains to present Antonio in a most flattering light: 'A kinder gentleman treads not the earth' (line 35). This description is clearly not accurate, as Antonio has already admitted to abusing Shylock (Act 1, Scene 3, lines 124–5).

- Salerio's account of the parting of Antonio and Bassanio is designed to win the sympathy of the audience for both men. Antonio's unselfishness, his love for Bassanio and his sentimental farewell to him – 'his eye being big with tears' (line 46) – make Antonio seem almost saintly (whereas Shylock has been presented as a devil).

Useful quotes

> *I never heard a passion so confused,*
> *So strange, outrageous, and so variable*
> *As the dog Jew did utter in the streets*
>
> (Solanio, lines 12–14)

> *Let good Antonio look he keep his day*
> *Or he shall pay for this.*
>
> (Solanio, lines 25–6)

> *I reasoned with a Frenchman yesterday,*
> *Who told me in the narrow seas that part*
> *The French and English there miscarrièd*
> *A vessel of our country richly fraught.*
> *I thought upon Antonio when he told me,*
> *And wished in silence that it were not his.*
>
> (Salerio, lines 27–32)

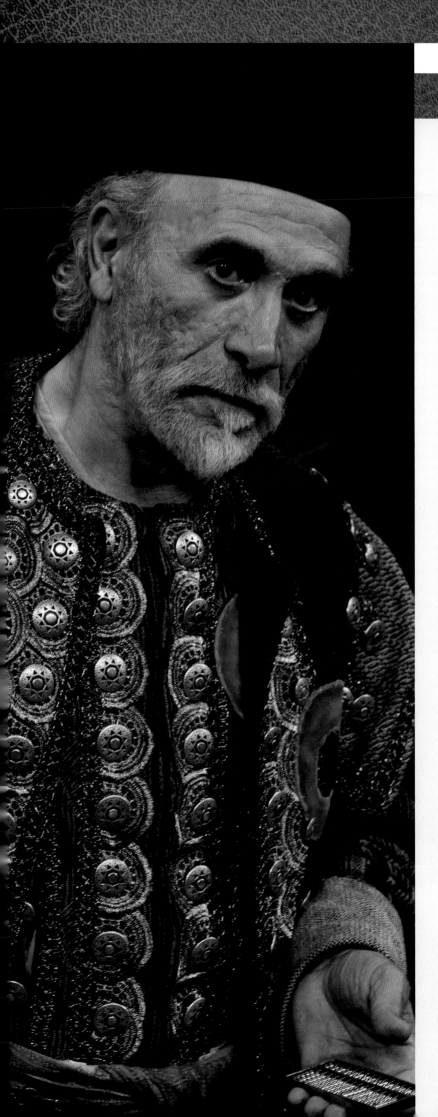

Questions ?

1 According to Solanio and Salerio, how has Shylock reacted to Jessica's elopement?

2 What prompted the Duke of Venice to go to search Bassanio's ship?

3 Solanio and Salerio are amused by Shylock's sufferings and losses. What does this tell us about these characters?

4 Do you think their behaviour might influence the audience to feel sympathy for Shylock? Give reasons for your answer.

5 Solanio refers to Shylock as 'the dog Jew' (line 14). What impact might such language have on the audience?

6 What new threats to Antonio's fortunes, and even to his life, emerge in this scene?

7 Describe Antonio's attitude to Bassanio as revealed in the account of their parting given in this scene.

8 Try to imagine what it might be like to be Shylock at this point in the play, and write about your feelings.

Talking point

Salerio and Solanio are delighted that Shylock is suffering, having lost his daughter and his valuables. Can you think of any modern examples of people rejoicing in the miseries of others, or in their downfall? Why, in your opinion, would people do this? Does it make them feel better?

ACT 2 ✝ Scene 9

Plot summary

The testing of Portia's suitors continues. The Prince of Arragon has taken the oath to abide by the rules of the lottery if he fails to choose the correct casket: he will not reveal which casket he chose, he will remain unmarried for life and he will leave immediately. He inspects the caskets, rejecting the lead one for being too common and the gold one for being too flashy. He opens the silver casket because he believes that he deserves to marry Portia. Inside he finds a picture of a fool and a scroll that tells him he is also a fool. He leaves as agreed.

Nerissa is confident that the right man for Portia will come along and choose the correct casket. We immediately get news that a handsome young suitor from Venice is on his way. Portia looks forward to his arrival and Nerissa hopes it will be Bassanio.

Did I deserve no more than a fool's head?
Is that my prize? Are my deserts no better?

ARRAGON, Act 2, Scene 9, 58–9

Belmont. A room in Portia's house.

Enter NERISSA and a SERVITOR.

Servitor: servant

NERISSA

Quick, quick, I pray thee draw the curtain straight:

The Prince of Arragon hath ta'en his oath,

And comes to his election presently.

Flourish of cornets. Enter the PRINCE OF ARRAGON, his TRAIN, and PORTIA.

PORTIA

Behold, there stand the caskets, noble prince.

If you choose that wherein I am contained,   5

Straight shall our nuptial rites be solemnized:

But if you fail, without more speech, my lord,

You must be gone from hence immediately.

ARRAGON

I am enjoined by oath to observe three things:

First, never to unfold to anyone   10

Which casket 'twas I chose; next, if I fail

Of the right casket, never in my life

To woo a maid in way of marriage;

Lastly, if I do fail in fortune of my choice,

Immediately to leave you, and be gone.   15

PORTIA

To these injunctions everyone doth swear

That comes to hazard for my worthless self.

ARRAGON

And so have I addressed me. Fortune now

To my heart's hope! Gold, silver and base lead.

'Who chooseth me, must give and hazard all he hath.'   20

You shall look fairer ere I give or hazard.

What says the golden chest? Ha, let me see!

'Who chooseth me, shall gain what many men desire.'

What many men desire — that 'many' may be meant

By the fool multitude that choose by show,   25

Not learning more than the fond eye doth teach,

Which pries not to th'interior but, like the martlet,

Builds in the weather on the outward wall,

Even in the force and road of casualty.

---

1 *draw ... straight:* pull back the curtain now

2 *Arragon:* a kingdom in Spain

3 *comes ... presently:* is to make his choice immediately

4 *Behold:* look, observe

6 *Straight ... solemnized:* our wedding will be celebrated immediately

8 *hence:* here

9 *enjoined:* obliged

10 *unfold to:* tell

11–12 *fail of:* fail to choose

14 *fail ... choice:* make an unlucky selection

16 *injunctions:* conditions

17 *hazard:* risk playing the lottery

18 *so ... me:* I have sworn as everyone else has

18–19 *Fortune ... hope:* may fortune help me to achieve my heart's desire

19 *base:* lowly, worthless

21 *You ... hazard:* the casket would need to be made of something more beautiful than lead before I would give and risk everything for it

24 *that ... meant:* the word 'many' may be taken to mean

25 *fool ... show:* stupid majority of the people who judge by appearances

26 *fond:* foolish

27–9 *pries ... casualty:* does not probe beneath the surface, but, like the house-martin ('martlet'), relies on the outer, exposed wall (to build its nest), which is open to damage

31 *jump ... spirits:* join with ordinary people

32 *rank ... multitudes:* include myself among the crowds of ignorant people

36–8 *who ... merit:* it would be wrong to try to cheat ('cozen') one's fate by seeking honours one does not deserve

40–42 *O ... wearer:* it would be wonderful if property, status and jobs were not given out in dishonest ways, and if rank were decided on merit

43 *should cover:* would put on hats. People in Shakespeare's day removed their hats in the presence of their superiors
bare: bare-headed

44 *be ... command:* who give orders would have to take them

45–8 *How much ... new-varnished:* how many low-born people would be removed from the ranks of the nobility, and how much more splendid the nobility would appear when inferior members were removed

50 *desert:* that I deserve to win

53 *blinking idiot:* fool with a winking eye

54 *schedule:* scroll

60 *To ... offices:* if you have committed a fault, you cannot expect to judge it fairly

30   I will not choose what many men desire,

Because I will not jump with common spirits

And rank me with the barbarous multitudes.

Why then to thee, thou silver treasure-house,

Tell me once more what title thou dost bear.

35   'Who chooseth me, shall get as much as he deserves.'

And well said too; for who shall go about

To cozen fortune and be honourable

Without the stamp of merit? Let none presume

To wear an undeservèd dignity.

40   O that estates, degrees and offices

Were not derived corruptly, and that clear honour

Were purchased by the merit of the wearer!

How many then should cover that stand bare!

How many be commanded that command!

45   How much low peasantry would then be gleaned

From the true seed of honour, and how much honour,

Picked from the chaff and ruin of the times,

To be new-varnished! Well, but to my choice.

'Who chooseth me, shall get as much as he deserves.'

50   I will assume desert. Give me a key for this,

And instantly unlock my fortunes here.

He opens the silver casket.

PORTIA

Too long a pause for that which you find there.

ARRAGON

What's here? The portrait of a blinking idiot

Presenting me a schedule! I will read it.

55   How much unlike art thou to Portia!

How much unlike my hopes and my deservings!

'Who chooseth me, shall have as much as he deserves.'

Did I deserve no more than a fool's head?

Is that my prize? Are my deserts no better?

PORTIA

60   To offend and judge are distinct offices,

And of opposèd natures.

ARRAGON

                  What is here?

'The fire seven times tried this:

Seven times tried that judgement is

That did never choose amiss.

Some there be that shadows kiss;   65

Such have but a shadow's bliss.

There be fools alive, Iwis,

Silvered o'er, and so was this.

Take what wife you will to bed,

I will ever be your head.   70

  So be gone, you are sped.'

Still more fool I shall appear

By the time I linger here.

With one fool's head I came to woo,

But I go away with two.   75

Sweet, adieu! I'll keep my oath,

Patiently to bear my wroth.

Exeunt ARRAGON and his TRAIN.

62–4 *The ... amiss:* to make silver pure it has to be treated seven times in fire. Perfect judgement is as rare and precious as silver

65–6 *Some ... bliss:* some people prefer illusions to real life, and these have only the appearance of happiness, not the reality

67–8 *There ... o'er:* a rich exterior can cover a stupid person

69–70 *Take ... head:* whatever woman you choose, you will always be a fool

71 *you are sped:* that's your fate; you are done for

77 *Patiently ... wroth:* to put up with my anger as patiently as I can

With one fool's head I came to woo,
But I go away with two.

ARRAGON, Act 2, Scene 9, 74–5

PORTIA

Thus, hath the candle singed the moth.

O these deliberate fools! When they do choose,

80 They have the wisdom by their wit to lose.

NERISSA

The ancient saying is no heresy:

Hanging and wiving goes by destiny.

PORTIA

Come, draw the curtain, Nerissa.

Enter MESSENGER.

MESSENGER

Where is my lady?

PORTIA

                                    Here, what would my lord?

MESSENGER

85 Madam, there is alighted at your gate

A young Venetian, one that comes before

To signify th'approaching of his lord,

From whom he bringeth sensible regreets;

To wit, besides commends and courteous breath,

90 Gifts of rich value. Yet I have not seen

So likely an ambassador of love.

A day in April never came so sweet

To show how costly summer was at hand

As this fore-spurrer comes before his lord.

PORTIA

95 No more I pray thee, I am half afeard

Thou wilt say anon he is some kin to thee,

Thou spend'st such high-day wit in praising him.

Come, come, Nerissa, for I long to see

Quick Cupid's post that comes so mannerly.

NERISSA

100 Bassanio, Lord Love, if thy will it be!

Exeunt.

79–80 *O . . . lose:* these fools who take a long time to make up their minds make bad choices

81–2 *The . . . destiny:* the old proverb that fate picks out those who will be hanged and those who will be married is true

84 *what would:* how can I help you

85 *alighted:* descended, dismounted

86–7 *before . . . lord:* ahead to advise of the arrival of his master

88 *sensible regreets:* sincere greetings

89–90 *To . . . value:* namely, compliments, gracious words and valuable gifts

90 *Yet:* as yet

91 *likely:* promising

93 *costly:* generous, abundant
at hand: approaching

94 *fore-spurrer:* forerunner, herald

95–6 *half . . . thee:* almost afraid you are about to say that he is your relative ('kin')

97 *Thou . . . him:* you are in such holiday spirits as you praise him

99 *Quick . . . mannerly:* the lively messenger of love that comes so courteously

100 *Bassanio . . . be:* Cupid, please let it be Bassanio

Key points

The second of three casket scenes sees the suitor incorrectly select the silver casket.

- Nerissa wants Arragon to make a quick choice. Perhaps she knows he will choose the wrong casket and wants him to do so and leave Belmont without delay.

- Like Morocco, Arragon makes a long speech as he examines the caskets, but this is all the two suitors have in common. While Morocco appeared noble and dignified, it seems clear that Arragon is to be regarded as a fool who is unduly proud of his birth and high rank, and who despises those below him in status. He is condescending, overly confident and, as his name hints at, arrogant.

- Arragon's choice of the silver casket is determined by his foolish belief that he is superior to others. He wants to 'get as much as he deserves' (line 35) because he believes that he deserves the very best. His reward for opening the wrong casket is humiliating: a 'portrait of a blinking idiot' (line 53) and a scroll telling him that he is a fool.

- The news of the arrival of an eligible suitor from Venice raises expectations that Bassanio is in Belmont. Portia makes her feelings clear to Nerissa. She sees his envoy as a messenger of love, 'Cupid's post' (line 99), outshining the other suitors in courtesy.

Useful quotes

> *I will not choose what many men desire,*
> *Because I will not jump with common spirits*
> *And rank me with the barbarous multitudes.*
>
> (Arragon, lines 30–32)

> *Come, come, Nerissa, for I long to see*
> *Quick Cupid's post that comes so mannerly.*
>
> (Portia, lines 98–9)

? Questions

1 What kind of husband might Arragon have been for Portia? Which of his qualities might she like or dislike?

2 What reasons does Arragon give for rejecting the lead and the gold caskets?

3 'Who chooseth me, shall get as much as he deserves' (line 35). Does this inscription prove to be true for Arragon?

4 Was it wise for Portia's father to make sure that a suitor who would choose the silver casket should not marry Portia? Give reasons for your answer.

5 Is Portia happy that Arragon chose the wrong casket? Give reasons for your answer.

6 What do lines 85–94 imply about how Bassanio has been spending the money he borrowed?

7 You are the social columnist for a Belmont newspaper. Your editor has asked you to write a special report on the recent attempts to win Portia in marriage. Compose a suitably catchy headline for your report.

8 You are the designer for a film version of *The Merchant of Venice*. Write a description and/or prepare a sketch of your design for each of the three caskets.

Talking point

Arragon is arrogant, thinking himself superior to 'the fool multitude' (line 25) or the common people. Is it okay to think you are better than everyone else? Have you ever come across someone who behaves like this? Do you think any person can afford to despise an entire class of people as Arragon does?

ACT 2 ⚔ Key moments

Scene 1
- The Prince of Morocco agrees to try his luck with the three caskets. He tells Portia that she should not dislike him for his colour.

Scene 2
- Launcelot Gobbo decides to leave Shylock's service. He also plays tricks on his half-blind father.
- Bassanio agrees to hire Launcelot as his servant. He also agrees to bring Gratiano with him to Belmont, but warns Gratiano to be on his best behaviour.

Scene 3
- Jessica, Shylock's daughter, is unhappy and plans to become a Christian and elope with Lorenzo. She asks Launcelot to deliver a letter to Lorenzo.

Scene 4
- Lorenzo tells Gratiano that Jessica has directed him to take her from her father's house. She will bring some of Shylock's gold and jewels, and be dressed as a page.

Scene 5
- Shylock accepts Bassanio's invitation to dinner. He instructs Jessica to lock the doors and stay away from the windows.

Scene 6
- Lorenzo and Jessica elope.

Scene 7
- The Prince of Morocco chooses the gold casket, which is incorrect.

Scene 8
- Solanio and Salerio joke about Shylock's distress following Jessica's betrayal, but express concern about the possibility that one of Antonio's ships may have been lost.

Scene 9
- The Prince of Arragon chooses the silver casket, which is incorrect.

ACT 2 ⚔ Speaking and listening

1 Select a student to play the part of Portia. Members of the class should interview Portia about her attitude to the test her father has devised involving the three caskets, her views on the various suitors who have come to Belmont to seek her hand in marriage, and whether or not she is nervous about the outcome of the lottery process.

2 Divide the class into pairs. One member of each pair should look back over the speeches of Jessica in this Act, and another should look back over Lorenzo's speeches. Each person should select and recite one speech that reflects the nature of his or her chosen character. Discuss the qualities that each speech reveals.

Q Revision quiz: plot summary

Use the words listed in the panel to fill in the blanks in this summary of Act 2:

Antonio
Arragon
Bassanio
casket
Christian
colour
daughter
fool
Gobbo
gold
Jessica
jewels
letter
lottery
masque
Morocco
page
Salerio
ships
silver
skull
torch
unmarried
Venice
weather

The key events of Act 2 are two casket scenes and the elopement of Jessica and Lorenzo.

Under the terms of the casket _____, the suitor must swear that if he chooses the wrong _____, he will not reveal which casket he chose, he will remain _____ and he will leave immediately.

The first to attempt to choose the correct casket is the Prince of _____. He argues that his skin _____ is not a valid reason for anyone to dislike him. He chooses the _____ casket, thinking that Portia's portrait must be in the most beautiful casket. Inside he finds a _____ and a scroll telling him he has made the wrong choice. He accepts his failure without complaint.

The second suitor to try the lottery is the Prince of _____. He selects the _____ casket because he believes that he deserves to marry Portia. Inside he finds a picture of a _____ and a scroll that tells him he is also a fool. He leaves immediately.

At the end of the Act, Portia is excited to hear that a promising suitor from _____ is on his way.

Launcelot _____ wants to leave Shylock's service because he finds him mean and unpleasant. It is agreed that he will work for _____ instead. Shylock's only child, _____, is also unhappy in Shylock's home and has decided to become a _____ and to elope with Lorenzo. She asks Launcelot to deliver a _____ to Lorenzo.

Bassanio's farewell party will provide an opportunity for Jessica to run away. Shylock is invited to dine with Bassanio so that he will be out of the house. Jessica will wear the clothes of a _____ and carry Lorenzo's _____ as he and his friends proceed to the masque. The elopement goes ahead and Jessica takes as much of Shylock's gold and _____ as she can carry with her. However, due to a change in the _____, Bassanio's ship must leave immediately and the _____ is cancelled.

Solanio and _____ gossip about, and mock, Shylock's distress and anger at the loss of his _____ and his valuables. They worry that _____ may suffer for it as there is news that one of his _____ may have been lost and he may not be able to repay the money borrowed from Shylock.

The loss of one of Antonio's ships is confirmed. Salerio and Solanio mock Shylock cruelly on his loss of Jessica, and then ask if he has heard about Antonio's misfortune. Shylock states that if Antonio fails to honour his bond, he will have his revenge by taking a pound of Antonio's flesh. Shylock's friend Tubal arrives. He has been searching for Jessica, but although he heard about her being in different places he did not find her. Shylock has suffered huge financial losses at the hands of his daughter, in terms of what she stole from him and the cost of the search to find her. Tubal tries to console Shylock with the news that Antonio has lost another ship and is likely to go bankrupt. This tactic works until Shylock hears that Jessica is being wasteful with his money and has bought a monkey using a ring that was of sentimental value to him. He wants revenge on his Christian enemies and will have Antonio arrested as soon as he defaults on the loan.

The villainy you teach me I will execute, and it shall go hard but I will better the instruction.

SHYLOCK, Act 3, Scene 1, 59–60

Venice. A street.

Enter SOLANIO and SALERIO.

SOLANIO

Now, what news on the Rialto?

SALERIO

Why yet it lives there unchecked that Antonio hath a ship of rich lading wracked on the narrow seas — the Goodwins, I think they call the place — a very dangerous flat, and fatal, where the carcases of many a tall ship lie buried, as they say, if my gossip Report be an honest woman of her word.

SOLANIO

I would she were as lying a gossip in that, as ever knapped ginger, or made her neighbours believe she wept for the death of a third husband. But it is true, without any slips of prolixity or crossing the plain highway of talk, that the good Antonio, the honest Antonio — O that I had a title good enough to keep his name company—

SALERIO

Come, the full stop.

SOLANIO

Ha! What sayest thou? Why, the end is he hath lost a ship.

SALERIO

I would it might prove the end of his losses.

SOLANIO

Let me say 'amen' betimes, lest the devil cross my prayer — for here he comes in the likeness of a Jew.

Enter SHYLOCK.

How now, Shylock! What news among the merchants?

SHYLOCK

You knew, none so well, none so well as you, of my daughter's flight.

SALERIO

That's certain: I, for my part, knew the tailor that made the wings she flew withal.

SOLANIO

And Shylock, for his own part, knew the bird was fledged, and then it is the complexion of them all to leave the dam.

Line numbers: 5, 10, 15, 20, 25

Glossary (left margin):

2–3 *yet ... seas:* no one denies the report that one of Antonio's ships, laden with rich cargo, is wrecked in the English Channel

5 *flat:* sandbank

6–7 *my ... word:* the rumours (described as a gossiping woman called 'Report') reaching me are correct

8–10 *I ... husband:* I wish the rumour to be false, like a woman who nibbled ginger to hide the smell of drink, or a woman who pretended to weep over the death of her third husband

10–11 *without ... talk:* to come to the point

12–13 *O ... company:* no words of mine can describe Antonio's excellence

14 *the full stop:* finish your sentence

15 *end:* point

17–18 *Let ... Jew:* I'll say 'amen' to that prayer immediately, in case the devil should interfere with it – and speaking of the devil, here he comes disguised as a Jew

21 *flight:* he means that she has run away from home

23 *withal:* with

24 *fledged:* feathered and ready for flight

25 *the complexion ... dam:* in the nature of fledglings to leave their mother ('dam')

SHYLOCK

She is damned for it.

SALERIO

That's certain, if the devil may be her judge.

SHYLOCK

My own flesh and blood to rebel!

SOLANIO

Out upon it, old carrion, rebels it at these years?

SHYLOCK

I say my daughter is my flesh and blood.   30

SALERIO

There is more difference between thy flesh and hers than
between jet and ivory; more between your bloods than
there is between red wine and Rhenish. But tell us, do you
hear whether Antonio have had any loss at sea or no?

SHYLOCK

There I have another bad match, a bankrupt, a prodigal,   35
who dare scarce show his head on the Rialto, a beggar
that was used to come so smug upon the mart; let him
look to his bond! He was wont to call me usurer; let
him look to his bond! He was wont to lend money for a
Christian courtesy; let him look to his bond!   40

SALERIO

Why I am sure, if he forfeit, thou wilt not take his flesh —
what's that good for?

SHYLOCK

To bait fish withal — if it will feed nothing else, it will feed
my revenge. He hath disgraced me, and hindered me
half a million, laughed at my losses, mocked at my gains,   45
scorned my nation, thwarted my bargains, cooled my
friends, heated mine enemies. And what's his reason? I am
a Jew. Hath not a Jew eyes? Hath not a Jew hands, organs,
dimensions, senses, affections, passions? Fed with the
same food, hurt with the same weapons, subject to the   50
same diseases, healed by the same means, warmed and
cooled by the same winter and summer as a Christian is?
If you prick us, do we not bleed? If you tickle us, do we not
laugh? If you poison us, do we not die? And if you wrong

29   *Out … years?* Shame on you, you rotten old
     fellow; are you having lustful desires at your age?
     Solanio pretends to believe that Shylock has been
     talking about his own rebellious flesh

32   *jet and ivory:* black and white

33   *Rhenish:* white wine

35   *match:* bargain
     prodigal: spendthrift, waster

37   *smug:* aware of his own cleverness
     mart: stock exchange

38   *look to:* beware of
     was wont: liked
     usurer: a person who lends money at extortionate
     rates of interest

39–40   *for … courtesy:* out of charity (i.e. free of interest)

43   *bait fish withal:* use as bait for fishing

44   *hindered me:* prevented me from making

46   *nation:* Jewishness
     thwarted my bargains: prevented me from doing
     deals

46–7   *cooled … enemies:* made my friends distant and
     my enemies more fired up

49   *dimensions:* bodily parts
     affections: feelings

56–7 *If … humility?* If a Jew harms a Christian, how does the humble Christian respond?

58 *sufferance:* hardship

59–60 *The … instruction:* Christians have taught Jews to take revenge when they are wronged and so I will take revenge, and even improve on the kind of revenge I have been taught

63 *up and down:* everywhere

64–5 *a third … Jew:* it would be impossible to find anyone as bad as these two Jews, unless the devil becomes a Jew

73 *would:* wish

74 *hearsed:* in her coffin

78–9 *no ill … shoulders:* nobody has bad luck except me
79–80 *no sighs … shedding:* nobody sighs or weeps but me

55 us, shall we not revenge? If we are like you in the rest, we will resemble you in that. If a Jew wrong a Christian, what is his humility? Revenge. If a Christian wrong a Jew, what should his sufferance be by Christian example? Why, revenge. The villainy you teach me I will execute, and it

60 shall go hard but I will better the instruction.

Enter SERVINGMAN.

SERVINGMAN

Gentlemen, my master Antonio is at his house and desires to speak with you both.

SALERIO

We have been up and down to seek him.

Enter TUBAL.

SOLANIO

Here comes another of the tribe — a third cannot be

65 matched, unless the devil himself turn Jew.

Exeunt SOLANIO, SALERIO and SERVINGMAN.

SHYLOCK

How now, Tubal! What news from Genoa? Hast thou found my daughter?

TUBAL

I often came where I did hear of her, but cannot find her.

SHYLOCK

Why there, there, there, there! A diamond gone cost me

70 two thousand ducats in Frankfort — the curse never fell upon our nation till now; I never felt it till now: two thousand ducats in that, and other precious, precious jewels. I would my daughter were dead at my foot, and the jewels in her ear. Would she were hearsed at my foot,

75 and the ducats in her coffin. No news of them? Why so — and I know not what's spent in the search. Why thou — loss upon loss: the thief gone with so much, and so much to find the thief, and no satisfaction, no revenge, nor no ill luck stirring but what lights o' my shoulders; no sighs but

80 o' my breathing; no tears but o' my shedding.

TUBAL

Yes, other men have ill luck too — Antonio, as I heard in Genoa—

SHYLOCK

What, what, what? Ill luck, ill luck?

TUBAL

— hath an argosy cast away, coming from Tripolis.

84   *an argosy cast away:* a big ship wrecked

SHYLOCK

I thank God, I thank God! Is it true, is it true?

85

TUBAL

I spoke with some of the sailors that escaped the wrack.

86   *wrack:* shipwreck

SHYLOCK

I thank thee, good Tubal: good news, good news! Ha, ha! Heard in Genoa!

TUBAL

Your daughter spent in Genoa, as I heard, one night fourscore ducats.

90

90   *fourscore:* eighty

SHYLOCK

Thou stick'st a dagger in me — I shall never see my gold again — fourscore ducats at a sitting, fourscore ducats!

92   *at a sitting:* in one go

TUBAL

There came divers of Antonio's creditors in my company to Venice that swear he cannot choose but break.

93   *divers … creditors:* a number of people to whom Antonio owes money
94   *break:* become a bankrupt

SHYLOCK

I am very glad of it — I'll plague him, I'll torture him — I am glad of it.

95

TUBAL

One of them showed me a ring that he had of your daughter for a monkey.

SHYLOCK

Out upon her! Thou torturest me, Tubal — it was my turquoise, I had it of Leah when I was a bachelor. I would not have given it for a wilderness of monkeys.

100

99   *Out upon her:* damn her, a curse on her
100 *turquoise:* a ring containing a rare and valuable blue-green mineral
       Leah: Shylock's late wife

102 *undone:* ruined, destroyed

103–4 *fee … officer:* pay for an officer of the law to arrest Antonio

104 *bespeak him:* book him, engage his services

105 *him:* Antonio

105–6 *for … will:* because if Antonio were not in Venice as my rival I could make all the profit I liked

TUBAL

But Antonio is certainly undone.

SHYLOCK

Nay, that's true, that's very true. Go, Tubal, fee me an officer; bespeak him a fortnight before. I will have the 105 heart of him if he forfeit, for, were he out of Venice, I can make what merchandise I will. Go, Tubal, and meet me at our synagogue — go, good Tubal — at our synagogue, Tubal.

Exeunt.

Key points

The mutual hatred between the Christians and Shylock increases, leading Shylock to seek revenge for his recent losses by punishing Antonio.

- Both Shylock and Antonio have suffered serious reversals in their fortunes. Shylock has lost his daughter to Lorenzo and his wealth has been greatly reduced. Antonio has lost two ships at sea and appears to be close to bankruptcy.

- Shylock has good reason to be angry: Jessica has made off with a diamond that cost him 2,000 ducats, is now spending his money freely and has exchanged a precious ring given to him by his late wife for a monkey.

- Shylock is angry enough to avenge himself on Antonio, who now seems to be at his mercy. He tells Antonio's friends, who are heaping insults on him, that if Antonio cannot pay back the money owed to him, he is prepared to demand his pound of flesh, which will 'feed' his revenge (lines 43–4).

- In order to speed up his revenge, Shylock later asks Tubal to pay an officer of the law to arrest Antonio as soon as the deadline passes for the repayment of the 3,000 ducats. Shylock is also aware of the advantages that getting rid of Antonio would have for his moneylending business.

- Shylock is given one of the most impressive speeches in the play at lines 43–60. The speech gives the actor playing Shylock an ideal opportunity to win sympathy for the character as the victim of hatred and prejudice, contempt and abuse. It is divided into three parts.

- In the first part of the speech (lines 43–8), Shylock explains why he wants to take revenge on Antonio, listing a number of abuses he has suffered at the hands of Antonio.

- In the second part (lines 48–55), he defends the right of Jews to be considered equal to Christians as members of the human race. This argument reminds us of Morocco's comments in Act 2, Scene 1.

- In the third part (lines 55–60), he puts forward a clever argument: Christianity teaches Christians to forgive wrongs done to them, but yet if Jews offend Christians, they take revenge. Shylock will follow the example given by Christians and also take revenge. Indeed he will better their example by making his revenge more terrible than that which Christians have inflicted on him.

- When Shylock tells Antonio's friends that 'The villainy you teach me I will execute' (line 59), he is suggesting that as the Christians have demonised him, he will behave towards them, in particular towards Antonio, as if he is really the devil they think he is.

Questions ?

1 Comment on the attitude of Salerio and Solanio to Shylock's loss of his daughter.

2 How does what they say affect your view of Shylock?

3 What does Shylock think about his Christian neighbours? See his speeches at lines 35–40 and 43–60.

4 How do these speeches influence your opinion of Shylock?

5 At what point does Shylock decide on his revenge?

6 Shylock defends his decision to take vengeance on Antonio. What is his defence?

7 Do you find Shylock's argument convincing?

8 Do you think Shylock sees any connection between Antonio and the conduct of Jessica and Lorenzo? Explain your answer.

9 One detail of Tubal's account of Jessica's behaviour is particularly offensive to Shylock. Mention this detail. Is he right to be offended? How does this detail influence your view of Jessica?

10 Shylock is searching for Jessica. What, do you think, are his reasons?

Useful quotes

I am a Jew. Hath not a Jew eyes? Hath not a Jew hands, organs, dimensions, senses, affections, passions? Fed with the same food, hurt with the same weapons, subject to the same diseases, healed by the same means, warmed and cooled by the same winter and summer as a Christian is?

(Shylock, lines 47–52)

Here comes another of the tribe — a third cannot be matched, unless the devil himself turn Jew.

(Solanio, lines 64–5)

Out upon her! Thou torturest me, Tubal — it was my turquoise, I had it of Leah when I was a bachelor. I would not have given it for a wilderness of monkeys.

(Shylock, lines 99–101)

I will have the heart of him if he forfeit, for, were he out of Venice, I can make what merchandise I will.

(Shylock, lines 104–6)

Talking point

Shylock wants to have revenge on his enemies. Desire for revenge is a strong human emotion, but is acting on that instinct ever justified? Who gains from revenge? Does it solve any problems? Is it self-destructive? Does an eye for an eye just end up making the whole world blind?

ACT 3 ✝ Scene 2

Plot summary

Portia attempts to delay Bassanio from taking part in the casket lottery. She loves him and is afraid that he may choose the wrong casket. He insists on going ahead. Portia arranges for music to be played while he makes his choice. Bassanio rejects the gold and silver caskets because he does not want to be influenced by outward appearance. He opens the lead casket and finds the portrait of Portia and a scroll telling him that he has won the right to marry her. Portia gives Bassanio a ring and declares that he is now her master and the master of all she has. If he parts with this ring it will mean that his love for her is at an end. He promises to guard it with his life. Gratiano announces that he and Nerissa also wish to marry.

Lorenzo, Jessica and Salerio arrive. Salerio has a letter from Antonio revealing that all his ships have been lost at sea. Antonio, who expects to lose his life to Shylock, wants to see Bassanio before he dies. With Portia's support, Bassanio decides to marry immediately and return to Venice to pay off the debt.

> *Let me choose,*
> *For as I am, I live upon the rack.*

BASSANIO, Act 3, Scene 2, 24–5

Belmont. A room in Portia's house.

Enter BASSANIO, PORTIA, GRATIANO, NERISSA, and all their TRAINS.

PORTIA

I pray you tarry, pause a day or two		1 *tarry:* delay
Before you hazard, for in choosing wrong		2 *hazard:* gamble (on the casket lottery)
I lose your company; therefore forbear a while.		3 *forbear:* be patient
There's something tells me — but it is not love —		
I would not lose you; and you know yourself,	5	5 *would not:* do not want to
Hate counsels not in such a quality.		6 *Hate ... quality:* such a statement cannot be influenced by feelings of dislike
But lest you should not understand me well —		7 *lest:* in case
And yet a maiden hath no tongue but thought —		8 *maiden ... thought:* girl must say what she thinks
I would detain you here some month or two		
Before you venture for me. I could teach you	10	10 *venture:* try to win the lottery
How to choose right, but I am then forsworn,		11–12 *forsworn ... be:* breaking my promise to my father, which I will never do
So will I never be — so may you miss me —		12 *miss:* fail to win
But if you do, you'll make me wish a sin,		13 *a sin:* I'd done something wrong
That I had been forsworn. Beshrew your eyes,		14 *been forsworn:* broken my word
They have o'erlooked me and divided me;	15	14–15 *Beshrew ... divided me:* shame on you for looking so attractive and causing such conflict within me
One half of me is yours, the other half yours —		
Mine own I would say: but if mine, then yours,		17 *would:* ought to
And so all yours. O these naughty times		18–19 *O ... rights:* we live in wicked times when we cannot have what belongs to us
Put bars between the owners and their rights!		
And so, though yours, not yours. Prove it so,	20	20 *Prove it so:* if it turns out that I cannot be your wife
Let fortune go to hell for it, not I.		
I speak too long, but 'tis to piece the time,		22 *piece:* fill out
To eke it, and to draw it out in length,		23 *eke:* add to
To stay you from election.		24 *stay ... election:* prevent you from choosing

BASSANIO

Let me choose,		
For as I am, I live upon the rack.	25	25 *live ... rack:* am tortured. The rack was an instrument for stretching suspected traitors to force them to confess

PORTIA

Upon the rack, Bassanio? Then confess		
What treason there is mingled with your love.		27 *treason:* betrayal, disloyalty

BASSANIO

None but that ugly treason of mistrust,		
Which makes me fear th'enjoying of my love —		
There may as well be amity and life	30	30–31 *There ... love:* just as there can never be friendship ('amity') between snow and fire, neither can there be any between my love and disloyalty
'Tween snow and fire, as treason and my love.		

PORTIA

Ay, but I fear you speak upon the rack,

Where men enforcèd do speak anything.

BASSANIO

Promise me life, and I'll confess the truth.

PORTIA

Well then, confess and live.

BASSANIO

35   'Confess and love'

Had been the very sum of my confession:

O happy torment, when my torturer

Doth teach me answers for deliverance!

But let me to my fortune and the caskets.

PORTIA

40 Away then. I am locked in one of them —

If you do love me, you will find me out.

Nerissa and the rest, stand all aloof.

Let music sound while he doth make his choice;

Then, if he lose, he makes a swan-like end,

45 Fading in music. That the comparison

May stand more proper, my eye shall be the stream

And wat'ry death-bed for him. He may win,

And what is music then? Then music is

Even as the flourish when true subjects bow

50 To a new-crownèd monarch: such it is

As are those dulcet sounds in break of day

That creep into the dreaming bridegroom's ear

And summon him to marriage. Now he goes

With no less presence, but with much more love,

55 Than young Alcides when he did redeem

The virgin tribute paid by howling Troy

To the sea-monster: I stand for sacrifice,

The rest aloof are the Dardanian wives,

With blearèd visages, come forth to view

60 The issue of th'exploit. Go, Hercules!

Live thou, I live — with much much more dismay

I view the fight than thou that mak'st the fray.

*A song to music whilst BASSANIO comments on the caskets
to himself.*

---

33   *enforcèd:* forced by suffering

35–6   *Confess . . . confession:* if I were to tell you the truth about my feelings, I would confess my love for you

37–8   *happy . . . deliverance:* I am in a happy state of suffering when my torturer (Portia) tells me how to escape from my torture

40   *Away:* go ahead

42   *all aloof:* well out of the way

43   *sound:* be heard

44   *swan-like end:* there was a belief that the swan sang one sweet song before its death

46   *stand more proper:* fit more accurately

46–7   *my . . . him:* she imagines that Bassanio will be a dying swan in a river of her tears if he loses her

49   *flourish:* fanfare of trumpets

50–53   *such . . . marriage:* Portia is referring to the custom of playing pleasant music ('dulcet sounds') to awaken a bridegroom on his wedding day

54   *presence:* nobility, dignity

55   *Alcides:* another name for the classical hero Hercules

55–7   *redeem . . . sea-monster:* save a Trojan princess from being sacrificed to a sea-monster by killing it. Hercules did not save her for love, but to get some horses offered by her father. Unlike Hercules, Bassanio is doing what he does for love

57   *stand for sacrifice:* am here to be sacrificed

58–60   *The . . . th'exploit:* the others standing over there are the Trojan women, who, with tear-stained faces, have come out to see what happens

61   *Live . . . live:* if you make the right choice, I shall live happily

61–2   *with . . . fray:* I who watch am much more nervous and alarmed than you are, although you have to do the choosing

SINGER

Tell me where is fancy bred,

Or in the heart, or in the head?

How begot, how nourishèd?   65

ALL

Reply, reply.

SINGER

It is engendered in the eyes,

With gazing fed, and fancy dies

In the cradle where it lies.

Let us all ring fancy's knell.   70

I'll begin it. Ding, dong, bell.

ALL

Ding, dong, bell.

BASSANIO

So may the outward shows be least themselves —

The world is still deceived with ornament.

In law, what plea so tainted and corrupt,   75

But, being seasoned with a gracious voice,

Obscures the show of evil? In religion,

What damnèd error, but some sober brow

Will bless it and approve it with a text,

Hiding the grossness with fair ornament?   80

There is no vice so simple, but assumes

Some mark of virtue on his outward parts.

How many cowards, whose hearts are all as false

As stairs of sand, wear yet upon their chins

The beards of Hercules and frowning Mars;   85

Who, inward searched, have livers white as milk?

And these assume but valour's excrement

To render them redoubted. Look on beauty

And you shall see 'tis purchased by the weight,

Which therein works a miracle in nature,   90

Making them lightest that wear most of it.

So are those crispèd, snaky, golden locks,

Which make such wanton gambols with the wind

Upon supposèd fairness, often known

To be the dowry of a second head,   95

The skull that bred them in the sepulchre.

---

63   *fancy:* love that is not serious, desire

65   *begot:* conceived
     nourishèd: fed

67–9   *It … lies:* desire depends on outward appearance, so that (unlike true love) it does not last long

70   *knell:* funeral bell

73–4   *So … ornament:* it is easy to be deceived by appearances – people always tend to make that mistake

75–7   *In … evil:* lawyers can often make a bad case sound good by means of smooth words

77–80   *In … ornament:* you will always find a serious-looking clergyman to defend errors by quoting from the Bible

81–2   *There … parts:* even something totally evil can be made to look good on the outside

83–8   *How … redoubted:* many cowards try to pose as heroes such as Hercules, or angry gods such as Mars (the Roman god of war), but test them and you will find out how cowardly they are. They take on a brave appearance to make themselves look threatening

87   *excrement:* beard

88   *redoubted:* feared

89   *by the weight:* Bassanio is thinking of beauty as depending on cosmetics that were bought by weight

90   *Which … nature:* cosmetics bring about miraculous changes in appearance

91   *Making … it:* those who wear cosmetics are not to be taken seriously

92   *crispèd:* curled
     locks: hair

93   *wanton gambols:* wild, playful movements designed to attract notice

95–6   *To … sepulchre:* to have been the property of someone else, who is now dead and buried in a tomb (i.e. it is a wig)

97	*guilèd:* attractive but deceptive
98	*beauteous:* beautiful
100	*seeming:* apparent
102	*Hard … Midas:* in Greek mythology, Midas wished that all he touched would turn to gold; eating became a problem for him
103–4	*pale … and man:* this is silver, which is pale in comparison to gold, and described as a drudge or slave because it was the commonest metal used in business deals
104	*meagre:* unattractive
105	*Which … aught:* your inscription seems to threaten rather than promise anything
106	*eloquence:* persuasive words
107	*joy … consequence:* may happiness follow my choice
108	*fleet to air:* vanish
109	*As … despair:* such as doubts and foolish lack of hope
111	*allay thy ecstasy:* keep the great joy I feel under control
112	*In … excess:* do not let the joy that falls on me like rain overflow
114	*surfeit:* become ill through having too much joy
115	*counterfeit:* portrait
115–16	*What … creation:* the artist must have been half a god to have painted such a good likeness
116–18	*Move … motion?* Are Portia's eyes moving? Or is it the movement of my own eyes that makes them seem to move?
118	*severed:* parted, slightly opened
119–20	*so … friends:* such a fragrant barrier separating such appealing lips
124–6	*Having … unfurnished:* the first painted eye could have blinded the painter with its beauty and left him unable to paint the second one
127–9	*The … the substance:* no words of praise from me can do this portrait ('shadow') justice, and no portrait can do the real Portia justice
130	*continent:* container
132	*Chance … true:* may your fortune be as fair and your judgement as true as Portia is

Thus, ornament is but the guilèd shore

To a most dangerous sea; the beauteous scarf

Veiling an Indian beauty; in a word,

100   The seeming truth which cunning times put on

To entrap the wisest. Therefore thou gaudy gold,

Hard food for Midas, I will none of thee;

Nor none of thee, thou pale and common drudge

'Tween man and man; but thou, thou meagre lead,

105   Which rather threaten'st than dost promise aught,

Thy paleness moves me more than eloquence,

And here choose I — joy be the consequence!

PORTIA [*aside*]

How all the other passions fleet to air,

As doubtful thoughts, and rash-embraced despair,

110   And shudd'ring fear, and green-eyed jealousy.

O love, be moderate; allay thy ecstasy,

In measure rain thy joy, scant this excess.

I feel too much thy blessing: make it less,

For fear I surfeit.

BASSANIO

           What find I here?

Opens the leaden casket.

115   Fair Portia's counterfeit. What demi-god

Hath come so near creation? Move these eyes?

Or whether, riding on the balls of mine,

Seem they in motion? Here are severed lips

Parted with sugar breath — so sweet a bar

120   Should sunder such sweet friends. Here in her hairs

The painter plays the spider and hath woven

A golden mesh t'entrap the hearts of men

Faster than gnats in cobwebs. But her eyes —

How could he see to do them? Having made one,

125   Methinks it should have power to steal both his

And leave itself unfurnished. Yet look how far

The substance of my praise doth wrong this shadow

In underprizing it, so far this shadow

Doth limp behind the substance. Here's the scroll,

130   The continent and summary of my fortune:

        'You that choose not by the view,

          Chance as fair and choose as true.

Since this fortune falls to you,

Be content and seek no new.

If you be well pleased with this   135

And hold your fortune for your bliss,

Turn you where your lady is,

And claim her with a loving kiss.'

A gentle scroll. Fair lady, by your leave,

I come by note to give and to receive.   140

Like one of two contending in a prize,

That thinks he hath done well in people's eyes,

Hearing applause and universal shout,

Giddy in spirit, still gazing in a doubt

Whether these pearls of praise be his or no.   145

So, thrice-fair lady, stand I even so,

As doubtful whether what I see be true,

Until confirmed, signed, ratified by you.

PORTIA

You see me, Lord Bassanio, where I stand,

Such as I am; though for myself alone   150

I would not be ambitious in my wish

To wish myself much better, yet for you

I would be trebled twenty times myself,

A thousand times more fair, ten thousand times more rich,

That only to stand high in your account,   155

I might in virtues, beauties, livings, friends

Exceed account. But the full sum of me

Is sum of something, which, to term in gross,

Is an unlessoned girl, unschooled, unpractisèd.

Happy in this, she is not yet so old   160

But she may learn; happier than this,

She is not bred so dull but she can learn;

Happiest of all, is that her gentle spirit

Commits itself to yours to be directed,

As from her lord, her governor, her king.   165

Myself and what is mine to you and yours

Is now converted. But now I was the lord

Of this fair mansion, master of my servants,

Queen o'er myself; and even now, but now,

This house, these servants and this same myself   170

Are yours — my lord's — I give them with this ring,

---

134 *new:* alternative

136 *hold … bliss:* think that your fortune is your happiness

140 *by note:* as the scroll tells me

141 *contending in:* competing for

145 *his or no:* for him or not

146 *even so:* just like that

148 *ratified:* made official

155 *account:* opinion

156 *livings:* property

157–9 *But … unpractisèd:* I amount to very little. To sum me up, I am a girl without learning, training or experience

167 *converted:* transferred
But: until

169 *even:* just

173 *presage:* predict

174 *be ... you:* give me the right to criticise you

175 *bereft:* deprived

177 *powers:* ability to speak and think

178–83 *As ... not expressed:* like when a popular prince makes a speech and there is a confused mixture of approving noises from his audience, but in spite of the confusion, there is no mistaking the happiness of the listeners

184 *hence:* here. Bassanio is pointing to himself

190 *joy ... wish:* happiness that you would wish for yourselves

191 *can ... me:* would not wish to deprive me of any of my own joy

192–3 *solemnize ... faith:* celebrate your marriage

193 *beseech:* beg, implore

195 *so:* provided that

199–200 *intermission ... you:* I wasted no more time in choosing a wife than you did

202 *the matter falls:* it happens

203–5 *For ... love:* I pleaded so hard that the effort made me sweat, and I swore so many oaths of love that my mouth was dry

---

Which when you part from, lose or give away,

Let it presage the ruin of your love

And be my vantage to exclaim on you.

BASSANIO

175 Madam, you have bereft me of all words,

Only my blood speaks to you in my veins,

And there is such confusion in my powers,

As after some oration fairly spoke

By a belovèd prince, there doth appear

180 Among the buzzing pleasèd multitude,

Where every something being blent together

Turns to a wild of nothing, save of joy

Expressed and not expressed. But when this ring

Parts from this finger, then parts life from hence —

185 O then be bold to say Bassanio's dead!

NERISSA

My lord and lady, it is now our time

That have stood by and seen our wishes prosper,

To cry good joy — good joy, my lord and lady!

GRATIANO

My Lord Bassanio, and my gentle lady,

190 I wish you all the joy that you can wish,

For I am sure you can wish none from me.

And when your honours mean to solemnize

The bargain of your faith, I do beseech you

Even at that time I may be married too.

BASSANIO

195 With all my heart, so thou canst get a wife.

GRATIANO

I thank your lordship, you have got me one.

My eyes, my lord, can look as swift as yours:

You saw the mistress, I beheld the maid;

You loved, I loved — for intermission

200 No more pertains to me, my lord, than you.

Your fortune stood upon the caskets there,

And so did mine too, as the matter falls;

For wooing here until I sweat again,

And swearing till my very roof was dry

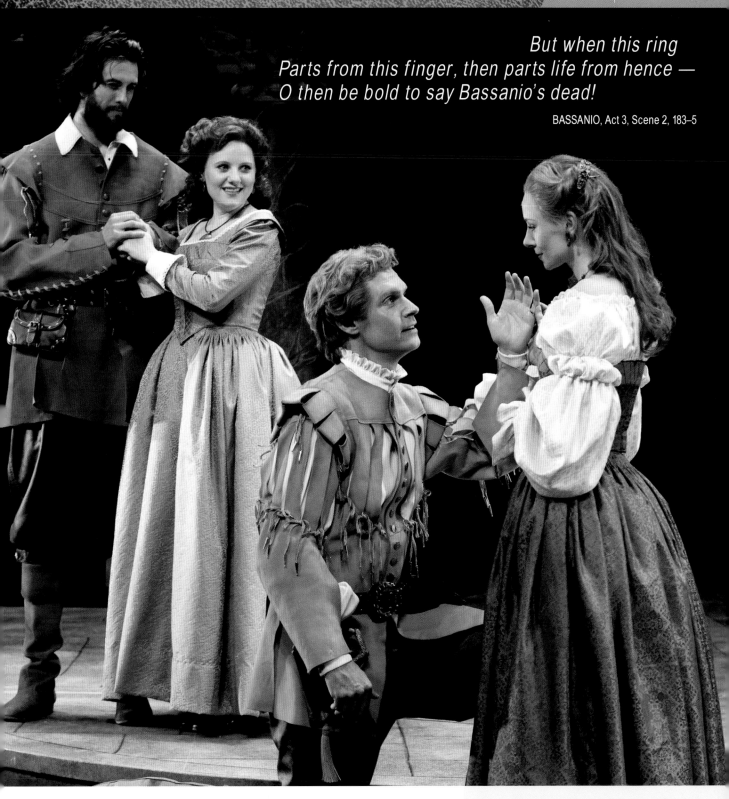

> *But when this ring*
> *Parts from this finger, then parts life from hence —*
> *O then be bold to say Bassanio's dead!*
>
> BASSANIO, Act 3, Scene 2, 183–5

With oaths of love, at last — if promise last —   205

I got a promise of this fair one here

To have her love, provided that your fortune

Achieved her mistress.

PORTIA

        Is this true, Nerissa?

NERISSA

Madam, it is, so you stand pleased withal.

205 *promise last:* we can trust promises to be kept

206 *this fair one:* Nerissa

208 *Achieved her mistress:* won Portia for yourself

209 *so … withal:* as long as you are happy with it

210 *mean good faith:* intend to be a good husband

211 *faith:* I promise

213 *play ... ducats:* bet them a thousand ducats that our son and heir will be born before theirs

214 *What ... down?* Do you want to put down our money on that bet in advance?

216 *infidel:* unbeliever; here, Jewess

219–20 *If ... welcome:* since I have only just become Lord of Belmont, I do not know if I have the right to welcome you
221 *very:* true

227 *past ... nay:* and would not take no for an answer

BASSANIO

210 And do you, Gratiano, mean good faith?

GRATIANO

Yes, faith, my lord.

BASSANIO

Our feast shall be much honoured in your marriage.

GRATIANO

We'll play with them the first boy for a thousand ducats.

NERISSA

What, and stake down?

GRATIANO

215 No, we shall ne'er win at that sport and stake down.

Enter LORENZO, JESSICA and SALERIO, a messenger from Venice.

But who comes here? Lorenzo and his infidel!

What, and my old Venetian friend Salerio?

BASSANIO

Lorenzo and Salerio, welcome hither;

If that the youth of my new int'rest here

220 Have power to bid you welcome. — By your leave,

I bid my very friends and countrymen,

Sweet Portia, welcome.

PORTIA

                                    So do I, my lord:

They are entirely welcome.

LORENZO

I thank your honour. For my part, my lord,

225 My purpose was not to have seen you here,

But meeting with Salerio by the way,

He did entreat me, past all saying nay,

To come with him along.

SALERIO

                                    I did, my lord,

And I have reason for it — Signior Antonio

Commends him to you.

Gives BASSANIO a letter.

BASSANIO

                 Ere I ope his letter   230

I pray you tell me how my good friend doth.

SALERIO

Not sick, my lord, unless it be in mind;

Nor well, unless in mind: his letter there

Will show you his estate.

BASSANIO opens the letter.

GRATIANO

Nerissa, cheer yond stranger, bid her welcome.   235

Your hand, Salerio — what's the news from Venice?

How doth that royal merchant, good Antonio?

I know he will be glad of our success;

We are the Jasons, we have won the fleece.

SALERIO

I would you had won the fleece that he hath lost.   240

PORTIA

There are some shrewd contents in yond same paper

That steals the colour from Bassanio's cheek —

Some dear friend dead, else nothing in the world

Could turn so much the constitution

Of any constant man. What, worse and worse?   245

With leave, Bassanio, I am half yourself,

And I must freely have the half of anything

That this same paper brings you.

BASSANIO

                    O sweet Portia,

Here are a few of the unpleasant'st words

That ever blotted paper. Gentle lady,   250

When I did first impart my love to you,

I freely told you all the wealth I had

Ran in my veins — I was a gentleman —

And then I told you true: and yet, dear lady,

Rating myself at nothing, you shall see   255

How much I was a braggart. When I told you

My state was nothing, I should then have told you

That I was worse than nothing; for indeed

I have engaged myself to a dear friend,

Glossary / Notes

230 *Ere I ope:* before I open

232 *Not … mind:* not physically sick, but depressed

233 *Nor … mind:* there is nothing well about him, except his brave spirit

234 *estate:* condition

235 *cheer yond stranger:* cheer up Jessica

239 *We are … fleece:* we have achieved what we sought (i.e. the love of Nerissa and Portia), just as Jason found the Golden Fleece

240 *I … lost:* I wish you had won the fleets (a pun on 'fleece') that Antonio has lost at sea

241 *There … paper:* that letter contains some bitter bad news

244–5 *turn … man:* cause a steady man to lose his self-control

246 *With leave:* permit me to say

251 *impart:* communicate, make known

252–3 *freely … veins:* openly admitted to you that though I had no wealth I was of noble blood

255 *Rating:* valuing, counting

256 *braggart:* boaster

257 *state:* estate, fortune

259 *engaged:* bound, pledged

260–61 *Engaged . . . means:* put Antonio at the mercy of his absolute enemy, Shylock, in order to get the money I wanted

262 *as:* is like

265 *What . . . hit?* Has not even one ship reached a port safely?

268 *scape:* avoided, escaped

269 *merchant-marring rocks:* rocks that wreck merchant ships

271–2 *present . . . it:* ready money to pay his debt, Shylock would not accept it

273 *bear . . . man:* look human

274 *keen . . . man:* ready, like a wild beast, to destroy a human being

275 *plies:* urges

276–7 *And . . . justice:* if he does not get his pound of flesh, Shylock is going to accuse Venice of discrimination. As a free city, Venice cannot practise discrimination

278–9 *magnificoes . . . port:* most important members of the ruling class in Venice

279 *persuaded:* pleaded

280 *envious plea:* malicious claim (that he is entitled to a pound of Antonio's flesh)

287 *deny not:* do not prevent it

288 *go hard with:* turn out badly for

291–2 *The . . . courtesies:* a man who never tires of helping others

293 *ancient Roman honour:* like Antonio, Romans placed a high value on loyalty to one's friends

260 Engaged my friend to his mere enemy,

To feed my means. Here is a letter, lady;

The paper as the body of my friend,

And every word in it a gaping wound

Issuing life-blood. But is it true, Salerio?

265 Have all his ventures failed? What, not one hit?

From Tripolis, from Mexico and England,

From Lisbon, Barbary and India,

And not one vessel scape the dreadful touch

Of merchant-marring rocks?

SALERIO

                              Not one, my lord.

270 Besides, it should appear that if he had

The present money to discharge the Jew,

He would not take it. Never did I know

A creature that did bear the shape of man

So keen and greedy to confound a man.

275 He plies the duke at morning and at night,

And doth impeach the freedom of the state

If they deny him justice. Twenty merchants,

The duke himself, and the magnificoes

Of greatest port, have all persuaded with him,

280 But none can drive him from the envious plea

Of forfeiture, of justice, and his bond.

JESSICA

When I was with him, I have heard him swear

To Tubal and to Chus, his countrymen,

That he would rather have Antonio's flesh

285 Than twenty times the value of the sum

That he did owe him; and I know, my lord,

If law, authority and power deny not,

It will go hard with poor Antonio.

PORTIA

Is it your dear friend that is thus in trouble?

BASSANIO

290 The dearest friend to me, the kindest man,

The best-conditioned and unwearied spirit

In doing courtesies, and one in whom

The ancient Roman honour more appears

Than any that draws breath in Italy.

PORTIA

What sum owes he the Jew?   295

BASSANIO

For me, three thousand ducats.

PORTIA

                                   What, no more?

Pay him six thousand, and deface the bond;

Double six thousand, and then treble that,

Before a friend of this description

Shall lose a hair through Bassanio's fault.   300

First, go with me to church and call me wife,

And then away to Venice to your friend;

For never shall you lie by Portia's side

With an unquiet soul. You shall have gold

To pay the petty debt twenty times over.   305

When it is paid, bring your true friend along.

My maid Nerissa and myself meantime

Will live as maids and widows. Come, away,

For you shall hence upon your wedding-day.

Bid your friends welcome, show a merry cheer: 310

Since you are dear bought, I will love you dear.

But let me hear the letter of your friend.

BASSANIO

[*reads*] 'Sweet Bassanio, my ships have all miscarried, my creditors grow cruel, my estate is very low, my bond to the Jew is forfeit, and, since in paying it, it is impossible   315 I should live, all debts are cleared between you and I if I might but see you at my death. Notwithstanding, use your pleasure — if your love do not persuade you to come, let not my letter.'

PORTIA

O love, dispatch all business and be gone!   320

BASSANIO

Since I have your good leave to go away,

I will make haste; but, till I come again,

No bed shall e'er be guilty of my stay,

No rest be interposer 'twixt us twain.

Exeunt.

297 *deface:* destroy

301 *call me wife:* marry me
302 *away:* travel

304 *unquiet:* uneasy
305 *petty:* small, insignificant
306 *along:* back here to Belmont

308 *maids:* virgins, unmarried women
309 *shall hence:* must leave here

311 *dear bought:* expensive, costing me a lot

313 *miscarried:* come to harm, been lost

317 *Notwithstanding:* however
317–18 *use your pleasure:* do what pleases you

320 *dispatch all business:* make the arrangements

324 *No . . . twain:* sleep will not get in the way between us two (i.e. he will not rest until he sees Portia again)

Key points

The third of three casket scenes sees the suitor correctly select the lead casket. However, the celebrations are interrupted by bad news from Venice.

- The romantic interest comes to a head in this scene. Bassanio chooses the right casket, and Gratiano announces that he wants to marry Nerissa at the same time as Portia and Bassanio are married. There is also the arrival of the third pair of lovers, Lorenzo and Jessica.

- Portia makes it clear to Bassanio that he is the suitor she prefers, but that, as much as she would like to, she cannot tell him 'how to choose right' (line 11). She must obey her father's wishes. However, it seems possible that Portia offers a hint to Bassanio about which casket he should choose through the song that she then arranges to be sung.

- The song begins: 'Tell me where is fancy bred, or in the heart, or in the head? How begot, how nourishèd?' (lines 63–5). The fact that the three rhyming words – *bred*, *head* and *nourishèd* – all rhyme with *lead* may well give Bassanio the necessary clue.

- Furthermore, the second verse states that 'fancy', which is lust or infatuation rather than genuine love, makes choices based on the 'eyes' (line 67), i.e. by what it sees. Bassanio takes this theme seriously when he points out that it is easy to be deceived by appearances, and that people always tend to make that mistake: 'So may the outward shows be least themselves — the world is still deceived with ornament' (lines 73–4) – he goes on to repeat this point for the next thirty or so lines.

- Before Bassanio attempted the casket lottery, Portia declared her love for him (lines 14–18). Her intense joy after he makes the correct choice of the humble lead casket confirms that her love for Bassanio is genuine (lines 149–74).

- The arrival of Jessica, Lorenzo and Salerio introduces a strange episode. While Lorenzo and Salerio are welcomed warmly, Jessica is largely ignored. Gratiano recognises Jessica's presence in a single comment: 'But who comes here? Lorenzo and his infidel!' (line 216). He calls her an 'infidel' (an unbeliever) even though he is well aware that Jessica has decided to become a Christian. Notice that he does not even give her a name. Gratiano, once it has been confirmed that Salerio requested Lorenzo and Jessica to accompany him, then has to tell Nerissa to welcome Jessica (line 235).

- The mood of the scene changes from joy to despair. The news Salerio brings is that all Antonio's ships are lost at sea. Worse still, even if Antonio could raise the money at this stage to honour the bond, Shylock would not accept it, preferring to take a pound of Antonio's flesh. The most powerful men in Venice, including the duke, cannot persuade Shylock to spare Antonio.

- Bassanio has a further problem as his debt to Antonio is about to be made public knowledge. He has failed to give Portia a true account of his financial position and is now forced by circumstances to do so. He admits that when he told her he was penniless, he was not telling the whole truth. He should have told her he is worse off than that as he is in debt.

- Portia offers to pay Shylock whatever he wants in order to cancel the debt and save Antonio. For Bassanio's sake, she is prepared to offer enough 'gold to pay the petty debt twenty times over' (lines 304–5). Portia's response not only confirms her love for Bassanio, it also indicates her enormous wealth.

- Having been ignored by the others, and having heard Salerio's abusive remarks about Shylock: 'Never did I know a creature that did bear the shape of man so keen and greedy to confound a man' (lines 272–4), Jessica's only speech in this scene (lines 282–8) is unfavourable to her father. She makes no attempt to defend him or justify his actions. She merely confirms that he will not be deterred from taking Antonio's flesh.

Useful quotes

But who comes here? Lorenzo and his infidel!

(Gratiano, line 216)

Beshrew your eyes,
They have o'erlooked me and divided me;
One half of me is yours, the other half yours —
Mine own I would say: but if mine, then yours,
And so all yours.

(Portia, lines 14–18)

When I was with him, I have heard him swear
To Tubal and to Chus, his countrymen,
That he would rather have Antonio's flesh
Than twenty times the value of the sum
That he did owe him

(Jessica, lines 282–6)

You see me, Lord Bassanio, where I stand,
Such as I am; though for myself alone
I would not be ambitious in my wish
To wish myself much better, yet for you
I would be trebled twenty times myself,
A thousand times more fair, ten thousand times more rich

(Portia, lines 149–54)

Pay him six thousand, and deface the bond;
Double six thousand, and then treble that,
Before a friend of this description
Shall lose a hair through Bassanio's fault.

(Portia, lines 297–300)

You saw the mistress, I beheld the maid;
You loved, I loved

GRATIANO, Act 3, Scene 2, 198–9

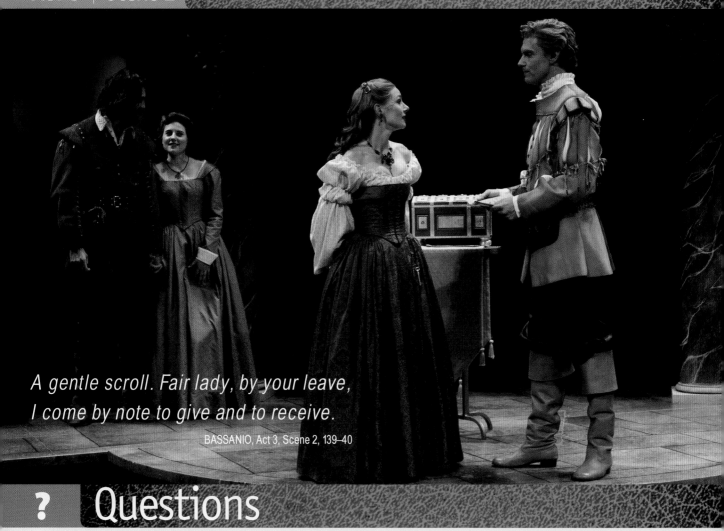

*A gentle scroll. Fair lady, by your leave,
I come by note to give and to receive.*

BASSANIO, Act 3, Scene 2, 139–40

? Questions

1 Lines 24–38 are dominated by an image of torture. In using such an image, what roles does Bassanio assign to Portia and himself? Is this a suitable image here?

2 Portia presents herself as a helpless victim in lines 40–62. Is she giving an accurate view of herself at this point? Explain your answer with reference to the text.

3 Bassanio is conscious of false appearances and considers them under four headings in lines 73–107. Identify three of these headings and briefly describe what Bassanio says under each one.

4 How is the theme of false appearances linked to what Bassanio is about to do?

5 The inscription on the lead casket is: 'Who chooseth me, must give and hazard all he hath.' Does this inscription prove to be true for Bassanio?

6 Was it wise for Portia's father to make sure that a suitor who would choose the lead casket should marry Portia? Give reasons for your answer.

7 What kind of husband is Bassanio likely to be for Portia? Which of his qualities might she like or dislike?

8 Portia gives Bassanio a ring. What conditions does she attach to it and what commitment does Bassanio make in response?

9 What is suggested by the treatment of Jessica in this scene?

10 How does this scene damage Shylock's reputation?

Talking point

Although Portia has been managing her household well, she tells Bassanio that, as her husband, he will be in control of her, of all she owns and of her servants. This is what her society required her to do. What does such an arrangement say about the positions of men and women in such a society? Who does best out of it? Would it be acceptable today?

ACT 3 ✝ Scene 3

Antonio is in the custody of a gaoler. He tries to plead with Shylock, but Shylock refuses to listen as he is determined to have Antonio's life. Antonio gives up hope: he recognises that Shylock wants him to die and that the law will be on Shylock's side. All he cares about now is seeing Bassanio again.

Thou call'dst me dog before thou hadst a cause;
But since I am a dog, beware my fangs.

SHYLOCK, Act 3, Scene 3, 6–7

Venice. A street.

Enter SHYLOCK, SOLANIO, ANTONIO and the GAOLER.

SHYLOCK
Gaoler, look to him — tell not me of mercy —
This is the fool that lent out money gratis.
Gaoler, look to him.

ANTONIO
                                   Hear me yet, good Shylock.

SHYLOCK
I'll have my bond, speak not against my bond —
5 I have sworn an oath that I will have my bond.
Thou call'dst me dog before thou hadst a cause;
But since I am a dog, beware my fangs.
The duke shall grant me justice. I do wonder,
Thou naughty gaoler, that thou art so fond
10 To come abroad with him at his request.

ANTONIO
I pray thee hear me speak.

SHYLOCK
I'll have my bond. I will not hear thee speak.
I'll have my bond, and therefore speak no more.
I'll not be made a soft and dull-eyed fool,
15 To shake the head, relent and sigh, and yield
To Christian intercessors. Follow not —
I'll have no speaking, I will have my bond.
Exit.

SOLANIO
It is the most impenetrable cur
That ever kept with men.

ANTONIO
                                   Let him alone.
20 I'll follow him no more with bootless prayers.
He seeks my life; his reason well I know —
I oft delivered from his forfeitures
Many that have at times made moan to me,
Therefore he hates me.

1 *look to him:* guard him closely

2 *gratis:* free of interest

9 *naughty:* bad, undisciplined
fond: foolish
10 *abroad:* out of prison

14 *dull-eyed:* easily deceived

16 *intercessors:* people who plead on Antonio's behalf

18–19 *It ... men:* Shylock is the most heartless dog ('cur') that ever lived among human beings

19 *Let:* leave

20 *bootless prayers:* pleas that will not be answered

22–3 *oft ... me:* often released people from his grasp by paying their debts when they pleaded with me

SOLANIO

I am sure the duke
Will never grant this forfeiture to hold.   25

ANTONIO

The duke cannot deny the course of law:
For the commodity that strangers have
With us in Venice, if it be denied,
Will much impeach the justice of the state,
Since that the trade and profit of the city   30
Consisteth of all nations. Therefore go —
These griefs and losses have so bated me
That I shall hardly spare a pound of flesh
Tomorrow to my bloody creditor.
Well, gaoler, on. Pray God Bassanio come   35
To see me pay his debt, and then I care not.

Exeunt.

25 *grant … hold:* allow the penalty in Shylock's bond to be imposed

26 *deny … law:* prevent the law from taking its course

27 *commodity:* trade and commercial dealings *strangers:* foreigners

28 *it:* Shylock's rights under the law

29 *impeach:* discredit

31 *Consisteth … nations:* involves people from all over the world

32 *bated me:* caused me to lose weight

Key points

This scene features an unequal contest between Antonio and Shylock. Shylock, who has the law on his side, has all the advantages.

- Antonio, who previously cursed and abused Shylock, now pleads for his life to 'good Shylock' (line 3). Shylock, who does not feel that he has to listen to Antonio, interrupts him as he tries to speak. Antonio once called him a dog for no reason and Shylock will now live up to Antonio's abusive remark by behaving like a dog and showing that he can bite (lines 6–7). Shylock appears to be enjoying having the upper hand for a change.

- The scene focuses on the theme of mercy and on Shylock's determination to stand by the letter of the law: 'I'll have my bond' (line 4). He has no time for the spirit of the law, however, and he refuses to listen to Antonio or to show the slightest sympathy for his suffering. Shylock's insistence on strict justice as a means of getting revenge on Antonio for the harm he has done him in the past does nothing to win the sympathy of the audience.

- Explaining why he thinks Shylock wants to end his life, Antonio recalls that he often released people from Shylock's grasp by paying their debts (lines 22–3). Indeed, Shylock himself refers to Antonio as 'the fool that lent out money gratis' (line 2). However, their commercial rivalry is not the only motive for Shylock's lack of mercy. Other reasons include Antonio's abuse of him in the past, Jewish–Christian divisions, and the fact that Lorenzo, who has eloped with Jessica, is among Antonio's circle of friends.

- Antonio knows that the law is on Shylock's side. Antonio has broken a contract and must pay the agreed penalty. If Shylock's rights are interfered with, then the legal system of Venice will not be trusted abroad, and trade with other places will suffer. By the end of the scene Antonio appears to have lost hope and accepted his fate.

Useful quotes

> *Gaoler, look to him — tell not me of mercy —*
> *This is the fool that lent out money gratis.*
>
> (Shylock, lines 1–2)

> *These griefs and losses have so bated me*
> *That I shall hardly spare a pound of flesh*
> *Tomorrow to my bloody creditor.*
>
> (Antonio, lines 32–4)

> *Thou call'dst me dog before thou hadst a cause;*
> *But since I am a dog, beware my fangs.*
> *The duke shall grant me justice.*
>
> (Shylock, lines 6–8)

> *Pray God Bassanio come*
> *To see me pay his debt, and then I care not.*
>
> (Antonio, lines 35–6)

? Questions

1 Antonio seems to have changed his tone at the start of this scene, referring to Shylock as 'good Shylock' (line 3). Why has he changed his tone? Is he being a hypocrite?

2 'I pray thee hear me speak' (line 11). What, do you think, did Antonio want to say to Shylock?

3 Why does Shylock keep repeating the word 'bond'? What effect does this repetition have?

4 Shylock reasons that since Antonio has treated him like a dog, he is entitled to behave like one and deal with his enemy as a dog would. Do you have any sympathy for Shylock's point of view? Explain.

5 How should Shylock deliver his two speeches in this scene (lines 4–10 and lines 12–17)? What movements or gestures should he make? What should his facial expressions be like?

6 Why does Antonio think that the Duke of Venice cannot intervene on his behalf against Shylock? What would happen if he did?

7 What impression do you get from Antonio's speech at lines 26–36? Does he mind giving up his life?

8 Does this scene win sympathy for Antonio? Give reasons for your answer.

9 What, do you think, is happening at Belmont while the events of this scene take place?

10 Imagine you are Shylock. Write a diary entry in which you look forward to your day in court.

Talking point

Shylock thinks that justice means enforcing the letter of the law and that it has nothing to do with mercy. Antonio has broken his bond so he must pay the penalty. Would you agree with Shylock? Do you think courts should have very precise rules about how to deal with cases or should there be room to consider the circumstances of each case?

ACT 3 ✟ Scene 4

Lorenzo praises Portia for helping out Antonio, and praises Antonio for his faithful friendship to Bassanio. Portia is happy to help as she assumes Antonio must be a similar person to Bassanio. She asks Lorenzo and Jessica to take charge of her household while she and Nerissa retreat to a monastery during their husbands' absence.

Portia has other plans, however. She sends her servant Balthazar to deliver a letter to her cousin Doctor Bellario in Padua. Balthazar is to bring papers and clothes from Bellario to the public ferry, where he will meet Portia. Portia then tells Nerissa that they will see their husbands again soon, but their husbands will not recognise them because they will be disguised as young men.

> *Come on, Nerissa, I have work in hand*
> *That you yet know not of; we'll see our husbands*
> *Before they think of us.*
>
> PORTIA, Act 3, Scene 4, 57–9

Belmont. A room in Portia's house.

Enter PORTIA, NERISSA, LORENZO, JESSICA and BALTHAZAR, a man of PORTIA's.

LORENZO

Madam, although I speak it in your presence,

You have a noble and a true conceit

Of godlike amity, which appears most strongly

In bearing thus the absence of your lord.

5   But if you knew to whom you show this honour,

How true a gentleman you send relief,

How dear a lover of my lord your husband,

I know you would be prouder of the work

Than customary bounty can enforce you.

PORTIA

10   I never did repent for doing good,

Nor shall not now: for in companions

That do converse and waste the time together,

Whose souls do bear an equal yoke of love,

There must be needs a like proportion

15   Of lineaments, of manners and of spirit,

Which makes me think that this Antonio,

Being the bosom lover of my lord,

Must needs be like my lord. If it be so,

How little is the cost I have bestowed

20   In purchasing the semblance of my soul

From out the state of hellish cruelty.

This comes too near the praising of myself,

Therefore no more of it. Hear other things.

Lorenzo, I commit into your hands

25   The husbandry and manage of my house

Until my lord's return. For mine own part,

I have toward heaven breathed a secret vow

To live in prayer and contemplation,

Only attended by Nerissa here,

30   Until her husband and my lord's return —

There is a monastery two miles off,

And there will we abide. I do desire you

Not to deny this imposition,

The which my love and some necessity

Now lays upon you.

---

2   *conceit:* understanding

3   *godlike amity:* the strongest friendship

4   *lord:* husband, Bassanio (who has left for Venice)

5   *whom:* i.e. Antonio

7   *lover:* friend

8–9 *the work ... you:* what you are doing for Antonio than you would be of one of your everyday good deeds

11–15 *in ... spirit:* among friends who spend time together, who are equally fond of each other, there are bound to be characteristics in common

17   *bosom lover:* intimate friend

19–20 *How ... soul:* I don't care how much it costs me to rescue Antonio. If I save him, I save my husband's image and therefore my own

25   *husbandry ... house:* running of my household

27   *toward ... vow:* sworn an oath to God

31   *off:* from here

32   *abide:* stay

33   *imposition:* task I have imposed on you

35   *lays:* places

LORENZO

Madam, with all my heart, 35

I shall obey you in all fair commands.

PORTIA

My people do already know my mind,

And will acknowledge you and Jessica

In place of Lord Bassanio and myself.

So fare you well till we shall meet again. 40

LORENZO

Fair thoughts and happy hours attend on you!

JESSICA

I wish your ladyship all heart's content.

PORTIA

I thank you for your wish, and am well pleased

To wish it back on you: fare you well, Jessica.

Exeunt JESSICA and LORENZO.

Now, Balthazar, 45

As I have ever found thee honest-true,

So let me find thee still. Take this same letter,

And use thou all th'endeavour of a man

In speed to Padua. See thou render this

Into my cousin's hand, Doctor Bellario, 50

And look what notes and garments he doth give thee —

Bring them I pray thee with imagined speed

Unto the traject, to the common ferry

Which trades to Venice. Waste no time in words

But get thee gone — I shall be there before thee. 55

BALTHAZAR

Madam, I go with all convenient speed.

Exit.

PORTIA

Come on, Nerissa, I have work in hand

That you yet know not of; we'll see our husbands

Before they think of us.

NERISSA

Shall they see us?

---

37 *My ... mind:* my staff have been told of my intentions

38 *acknowledge:* recognise the authority of

46 *ever:* always

48–9 *use ... speed:* go as fast as your man's legs will carry you

49 *render:* give

51 *look:* take care of

52 *imagined:* all possible

53–4 *Unto ... trades:* to the boarding-place for the public ferry that crosses

56 *convenient:* appropriately urgent

57 *work in hand:* things to do

59 *think of:* miss

60	*habit:* costume, outfit
61	*accomplished:* equipped
62	*hold . . . wager:* bet you anything you like
63	*accoutered:* dressed
64	*prettier:* more fashionably dressed
65	*with . . . grace:* more like a show-off
67	*reed:* squeaky *mincing:* dainty
68	*frays:* battles
69	*quaint:* cunning
71	*I denying:* when I refused them
72	*do withal:* fulfil their wishes
74	*puny:* pathetic
76	*twelvemonth:* year
77	*raw . . . Jacks:* immature tricks often played by these boastful fellows
78	*turn to men:* disguise ourselves as men, change into men
80	*lewd interpreter:* low-minded person who might take a crude meaning from your words
81	*device:* plan
82	*stays:* waits
83	*haste:* hurry
84	*measure:* cover, travel

PORTIA

60 They shall, Nerissa, but in such a habit
That they shall think we are accomplished
With that we lack. I'll hold thee any wager,
When we are both accoutered like young men,
I'll prove the prettier fellow of the two,
65 And wear my dagger with the braver grace,
And speak between the change of man and boy
With a reed voice, and turn two mincing steps
Into a manly stride, and speak of frays
Like a fine bragging youth, and tell quaint lies
70 How honourable ladies sought my love,
Which I denying, they fell sick and died:
I could not do withal — then I'll repent,
And wish for all that, that I had not killed them;
And twenty of these puny lies I'll tell,
75 That men shall swear I have discontinued school
Above a twelvemonth. I have within my mind
A thousand raw tricks of these bragging Jacks,
Which I will practise.

NERISSA

                  Why shall we turn to men?

PORTIA

Fie, what a question's that,
80 If thou wert near a lewd interpreter!
But come, I'll tell thee all my whole device
When I am in my coach, which stays for us
At the park gate; and therefore haste away,
For we must measure twenty miles today.

Exeunt.

Key points

Portia now becomes the active agent in the plot, since no one else can help Antonio.

- Lorenzo seems to think it necessary to convince Portia of Antonio's great merits. Portia feels that Antonio, whom she does not know, must be a mirror image of Bassanio, and therefore deserving of whatever help she can give him. She also thinks that the money she has offered to take Antonio out of 'the state of hellish cruelty' (line 21) seems small because it will mean, as she puts it, 'purchasing the semblance of my soul' (line 20). Her 'soul' here is Bassanio; the 'semblance' of her soul (the image of Bassanio) is Antonio.

- We already know that Antonio is in a desperate situation, and now we see Portia preparing a practical plan to save him from Shylock. She leaves Lorenzo and Jessica in charge of her household, claiming that she and Nerissa will be staying at a monastery while their husbands are away. This is a pretence.

- Portia then sends Balthazar to Padua to obtain expert legal advice from her cousin Doctor Bellario on the case, and to borrow lawyers' robes from him. When this has been done, she and Nerissa will travel to Venice disguised as young men: Nerissa as a legal clerk, and Portia as a young lawyer. Although not stated in the scene, it seems clear that Portia plans to pretend to be a lawyer in order to challenge Shylock's case in the Venetian courts and save Antonio's life.

Useful quotes

But if you knew to whom you show this honour,
How true a gentleman you send relief,
How dear a lover of my lord your husband,
I know you would be prouder of the work
Than customary bounty can enforce you.

(Lorenzo, lines 5–9)

I never did repent for doing good,
Nor shall not now

(Portia, lines 10–11)

I have toward heaven breathed a secret vow
To live in prayer and contemplation,
Only attended by Nerissa here,
Until her husband and my lord's return

(Portia, lines 27–30)

Take this same letter,
And use thou all th'endeavour of a man
In speed to Padua. See thou render this
Into my cousin's hand, Doctor Bellario,
And look what notes and garments he doth give thee

(Portia, lines 47–51)

? Questions

1 Does Lorenzo's speech, especially lines 1–4, sound sincere to you? Explain.

2 What motive might Lorenzo have for flattering Portia?

3 What reasons does Portia give for wanting to help Antonio?

4 Is Portia correct in assuming that, given their close friendship, Antonio and Bassanio must be alike? Give reasons for your answer.

5 Portia acknowledges Jessica by name (line 38), which represents a change in her attitude since Act 3, Scene 2. Can you explain this change?

6 Do you think Jessica will find her new role as temporary mistress of Belmont a pleasant one? What might make it difficult?

7 What instructions does Portia give to Balthazar?

8 Describe Portia's plan to save Antonio's life, as it appears at this point in the play.

9 What does Portia's plan say about her character?

10 Imagine you are Nerissa. Write a diary entry setting out your thoughts on the recent events at Belmont.

Talking point

Lorenzo praises Portia at the start of this scene. She acknowledges the praise but then feels embarrassed that she may be flattering herself. How do you react when someone praises you? Are you grateful for the compliment or do you shrug it off? Does it inspire you or make you feel uncomfortable?

Plot summary

Launcelot tells Jessica that she is damned because her father is a Jew, and if her father is not a Jew then that would mean that her mother was unfaithful and Jessica will be damned for that instead. Jessica claims that Lorenzo has saved her by making her a Christian; Launcelot complains that there will be too many Christians and the price of pork will rise.

Lorenzo accuses Launcelot of fathering a child with a Moor. He struggles to get Launcelot to go inside and order dinner to be served as Launcelot insists on making puns.

Jessica praises Portia and says that Bassanio is lucky to have found her. Lorenzo suggests that Jessica is equally lucky to have married him.

I shall be saved by my husband — he hath made me a Christian.

JESSICA, Act 3, Scene 5, 15–16

Belmont. A garden.

Enter LAUNCELOT and JESSICA.

LAUNCELOT

Yes, truly, for look you, the sins of the father are to be laid upon the children, therefore, I promise you, I fear you. I was always plain with you, and so now I speak my agitation of the matter: therefore be o' good cheer, for truly I think you
5   are damned. There is but one hope in it that can do you any good, and that is but a kind of bastard hope neither.

JESSICA

And what hope is that I pray thee?

LAUNCELOT

Marry, you may partly hope that your father got you not, that you are not the Jew's daughter.

JESSICA

10   That were a kind of bastard hope indeed — so the sins of my mother should be visited upon me.

LAUNCELOT

Truly then, I fear you are damned both by father and mother. Thus, when I shun Scylla, your father, I fall into Charybdis, your mother; well, you are gone both ways.

JESSICA

15   I shall be saved by my husband — he hath made me a Christian.

LAUNCELOT

Truly, the more to blame he: we were Christians enough before, e'en as many as could well live one by another. This making Christians will raise the price of hogs: if we grow
20   all to be pork-eaters, we shall not shortly have a rasher on the coals for money.

Enter LORENZO.

JESSICA

I'll tell my husband, Launcelot, what you say — here he comes.

LORENZO

I shall grow jealous of you shortly, Launcelot, if you thus
25   get my wife into corners.

JESSICA

Nay, you need not fear us, Lorenzo: Launcelot and I are out. He tells me flatly there's no mercy for me in heaven

---

2   *fear you:* fear for you

3   *plain:* honest
    agitation: he means 'cogitation' or thought

6   *bastard hope:* false hope, and also the hope that she may be illegitimate and not Shylock's daughter at all

8   *got you not:* is not really your father

10–11   *so ... me:* then I am bound to inherit my mother's sin (of having another man's child)

13–14   *when ... Charybdis:* Scylla lived on a rock, and Charybdis near a whirlpool, in a dangerous stretch of sea between Italy and Sicily. Both were monsters. Sailors who avoided one of them were captured by the other

14   *gone both ways:* damned either way

17–21   *Truly ... money:* Launcelot has second thoughts about Jessica becoming a Christian. If too many people give up being Jews, there will be a scarcity of pork, and its price will rise. Jews are forbidden to eat pork

25   *get ... corners:* have secret chats with my wife

26–7   *are out:* have fallen out

because I am a Jew's daughter; and he says you are no good member of the commonwealth, for in converting Jews to Christians you raise the price of pork.

LORENZO

I shall answer that better to the commonwealth than you can the getting up of the negro's belly: the Moor is with child by you, Launcelot.

LAUNCELOT

It is much that the Moor should be more than reason: but if she be less than an honest woman, she is indeed more than I took her for.

LORENZO

How every fool can play upon the word! I think the best grace of wit will shortly turn into silence, and discourse grow commendable in none only but parrots. Go in, sirrah; bid them prepare for dinner.

LAUNCELOT

That is done, sir; they have all stomachs.

LORENZO

Goodly lord, what a wit-snapper are you! Then bid them prepare dinner.

LAUNCELOT

That is done too, sir; only 'cover' is the word.

LORENZO

Will you cover then, sir?

LAUNCELOT

Not so, sir, neither; I know my duty.

LORENZO

Yet more quarrelling with occasion! Wilt thou show the whole wealth of thy wit in an instant? I pray thee understand a plain man in his plain meaning: go to thy fellows, bid them cover the table, serve in the meat, and we will come in to dinner.

LAUNCELOT

For the table, sir, it shall be served in; for the meat, sir, it shall be covered; for your coming in to dinner, sir, why let it be as humours and conceits shall govern.

Exit.

30

35

40

45

50

---

29 *commonwealth:* state of Venice

31–3 *I … by you:* I have a better chance of explaining myself to the state than you have of explaining how a Moorish woman is pregnant by you

34–6 *It … for:* it's a big deal that the Moor is larger than she should be: but if she is not a virtuous woman, that's still more than I thought of her in the first place. In Shakespeare's day 'Moor' was pronounced 'more', which explains Launcelot's play on the words 'much', 'more' and 'Moor'

37–9 *the best … parrots:* the only thing intelligent people can do is to remain silent and leave speaking to parrots

41 *stomachs:* appetites

42 *wit-snapper:* smart alec

44 *only … word:* they only need to be told to lay the table

45 *cover:* order the servants to lay the table

46 *duty:* Launcelot misunderstands 'cover' to mean putting on his hat, which was an unmannerly thing to do in the presence of superiors

47 *quarrelling with occasion:* quibbling at every opportunity

54 *as … govern:* just as you please

LORENZO	
55	O dear discretion, how his words are suited!
	The fool hath planted in his memory
	An army of good words, and I do know
	A many fools that stand in better place,
	Garnished like him, that for a tricksy word
60	Defy the matter. How cheer'st thou, Jessica?
	And now, good sweet, say thy opinion:
	How dost thou like the Lord Bassanio's wife?

LORENZO

55   O dear discretion, how his words are suited!

The fool hath planted in his memory

An army of good words, and I do know

A many fools that stand in better place,

Garnished like him, that for a tricksy word

60   Defy the matter. How cheer'st thou, Jessica?

And now, good sweet, say thy opinion:

How dost thou like the Lord Bassanio's wife?

JESSICA

Past all expressing. It is very meet

The Lord Bassanio live an upright life;

65   For, having such a blessing in his lady,

He finds the joys of heaven here on earth;

And if on earth he do not merit it,

In reason he should never come to heaven.

Why, if two gods should play some heavenly match,

70   And on the wager lay two earthly women,

And Portia one, there must be something else

Pawned with the other, for the poor rude world

Hath not her fellow.

LORENZO

                 Even such a husband

Hast thou of me, as she is for a wife.

JESSICA

75   Nay, but ask my opinion too of that.

LORENZO

I will anon — first, let us go to dinner.

JESSICA

Nay, let me praise you while I have a stomach.

LORENZO

No, pray thee let it serve for table-talk;

Then, howsome'er thou speak'st, 'mong other things

I shall digest it.

JESSICA

80   Well, I'll set you forth.

Exeunt.

Marginal glosses:

55 *discretion:* good sense
suited: dressed up

58 *A many:* several
stand ... place: have better positions

59 *Garnished:* dressed (in the traditional garments of a fool)

59–60 *that ... matter:* who in order to show off, talk nonsense

60 *How cheer'st thou:* a greeting

63 *Past all expressing:* more than words can say
meet: proper, suitable

68 *In reason:* it is only reasonable that

69–73 *Why ... fellow:* if two gods made a bet and one used Portia as a stake, then the other god would need to add in something more as no one could equal Portia. This is a roundabout way of saying that no woman can compare to Portia

76 *anon:* shortly

77 *have a stomach:* am still inclined to

78 *table-talk:* meal-time conversation

79–80 *howsome'er ... it:* whatever way you say it, I shall digest your praise of me along with my meal

80 *set you forth:* list your good qualities

Key points

This is the weakest scene in the play, containing a number of Launcelot's childish insults, poor jokes and weak puns.

- The previous four scenes dealt with serious matters. This scene is almost entirely trivial. However, Shakespeare needed to allow Portia and Nerissa time to get to Venice.

- Launcelot, the official clown in the play, amuses himself by mockingly preaching a sermon to Jessica. He thinks Jessica is damned because she is Shylock's daughter and she will inherit the results of her father's sins. In this exchange with Jessica (lines 1–21), Launcelot reflects the view taken by Christians in the play that Shylock is a devil and therefore damned. Notice that he cannot bring himself to mention Shylock's name: Jessica is 'the Jew's daughter' (line 9).

- Launcelot criticises Lorenzo for adding to the number of Christians by converting Jessica to Christianity. If this trend continues, and more Jews become Christians and therefore 'pork-eaters' (line 20), Launcelot claims that the price of pork will rise and people will not be able to afford rashers.

- Launcelot is mocked by Lorenzo for having made a Moorish woman pregnant. He does not give her a name: instead, he refers to her as 'the negro' and 'the Moor' (line 32). Once again, this exchange reflects the Christian characters' tendency to dislike the outsider, whether Jewish or Moorish. Differences in religion and race are rarely tolerated. Launcelot shows his base nature by revealing that he never thought much of the Moorish woman's virtue (lines 34–6).

- Launcelot is constantly repeating words and misunderstanding them. Playing with language and the different meanings and sounds of words was a popular pastime in Shakespeare's day and would have appealed to many people in his audiences.

- Jessica appears to have more patience than Lorenzo for Launcelot's humour, even though Launcelot is using it to condemn her. She is also full of praise for Portia and ready to praise her husband. She seems happy in her new environment and marriage.

Useful quotes

> Marry, you may partly hope that your father got you not, that you are not the Jew's daughter.
>
> (Launcelot, lines 8–9)

> It is very meet
> The Lord Bassanio live an upright life;
> For, having such a blessing in his lady,
> He finds the joys of heaven here on earth
>
> (Jessica, lines 63–6)

? Questions

1 Stage directions in the play refer to Launcelot as 'the clown'. Here he is treating Jessica to a clownish sermon based on the old belief that children are punished for the sins of their parents. What conclusion does Launcelot draw from this theory?

2 How does Jessica deal with Launcelot's argument?

3 Why does Lorenzo mention Launcelot's relationship with the Moorish woman?

4 How do you account for Jessica's lavish praise of Portia, a woman she hardly knows?

5 Do Jessica and Lorenzo appear to be a happy couple? Give reasons for your answer.

6 What do we learn about Launcelot in this scene?

7 What do we learn about Jessica in this scene?

8 What do we learn about Lorenzo in this scene?

9 Imagine you are the pregnant Moor. Write a letter to Launcelot explaining how you feel about him and your present situation.

10 What, do you think, is happening with the main characters (i.e. Portia, Shylock, Antonio and Bassanio) while the events of this scene take place?

Talking point

This is one of the play's comic scenes. Do you think it succeeds as comedy? What qualities do you look for in a comedy? Which comic writers and performers do you enjoy? Have you seen or heard any comedy sketches from before you were born? Are they still funny or have tastes changed?

ACT 3 ⚔ Key moments

Scene 1

- News comes that first one and then another of Antonio's ships have been lost at sea.
- Shylock laments the loss of his daughter, while his Christian enemies mock him. He vows to have revenge on Antonio if he cannot repay his loan.

Scene 2

- Bassanio chooses the correct (lead) casket. Portia gives him a ring as a token of their love. If he parts with this ring, it will mean that their love is at an end.
- Gratiano and Nerissa arrange to be married at the same time as Bassanio and Portia.
- Bassanio gets news that Antonio was unable to pay his debt to Shylock and so may lose his life. Portia tells Bassanio to pay Shylock whatever money he wants to cancel the debt.

Scene 3

- Antonio pleads for mercy, but Shylock insists that he will get justice by having his pound of flesh.

Scene 4

- Portia leaves Lorenzo and Jessica in charge of her house, telling them that she and Nerissa are going to a monastery until their husbands return.
- Portia sends a servant to Padua to ask her cousin Doctor Bellario to provide expert legal opinion on Antonio's case and to supply lawyers' robes.

Scene 5

- Launcelot tells Jessica that she is damned for being Shylock's daughter, while Lorenzo taunts Launcelot for getting a Moorish woman pregnant.

ACT 3 ⚔ Speaking and listening

1 In groups of three, select a student to play Bassanio. The other two students should prepare a list of questions to ask Bassanio. For example, they might ask him about his feelings after he read Antonio's letter describing his losses at sea and the dangers he faces at Shylock's hands. Does he feel guilty about getting Antonio into this situation? How did he decide which casket to choose? Did he get any help from Portia in making his choice? The group should then discuss whether Bassanio is a likeable character or not.

2 Divide into small groups to enact two versions of the casket selection episode in Act 3, Scene 2 (lines 40–148). In the first, Portia will do everything she can to help Bassanio to make the correct choice; and in the second, Portia will not influence his choice in any way. Consider where the actors might take up their positions on the stage, how they should move about, the gestures they might make, how they should speak their lines, what facial expressions they should adopt, etc. Act out the two versions (reading the lines) to see how your ideas work in practice.

Q Revision quiz: plot summary

Use the words listed in the panel to fill in the blanks in this summary of Act 3:

Antonio
arrested
Balthazar
Bassanio
Bellario
Belmont
bond
casket
gaoler
Gratiano
Jessica
justice
law
lead
Lorenzo
marry
master
monkey
Nerissa
Portia
pound
revenge
ring
song
Venice

The action in Act 3 is split between Venice and ▭.

In Venice, Shylock continues to suffer over the loss of ▭ and the money and valuables she took with her. He is distraught to hear that she has swapped a ring that was given to him by his late wife for a ▭.

News of Antonio's losses at sea lifts Shylock's spirits and shifts his focus to one of ▭. If Antonio fails to honour his ▭, i.e. to repay the 3,000 ducats given to Bassanio on time, then Shylock will insist that he forfeit a ▭ of his flesh. He arranges to have Antonio ▭ as soon as he defaults.

Next time we meet Antonio he is in the custody of a ▭. He pleads for mercy, but Shylock refuses to listen. As far as Shylock is concerned, the bond has been broken and he is entitled to get ▭. Antonio realises that the ▭ will be on Shylock's side. He wishes to see ▭ again before he dies.

In Belmont, a loving relationship has formed between Bassanio and Portia. Despite Portia's worries, Bassanio wants to try the ▭ lottery. Portia arranges for a helpful ▭ to accompany his choice. Bassanio chooses the ▭ casket and finds a portrait of ▭ and a scroll telling him that he has won the right to ▭ Portia.

Portia gives Bassanio a ▭ as a token of their love. She declares that he is now her ▭ and will control all she has. He promises that he will never part with the ring. ▭ and Nerissa arrange to be married at the same time as Bassanio and Portia.

Salerio arrives with a letter in which Antonio explains his misfortunes to Bassanio and asks to see him before he dies. Portia insists that Bassanio pay Shylock whatever money he wants to cancel the debt. Bassanio will marry Portia and then return to ▭ immediately.

Portia hatches a plan of her own to save ▭. She leaves ▭ and Jessica in charge of her household, and sends her servant ▭ to Padua to obtain legal advice and robes from her cousin Doctor ▭. Portia and ▭ set off for Venice.

ACT 4 † Scene 1

The Duke of Venice wants to save Antonio and tries to persuade Shylock not to seek his deadly vengeance. Bassanio offers to pay more money than is owed. Shylock refuses and continues to sharpen his knife. Doctor Bellario is expected to decide the case, but 'Balthazar' arrives in his place. Balthazar is Portia dressed as a doctor of laws and accompanied by Nerissa dressed as a clerk.

Portia/Balthazar advises Shylock to be merciful, but he insists on getting justice. Portia agrees that he is entitled to a pound of flesh. Shylock celebrates. Antonio bares his chest in preparation. Then Portia states that Shylock is entitled to exactly one pound of flesh only and may not shed a drop of blood. This is impossible, so Shylock says he will accept Bassanio's offer of 9,000 ducats instead. Portia does not allow this;

Shylock will get justice only, as he demanded. Shylock is declared guilty of attempting to end the life of Antonio, for which he could lose his possessions and his life. It is agreed that Antonio will hold half of Shylock's wealth on behalf of Lorenzo and Jessica, and Shylock may retain the other half if he becomes a Christian and agrees to leave all he has to his daughter and new son-in-law. Shylock leaves the court a broken man.

Portia will not take a fee, but asks Bassanio to give her the ring he is wearing. He refuses. Antonio persuades him to part with it.

I am sorry for thee — thou art come to answer
A stony adversary, an inhuman wretch
Uncapable of pity, void and empty
From any dram of mercy.

DUKE, Act 4, Scene 1, 3–6

Venice. A court of justice.

Enter the DUKE, the MAGNIFICOES, ANTONIO, BASSANIO, GRATIANO, SALERIO and OTHERS.

DUKE
What, is Antonio here?

ANTONIO
Ready, so please your grace.

DUKE
I am sorry for thee — thou art come to answer
A stony adversary, an inhuman wretch
5 Uncapable of pity, void and empty
From any dram of mercy.

ANTONIO
                I have heard
Your grace hath ta'en great pains to qualify
His rigorous course, but since he stands obdurate,
And that no lawful means can carry me
10 Out of his envy's reach, I do oppose
My patience to his fury, and am armed
To suffer with a quietness of spirit
The very tyranny and rage of his.

DUKE
Go one and call the Jew into the court.

SALERIO
15 He is ready at the door — he comes, my lord.
Enter SHYLOCK.

DUKE
Make room, and let him stand before our face.
Shylock, the world thinks, and I think so too,
That thou but leadest this fashion of thy malice
To the last hour of act, and then 'tis thought
20 Thou'lt show thy mercy and remorse more strange
Than is thy strange apparent cruelty,
And where thou now exact'st the penalty —
Which is a pound of this poor merchant's flesh —
Thou wilt not only loose the forfeiture,
25 But, touched with human gentleness and love,
Forgive a moiety of the principal,

---

4 *stony adversary:* hard-hearted enemy

5–6 *void ... mercy:* lacking even the smallest particle of mercy

7–8 *qualify ... course:* soften the harsh measures he insists upon

8 *obdurate:* unchanging, unmoved

10 *his envy's reach:* the reach of his hatred

10–11 *I ... fury:* I will put my calm composure up against his violent rage

11 *armed:* prepared

13 *The ... his:* the absolute violence and anger of his spirit

14 *Go one:* let someone go

18–19 *thou ... act:* you want to keep up an appearance of hatred against Antonio until the very last moment

20 *Thou'lt ... strange:* you will demonstrate a more extraordinary pity

21 *strange apparent:* strangely obvious

22 *exact'st:* demand

24 *loose the forfeiture:* give up your demand for Antonio's flesh

26 *Forgive ... principal:* not demand all the money he owes you

Glancing an eye of pity on his losses

That have of late so huddled on his back,

Enough to press a royal merchant down,

And pluck commiseration of his state   30

From brassy bosoms and rough hearts of flint,

From stubborn Turks and Tartars never trained

To offices of tender courtesy.

We all expect a gentle answer, Jew.

SHYLOCK

I have possessed your grace of what I purpose,   35

And by our holy Sabbath have I sworn

To have the due and forfeit of my bond —

If you deny it, let the danger light

Upon your charter and your city's freedom.

You'll ask me why I rather choose to have   40

A weight of carrion flesh than to receive

Three thousand ducats: I'll not answer that,

But say it is my humour. Is it answered?

What if my house be troubled with a rat

And I be pleased to give ten thousand ducats   45

To have it baned? What, are you answered yet?

Some men there are love not a gaping pig,

Some that are mad if they behold a cat,

And others, when the bagpipe sings i' th' nose,

Cannot contain their urine — for affection,   50

Mistress of passion, sways it to the mood

Of what it likes or loathes. Now, for your answer:

As there is no firm reason to be rendered

Why he cannot abide a gaping pig;

Why he, a harmless necessary cat;   55

Why he, a woollen bagpipe; but of force

Must yield to such inevitable shame

As to offend, himself being offended;

So can I give no reason, nor I will not,

More than a lodged hate and a certain loathing   60

I bear Antonio, that I follow thus

A losing suit against him. Are you answered?

BASSANIO

This is no answer, thou unfeeling man,

To excuse the current of thy cruelty.

30–31 *pluck … flint:* draw pity for his condition from even the hardest-hearted people

32–3 *Turks … courtesy:* pagans who would not be familiar with deeds of gentle kindness

35 *possessed:* told
purpose: intend to do

37 *the … bond:* what I am owed and what Antonio is bound to give me (i.e. a pound of flesh)

38–9 *If … freedom:* if you decide against me, it will make a dangerous mockery of the legal system on which Venice is founded

41 *carrion:* rotting

43 *is my humour:* pleases me
Is it answered? Is that answer enough for you?

46 *baned:* poisoned

47 *gaping pig:* roasted pig served up with fruit in its mouth

49 *sings i' th' nose :* drones

50–52 *affection … loathes:* the feelings we are born with decide the way we react to different things, what we like or hate

53 *rendered:* given

54–6 *he … he … he:* one man … another man … yet another man

56–8 *of … offended:* each is bound to give offence to others if he is offended by things they like

60–62 *More … him:* beyond that I have a deep ('lodged') and fixed ('certain') hatred for Antonio, which makes me pursue a case against him that I cannot win money on

64 *current:* movement, behaviour

SHYLOCK

65   I am not bound to please thee with my answers.

BASSANIO

Do all men kill the things they do not love?

SHYLOCK

Hates any man the thing he would not kill?

BASSANIO

Every offence is not a hate at first.

SHYLOCK

What, wouldst thou have a serpent sting thee twice?

ANTONIO

70   I pray you think you question with the Jew —

You may as well go stand upon the beach

And bid the main flood bate his usual height;

You may as well use question with the wolf

Why he hath made the ewe bleat for the lamb;

75   You may as well forbid the mountain pines

To wag their high tops and to make no noise

When they are fretten with the gusts of heaven;

You may as well do anything most hard

As seek to soften that — than which what's harder? —

80   His Jewish heart! Therefore I do beseech you

Make no more offers, use no farther means,

But with all brief and plain conveniency

Let me have judgement, and the Jew his will.

BASSANIO

For thy three thousand ducats, here is six.

SHYLOCK

85   If every ducat in six thousand ducats

Were in six parts, and every part a ducat,

I would not draw them; I would have my bond!

DUKE

How shalt thou hope for mercy, rend'ring none?

SHYLOCK

What judgement shall I dread, doing no wrong?

90   You have among you many a purchased slave,

Which, like your asses and your dogs and mules,

You use in abject and in slavish parts

---

68 *Every . . . first:* not every crime immediately causes the victim to hate the offender

70 *I . . . Jew:* please remember that you are arguing with Shylock, a merciless Jew

72 *bid . . . height:* ask the high tide ('main flood') not to reach its normal height

73 *use question:* discuss, debate

74 *bleat:* cry (because her lamb has been killed)

77 *fretten with:* shaken by

78 *most hard:* almost impossible

79 *than . . . harder:* which nothing is harder than

82 *with . . . conveniency:* as quickly and briefly as possible

83 *judgement:* the court's decision
will: wish

87 *draw:* take up, receive

88 *How . . . none?* Since you show no mercy to Antonio, how can you hope that mercy will be shown to you?

89 *What . . . wrong?* Why would I worry about being shown mercy when I haven't any need of it?

92 *in abject . . . parts:* for the worst and lowest jobs

Because you bought them — shall I say to you,
'Let them be free, marry them to your heirs?
Why sweat they under burthens? Let their beds   95
Be made as soft as yours, and let their palates
Be seasoned with such viands'? You will answer,
'The slaves are ours' — so do I answer you:
The pound of flesh which I demand of him
Is dearly bought; 'tis mine and I will have it.   100
If you deny me, fie upon your law:
There is no force in the decrees of Venice.
I stand for judgement — answer: shall I have it?

DUKE
Upon my power I may dismiss this court,
Unless Bellario, a learnèd doctor,   105
Whom I have sent for to determine this,
Come here today.

SALERIO
                    My lord, here stays without
A messenger with letters from the doctor,
New come from Padua.

DUKE
Bring us the letters; call the messenger.   110

BASSANIO
Good cheer, Antonio! What, man, courage yet!
The Jew shall have my flesh, blood, bones and all,
Ere thou shalt lose for me one drop of blood.

ANTONIO
I am a tainted wether of the flock,
Meetest for death — the weakest kind of fruit   115
Drops earliest to the ground, and so let me.
You cannot better be employed, Bassanio,
Than to live still and write mine epitaph.

Enter NERISSA, dressed as a lawyer's clerk.

DUKE
Came you from Padua, from Bellario?

NERISSA
From both, my lord. Bellario greets your grace.   120

Presents a letter.

95 *burthens:* burdens, heavy loads
96–7 *let ... viands:* let them have the same food as you eat
100 *Is dearly bought:* has cost me a lot
101–2 *If ... Venice:* if you refuse my request, a curse on your law: there is no power in the laws of Venice
103 *I ... it?* I am waiting for the court's decision; tell me now, am I to get it?
104 *Upon ... may:* I have the power to
105 *learnèd doctor:* legal expert
106 *determine this:* decide this case
107 *stays without:* waits outside
109 *New come:* newly arrived
111 *What ... yet:* stay strong, don't give up
113 *Ere:* before
114 *tainted wether:* sick ram
115 *Meetest:* most suitable
118 *mine epitaph:* words in tribute to me

121 *whet:* sharpen

122 *forfeiture . . . there:* pound of flesh that Antonio the bankrupt owes me

123 *sole:* Shylock is sharpening his knife on the sole of his shoe
soul: Shylock is risking damnation for his soul

124 *keen:* sharp

125 *hangman's:* executioner's

126 *sharp envy:* bitter, malicious hatred
pierce thee: get through to you

127 *wit:* intelligence

128 *inexecrable:* absolutely hateful

129 *And . . . accused:* the fact that you exist makes one wonder if there can be a just world

130–33 *Thou . . . men:* you almost make me lose my belief in the Christian religion and tempt me to believe that the souls of dead animals find their way into the bodies of men, making these men behave like animals. Pythagoras was a Greek philosopher

133–4 *thy . . . slaughter:* the soul you now have was once that of a wolf, which was hanged for killing human beings

135 *fell:* murderous, savage
fleet: race away

136 *unhallowed dam:* unholy mother

137 *Infused . . . thee:* gained entry to your body

138 *ravenous:* predatory

139 *Till . . . bond:* until you can make my bond worthless by shouting abuse

140 *Thou . . . loud:* you are only hurting your lungs by shouting

141–2 *Repair . . . ruin:* you had better improve your mind or it will be ruined beyond repair

143 *doth commend:* recommends

145 *He . . . by:* he is waiting close at hand

148 *give . . . conduct:* guide him politely

BASSANIO
Why dost thou whet thy knife so earnestly?

SHYLOCK
To cut the forfeiture from that bankrupt there.

GRATIANO
Not on thy sole, but on thy soul, harsh Jew,
Thou mak'st thy knife keen; but no metal can —
125 No, not the hangman's axe — bear half the keenness
Of thy sharp envy. Can no prayers pierce thee?

SHYLOCK
No, none that thou hast wit enough to make.

GRATIANO
O be thou damned, inexecrable dog!
And for thy life let justice be accused.
130 Thou almost mak'st me waver in my faith,
To hold opinion with Pythagoras
That souls of animals infuse themselves
Into the trunks of men: thy currish spirit
Governed a wolf, who, hanged for human slaughter,
135 Even from the gallows did his fell soul fleet,
And, whilst thou lay'st in thy unhallowed dam,
Infused itself in thee; for thy desires
Are wolvish, bloody, starved and ravenous.

SHYLOCK
Till thou canst rail the seal from off my bond,
140 Thou but offend'st thy lungs to speak so loud.
Repair thy wit, good youth, or it will fall
To cureless ruin. I stand here for law.

DUKE
This letter from Bellario doth commend
A young and learnèd doctor to our court.
Where is he?

NERISSA
145   He attendeth here hard by,
To know your answer — whether you'll admit him.

DUKE
With all my heart. Some three or four of you
Go give him courteous conduct to this place.

Meantime the court shall hear Bellario's letter:

[reads] 'Your grace shall understand that at the receipt   150
of your letter I am very sick, but in the instant that your
messenger came, in loving visitation was with me a
young doctor of Rome; his name is Balthazar. I acquainted
him with the cause in controversy between the Jew
and Antonio the merchant; we turned o'er many books   155
together; he is furnished with my opinion, which, bettered
with his own learning — the greatness whereof I cannot
enough commend — comes with him at my importunity
to fill up your grace's request in my stead. I beseech you
let his lack of years be no impediment to let him lack a   160
reverend estimation, for I never knew so young a body
with so old a head. I leave him to your gracious acceptance,
whose trial shall better publish his commendation.'

Enter PORTIA, dressed as a doctor of laws.

You hear the learn'd Bellario, what he writes,
And here, I take it, is the doctor come.   165

[*to PORTIA*] Give me your hand. Come you from old
 Bellario?

PORTIA
I did, my lord.

DUKE
            You are welcome; take your place.
Are you acquainted with the difference
That holds this present question in the court?

PORTIA
I am informèd throughly of the cause.   170
Which is the merchant here, and which the Jew?

DUKE
Antonio and old Shylock, both stand forth.

PORTIA
Is your name Shylock?

SHYLOCK
            Shylock is my name.

PORTIA
Of a strange nature is the suit you follow,
Yet in such rule that the Venetian law   175

154 *cause in controversy:* matter in dispute
155 *turned o'er:* consulted, referred to
156 *furnished ... opinion:* supplied with my thoughts on the case
156–7 *bettered ... learning:* improved by Balthazar's scholarly advice
158–9 *comes ... stead:* Balthazar comes with your messenger, at your urgent request, to act in my place
160–62 *let his ... head:* do not let his youth prevent you from giving him the respect due to an older person, since I never knew anybody so young and still so wise
162–3 *I ... commendation:* I recommend him to your grace, and if you accept him you will realise why I have recommended him

168–9 *difference ... court:* dispute that has led to this trial

170 *throughly:* fully

172 *forth:* forward

174 *suit:* case, claim
175 *in ... law:* your case is so properly made that the laws of Venice

176 *impugn . . . proceed:* overturn your charges

177 *stand . . . danger:* face his claim to harm you

178 *confess the bond:* admit having made the agreement

180 *On . . . I?* Who can make me?

181 *strained:* forced

185 *'Tis . . . the mightiest:* mercy is at its strongest when it is shown by those in power

185–6 *it . . . crown:* mercy is a finer ornament for a king than even his crown

187–8 *His . . . majesty:* the sceptre or rod held by kings is the symbol of their power on earth, and inspires worship and respect in their subjects

189 *Wherein . . . kings:* which makes the people fear kings

190 *sceptred sway:* power of kings

192 *an attribute to:* a quality of

193 *show likest:* appear most like

194 *seasons:* flavours

196–7 *in . . . salvation:* if God applied strict justice without mercy to human beings, all would be damned, since all are sinners

197–9 *pray . . . of mercy:* Portia is referring to the Lord's Prayer – forgive us our trespasses as we forgive those who trespass against us'

200 *mitigate:* soften

202 *Must needs:* will have to

203 *My . . . law:* I will accept the consequences of my actions. I beg that the law may take its course

Cannot impugn you as you do proceed.

[*to ANTONIO*] You stand within his danger, do you not?

ANTONIO
Ay, so he says.

PORTIA
                Do you confess the bond?

ANTONIO
I do.

PORTIA
        Then must the Jew be merciful.

SHYLOCK
180   On what compulsion must I? Tell me that.

PORTIA
The quality of mercy is not strained,
It droppeth as the gentle rain from heaven
Upon the place beneath; it is twice blest:
It blesseth him that gives and him that takes.
185   'Tis mightiest in the mightiest: it becomes
The thronèd monarch better than his crown;
His sceptre shows the force of temporal power,
The attribute to awe and majesty,
Wherein doth sit the dread and fear of kings;
190   But mercy is above this sceptred sway,
It is enthronèd in the hearts of kings,
It is an attribute to God himself;
And earthly power doth then show likest God's
When mercy seasons justice. Therefore, Jew,
195   Though justice be thy plea, consider this:
That in the course of justice none of us
Should see salvation; we do pray for mercy,
And that same prayer doth teach us all to render
The deeds of mercy. I have spoke thus much
200   To mitigate the justice of thy plea,
Which if thou follow, this strict court of Venice
Must needs give sentence 'gainst the merchant there.

SHYLOCK
My deeds upon my head! I crave the law,
The penalty and forfeit of my bond.

My deeds upon my head! I crave the law,
The penalty and forfeit of my bond.

SHYLOCK, Act 4, Scene 1, 203–4

PORTIA

Is he not able to discharge the money?   205

205 *discharge:* pay back

BASSANIO

Yes, here I tender it for him in the court;

Yea, twice the sum — if that will not suffice,

I will be bound to pay it ten times o'er

On forfeit of my hands, my head, my heart —

If this will not suffice, it must appear   210

That malice bears down truth. And I beseech you

Wrest once the law to your authority —

To do a great right, do a little wrong —

And curb this cruel devil of his will.

PORTIA

It must not be; there is no power in Venice   215

Can alter a decree establishèd:

206 *tender it:* offer money in payment

207 *suffice:* be enough

208 *be bound:* take an oath

211 *malice . . . truth:* Shylock's hatred overpowers truth
      or honesty

211–12 *beseech . . . authority:* beg you, use the power you
          have to bend or twist the law in favour of Antonio

214 *curb . . . will:* prevent Shylock from having his way

216 *a decree establishèd:* an existing law

217–19 *'Twill . . . state:* it will be an example when similar cases are heard, and cause errors to enter the laws of Venice

220 *Daniel:* a wise and intelligent judge in the Old Testament

224 *thrice:* three times

225–6 *I . . . soul:* I have taken an oath to have a pound of flesh – I would commit perjury (i.e. tell a lie under oath) if I let Antonio off

231 *tear:* break, destroy

232 *according . . . tenour:* exactly as it is stated in the bond

234 *exposition:* explanation

239 *alter . . . bond:* change my mind – I am sticking to my position

'Twill be recorded for a precedent,

And many an error by the same example

Will rush into the state — it cannot be.

SHYLOCK

220 A Daniel come to judgement! Yea, a Daniel!

O wise young judge, how I do honour thee!

PORTIA

I pray you let me look upon the bond.

SHYLOCK

Here 'tis, most reverend doctor, here it is.

PORTIA

Shylock, there's thrice thy money offered thee.

SHYLOCK

225 An oath, an oath, I have an oath in heaven —

Shall I lay perjury upon my soul?

No, not for Venice.

PORTIA

               Why this bond is forfeit,

And lawfully by this the Jew may claim

A pound of flesh, to be by him cut off

230 Nearest the merchant's heart. [*to SHYLOCK*] Be merciful:

Take thrice thy money; bid me tear the bond.

SHYLOCK

When it is paid according to the tenour.

It doth appear you are a worthy judge,

You know the law, your exposition

235 Hath been most sound: I charge you by the law,

Whereof you are a well-deserving pillar,

Proceed to judgement. By my soul I swear

There is no power in the tongue of man

To alter me — I stay here on my bond.

ANTONIO

240 Most heartily I do beseech the court

To give the judgement.

PORTIA

              Why then thus it is —

You must prepare your bosom for his knife.

SHYLOCK

O noble judge! O excellent young man!

PORTIA

For the intent and purpose of the law

Hath full relation to the penalty   245

Which here appeareth due upon the bond.

SHYLOCK

'Tis very true: O wise and upright judge,

How much more elder art thou than thy looks!

PORTIA

Therefore lay bare your bosom.

SHYLOCK

                                        Ay, his breast,

So says the bond, doth it not, noble judge?   250

'Nearest his heart' — those are the very words.

PORTIA

It is so. Are there balance here to weigh

The flesh?

SHYLOCK

                    I have them ready.

PORTIA

Have by some surgeon, Shylock, on your charge,

To stop his wounds, lest he do bleed to death.   255

SHYLOCK

Is it so nominated in the bond?

PORTIA

It is not so expressed, but what of that?

'Twere good you do so much for charity.

SHYLOCK

I cannot find it, 'tis not in the bond.

PORTIA

You, merchant, have you anything to say?   260

ANTONIO

But little; I am armed and well prepared.

Give me your hand, Bassanio; fare you well,

Grieve not that I am fall'n to this for you;

For herein Fortune shows herself more kind

244–5 *For … penalty:* the law fully backs up the penalty demanded by Shylock

251 *very:* exact

252 *balance:* weighing-scales

254 *Have … charge:* call in a surgeon, Shylock, at your own expense
255 *stop:* close up

256 *nominated:* stated

257–8 *It … charity:* it is not specified in the bond, but that does not matter; it is best to be humane

260 *merchant:* Antonio

261 *armed:* ready

264 *For … kind:* in granting me my death, fortune is being kinder to me

265–6 *it . . . wealth:* since she often lets miserable men suffer after losing their wealth

268 *An . . . poverty:* a poor old age
ling'ring penance: a long period of suffering

270 *Commend me:* give my regards

271 *the . . . end:* how Antonio died (the manner of his death and the legal process that led to it)

272 *me . . . death:* well of me when I am dead

274 *love:* dear friend

275–6 *Repent . . . debt:* if only you are sorry that you are losing me by my death, I will not be sorry that I am paying your debt to Shylock

278 *pay . . . heart:* willingly pay your debt. This is a sad, cruel pun as he will be literally paying Shylock with his heart

282 *esteemed:* valued, honoured

284 *deliver:* liberate, release

285–6 *Your . . . offer:* if your wife were here, she would not thank you for what you have just said

288–9 *would . . . Jew:* wish she were dead so that she might beg some heavenly power to soften Shylock's heart

291 *make . . . house:* otherwise create a house in which husband and wife do not get on well

292–4 *These . . . a Christian:* these are fine examples of Christian husbands. I wish my daughter had married any kind of Jew, even someone descended from evil (Barabbas was the murderer who was released when Christ was crucified), instead of marrying the Christian Lorenzo

295 *trifle:* are wasting

265 Than is her custom: it is still her use
To let the wretched man outlive his wealth,
To view with hollow eye and wrinkled brow
An age of poverty, from which ling'ring penance
Of such misery doth she cut me off.

270 Commend me to your honourable wife,
Tell her the process of Antonio's end,
Say how I loved you, speak me fair in death;
And, when the tale is told, bid her be judge
Whether Bassanio had not once a love.

275 Repent but you that you shall lose your friend
And he repents not that he pays your debt;
For if the Jew do cut but deep enough,
I'll pay it instantly with all my heart.

BASSANIO
Antonio, I am married to a wife
280 Which is as dear to me as life itself,
But life itself, my wife, and all the world
Are not with me esteemed above thy life.
I would lose all, ay, sacrifice them all
Here to this devil, to deliver you.

PORTIA
285 Your wife would give you little thanks for that
If she were by to hear you make the offer.

GRATIANO
I have a wife who I protest I love —
I would she were in heaven so she could
Entreat some power to change this currish Jew.

NERISSA
290 'Tis well you offer it behind her back;
The wish would make else an unquiet house.

SHYLOCK
[*aside*] These be the Christian husbands. I have a daughter;
Would any of the stock of Barrabas
Had been her husband rather than a Christian!
295 [*aloud*] We trifle time, I pray thee pursue sentence.

PORTIA
A pound of that same merchant's flesh is thine,
The court awards it, and the law doth give it.

SHYLOCK

Most rightful judge!

PORTIA

And you must cut this flesh from off his breast,

The law allows it, and the court awards it.   300

SHYLOCK

Most learnèd judge! A sentence! Come, prepare!

PORTIA

Tarry a little, there is something else.

This bond doth give thee here no jot of blood,

The words expressly are 'a pound of flesh':

Take then thy bond, take thou thy pound of flesh,   305

But in the cutting it, if thou dost shed

One drop of Christian blood, thy lands and goods

Are by the laws of Venice confiscate

Unto the state of Venice.

302   *Tarry a little:* take your time

303   *jot:* drop

308   *confiscate:* seized

309   *Unto:* on behalf of

This bond doth give thee here no jot of blood,
The words expressly are 'a pound of flesh'

PORTIA, Act 4, Scene 1, 303–4

GRATIANO

310   O upright judge! Mark, Jew: O learnèd judge!

SHYLOCK

Is that the law?

PORTIA

            Thyself shalt see the act:

For as thou urgest justice, be assured

Thou shalt have justice more than thou desir'st.

GRATIANO

O learnèd judge! Mark, Jew: a learnèd judge!

SHYLOCK

315   I take this offer then — pay the bond thrice

And let the Christian go.

BASSANIO

                 Here is the money.

PORTIA

Soft!

The Jew shall have all justice — soft, no haste!

He shall have nothing but the penalty.

GRATIANO

320   O Jew, an upright judge, a learnèd judge!

PORTIA

Therefore prepare thee to cut off the flesh.

Shed thou no blood, nor cut thou less nor more

But just a pound of flesh. If thou tak'st more

Or less than a just pound, be it but so much

325   As makes it light or heavy in the substance,

Or the division of the twentieth part

Of one poor scruple — nay, if the scale do turn

But in the estimation of a hair,

Thou diest and all thy goods are confiscate.

GRATIANO

330   A second Daniel, a Daniel, Jew!

Now, infidel, I have you on the hip.

PORTIA

Why doth the Jew pause? Take thy forfeiture.

SHYLOCK

Give me my principal, and let me go.

---

311 *act:* law that lays down these conditions

317 *Soft:* wait, hold on

327 *scruple:* the smallest measure of weight used by apothecaries or chemists. One-twentieth of a scruple would be impossible to weigh or measure

327–8 *if . . . hair:* if the weight of flesh removed is a hair's breadth greater or less than a pound

331 *infidel:* unbeliever; in this case, Jew
on the hip: at a disadvantage

333 *principal:* the money I lent Antonio

BASSANIO

I have it ready for thee; here it is.

PORTIA

He hath refused it in the open court.   335

He shall have merely justice and his bond.

GRATIANO

A Daniel, still say I, a second Daniel!

I thank thee, Jew, for teaching me that word.

SHYLOCK

Shall I not have barely my principal?

PORTIA

Thou shalt have nothing but the forfeiture,   340

To be so taken at thy peril, Jew.

SHYLOCK

Why then the devil give him good of it!

I'll stay no longer question.

PORTIA

                Tarry, Jew,

The law hath yet another hold on you.

It is enacted in the laws of Venice,   345

If it be proved against an alien

That by direct or indirect attempts

He seek the life of any citizen,

The party 'gainst the which he doth contrive

Shall seize one half his goods, the other half   350

Comes to the privy coffer of the state,

And the offender's life lies in the mercy

Of the duke only, 'gainst all other voice —

In which predicament I say thou stand'st;

For it appears by manifest proceeding   355

That indirectly, and directly too,

Thou hast contrived against the very life

Of the defendant; and thou hast incurred

The danger formerly by me rehearsed.

Down therefore and beg mercy of the duke.   360

GRATIANO

Beg that thou mayst have leave to hang thyself —

And yet, thy wealth being forfeit to the state,

---

335 *open:* public

339 *barely my principal:* my money back, even without the interest

343 *I'll ... question:* I will not stay to prolong this case

343 *Tarry:* wait

345 *enacted:* set out

346 *an alien:* anyone who is not a citizen of Venice

349 *party ... contrive:* person whom he has plotted to kill

351 *privy ... state:* treasury of Venice

352–3 *lies ... voice:* can be spared by the duke, and by nobody else

354 *In ... stand'st:* I say you are now in this position

355 *manifest proceeding:* everything you have publicly done

357 *contrived:* plotted, schemed

358–9 *incurred ... rehearsed:* brought on yourself the penalty I have just explained

360 *Down:* get down on your knees

361 *leave:* permission

363	*value ... cord:* price of a rope (for Shylock to hang himself with)
364	*charge:* expense
365–6	*That ... it:* to let you see the difference between charitable Christians and vengeful Jews like yourself, I spare your life before you even ask me to
368–9	*comes ... fine:* becomes the property of Venice, but if you accept your punishment humbly, I might fine you instead of taking all you have left
370	*Ay ... Antonio:* make sure that it is only the state's half of Shylock's money that is reduced to a fine, and that Antonio gets his half without reduction
372–3	*prop ... house:* money, the one thing that holds my household together
375	*render:* show, offer
376	*halter gratis:* free hangman's rope
378	*quit:* release Shylock from
380–82	*The ... daughter:* the use of my own half of the estate, to hold in trust for the benefit of Lorenzo and Jessica
383	*Two ... more:* I have two more requirements
384	*presently:* immediately
386	*all ... possessed:* everything he owns at the time of death
387	*son:* son-in-law
388	*recant:* withdraw
389	*late:* just now
390	*contented:* satisfied

Thou hast not left the value of a cord,

Therefore thou must be hanged at the state's charge.

DUKE

365   That thou shalt see the difference of our spirit,

I pardon thee thy life before thou ask it:

For half thy wealth, it is Antonio's;

The other half comes to the general state,

Which humbleness may drive unto a fine.

PORTIA

370   Ay, for the state, not for Antonio.

SHYLOCK

Nay, take my life and all; pardon not that —

You take my house, when you do take the prop

That doth sustain my house; you take my life,

When you do take the means whereby I live.

PORTIA

375   What mercy can you render him, Antonio?

GRATIANO

A halter gratis; nothing else, for God's sake.

ANTONIO

So please my lord the duke, and all the court,

To quit the fine for one half of his goods,

I am content, so he will let me have

380   The other half in use, to render it

Upon his death unto the gentleman

That lately stole his daughter.

Two things provided more: that, for this favour,

He presently become a Christian;

385   The other, that he do record a gift,

Here in the court, of all he dies possessed

Unto his son, Lorenzo, and his daughter.

DUKE

He shall do this, or else I do recant

The pardon that I late pronouncèd here.

PORTIA

390   Art thou contented, Jew? What dost thou say?

SHYLOCK

I am content.

PORTIA

> Clerk, draw a deed of gift.

391   *draw:* draw up, prepare

SHYLOCK

I pray you give me leave to go from hence;

I am not well — send the deed after me,

And I will sign it.

392   *hence:* here

DUKE

> Get thee gone, but do it.

394   *do it:* make sure you carry out what has been agreed

GRATIANO

In christ'ning shalt thou have two godfathers —

Had I been judge, thou shouldst have had ten more,

To bring thee to the gallows, not to the font.

Exit SHYLOCK.

395

395–7   *In … font:* when he is being christened, Shylock will have the usual two godfathers. If it had been up to me, there would be another ten to send him to the place of execution rather than the baptismal font. Gratiano's cruel joke depends on the fact that the twelve members of a jury were also known as godfathers

DUKE

Sir, I entreat you home with me to dinner.

398   *entreat … dinner:* beg you to dine at home with me

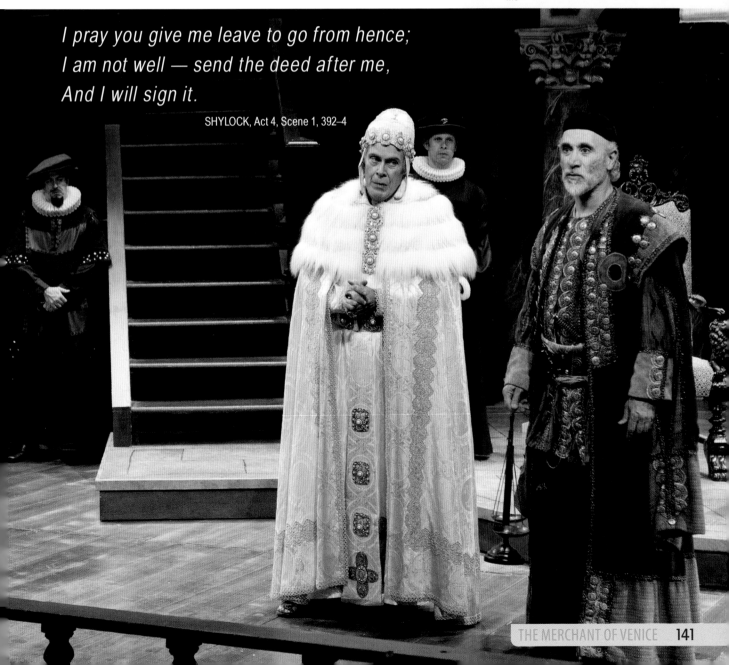

I pray you give me leave to go from hence;
I am not well — send the deed after me,
And I will sign it.

SHYLOCK, Act 4, Scene 1, 392–4

399	*I . . . pardon:* please excuse me
400	*away:* go away, leave
401	*it . . . forth:* it is fitting that I set out immediately
402	*your . . . not:* you do not have the time
403	*gratify:* reward
404	*much . . . him:* owe him a lot
406	*acquitted:* set free
407	*in lieu whereof:* as a payment for this
409	*cope . . . withal:* give you as a reward for your kind services on our behalf
413	*delivering:* rescuing
414	*account:* consider
415	*My . . . mercenary:* I have never sought payment (other than the personal satisfaction I get from helping others)
418	*of . . . further:* I really must again try to persuade you
419	*remembrance:* memento, token *tribute:* sign of esteem or gratitude
421	*deny:* refuse
422	*press me far:* are very insistent *yield:* give in
423	*for your sake:* in return for your politeness
424	*for your love:* to acknowledge your friendship

PORTIA

I humbly do desire your grace of pardon,

400   I must away this night toward Padua,

And it is meet I presently set forth.

DUKE

I am sorry that your leisure serves you not.

Antonio, gratify this gentleman,

For in my mind you are much bound to him.

Exeunt the DUKE and his TRAIN.

BASSANIO

405   Most worthy gentleman, I and my friend

Have by your wisdom been this day acquitted

Of grievous penalties, in lieu whereof

Three thousand ducats due unto the Jew

We freely cope your courteous pains withal.

ANTONIO

410   And stand indebted over and above

In love and service to you evermore.

PORTIA

He is well paid that is well satisfied,

And I, delivering you, am satisfied,

And therein do account myself well paid —

415   My mind was never yet more mercenary.

I pray you know me when we meet again.

I wish you well, and so I take my leave.

BASSANIO

Dear sir, of force I must attempt you further —

Take some remembrance of us as a tribute,

420   Not as a fee. Grant me two things I pray you:

Not to deny me, and to pardon me.

PORTIA

You press me far, and therefore I will yield.

[*to ANTONIO*] Give me your gloves, I'll wear them for your sake.

[*to BASSANIO*] And for your love, I'll take this ring from you —

425   Do not draw back your hand, I'll take no more,

And you in love shall not deny me this.

BASSANIO

This ring, good sir, alas, it is a trifle.

I will not shame myself to give you this.

PORTIA

I will have nothing else, but only this;

And now methinks I have a mind to it! 430

BASSANIO

There's more depends on this than on the value.

The dearest ring in Venice will I give you,

And find it out by proclamation —

Only for this, I pray you pardon me.

PORTIA

I see, sir, you are liberal in offers — 435

You taught me first to beg, and now methinks

You teach me how a beggar should be answered.

BASSANIO

Good sir, this ring was given me by my wife,

And when she put it on she made me vow

That I should neither sell, nor give, nor lose it. 440

PORTIA

That 'scuse serves many men to save their gifts.

And if your wife be not a madwoman,

And know how well I have deserved the ring,

She would not hold out enemy for ever

For giving it to me. Well, peace be with you! 445

Exeunt PORTIA and NERISSA.

ANTONIO

My Lord Bassanio, let him have the ring,

Let his deservings and my love withal

Be valued 'gainst your wife's commandëment.

BASSANIO

Go, Gratiano, run and overtake him;

Give him the ring, and bring him, if thou canst, 450

Unto Antonio's house — away, make haste.

Exit GRATIANO.

Come, you and I will thither presently,

And in the morning early will we both

Fly toward Belmont — come, Antonio.

Exeunt.

427	*trifle:* small, insignificant thing
428	*shame:* embarrass
430	*now … it:* it seems to me I really want it now
431	*the value:* what it cost
433	*proclamation:* public announcement
434	*Only … me:* but in the case of this ring, please forgive me for not letting you have it
435	*liberal in:* very generous in making
436–7	*taught … answered:* wanted me to ask you for something, like a beggar, and you now treat me like a beggar by refusing it
439	*vow:* swear
441	*'scuse serves:* excuse helps
444	*hold out enemy:* stay angry with you
447	*deservings:* entitlement *withal:* as well
448	*commandëment:* instructions not to part with her ring
452	*thither presently:* go there immediately
454	*Fly:* rush

Key points

In the most powerful scene in the play, the highest court in Venice must decide whether Antonio should lose a pound of his flesh, which is the penalty he agreed with Shylock if he did not pay the debt in time.

- The Duke of Venice immediately shows that he is not impartial. He makes it clear that his sympathies are with Antonio and that he has contempt for Shylock, whom he calls 'an inhuman wretch' (line 4). The dialogue suggests that the duke has already made efforts to change Shylock's mind.

- Shylock is given various opportunities to show mercy to Antonio. He refuses, basing his case on the laws of Venice, and warning the court not to undermine those laws in order to spare Antonio. There is a sense that he is enjoying his day in court; he feels in control of the proceedings and knows that the law is on his side.

- Despite Bassanio's support, Antonio gives up all hope of mercy from Shylock. He wants the trial to come to a speedy end. He has a low opinion of his own value as a human being and sees himself as a weak or sick member of the human race, and fit for death.

- The arrival of Nerissa, disguised as a lawyer's clerk, to ask the court to admit a 'young and learnèd doctor' (line 144), i.e. Portia disguised as Balthazar, marks a turning point in the proceedings. Indeed, the intervention of the disguised Portia will prove to be the turning point of the play as a whole.

- The letter from Doctor Bellario describing the amazing legal abilities of 'Balthazar' is really part of Portia's disguise. She is dressed not only as a male lawyer, but also in the reputation given to her in Bellario's letter. This letter is designed to give the court the impression that Balthazar's/Portia's views on the case should carry considerable weight.

- In a speech on the need to show mercy even to enemies, Portia suggests that Shylock, a Jew, should observe the Christian teaching on mercy. She refers to the Lord's Prayer, in which Christians ask for God's mercy and forgiveness and are taught to grant the same forgiveness to

those who have offended them. Her words make no impression on Shylock, who insists on revenge. He wants justice (which he calls the law) and will not be denied this by people who talk of mercy. Shylock's outlook is based on the Old Testament notion of an eye for an eye.

- Portia reviews the bond and, when Shylock refuses an offer of 9,000 ducats, she declares that the law allows him to cut a pound of flesh from Antonio's breast. Shylock heaps praise on this 'rightful judge' (line 298). Just as Antonio's death seems inevitable, however, Portia decrees that Shylock must not 'shed one drop of Christian blood' (lines 306–7). It is now Gratiano's turn to praise the 'upright judge' (line 310).

- Realising that he cannot proceed, Shylock agrees to accept the 9,000 ducats he was offered. Portia, however, declares that he has no choice now but to take 'the penalty' (line 319) he demanded, i.e. a pound of Antonio's flesh. Shylock faces an impossible task: to cut flesh without shedding a drop of blood, and at the same time to ensure that the quantity of flesh he removes weighs an exact pound. If he fails, the penalty of death will be imposed on him and all his goods will be confiscated.

- Shylock's situation gets worse when Portia comes up with another law of Venice that applies to an 'alien' or non-citizen (i.e. Shylock as a Jew) who directly or indirectly seeks the life of a citizen of Venice. That citizen (i.e. Antonio) can seize half of the alien's goods, the other half going to the treasury of Venice, while the Duke of Venice has the power to decide whether the offender should live or die.

- The duke spares Shylock's life, but the other penalties leave him in poverty. Shylock cannot accept this. If he loses the bulk of his wealth, his way of life will collapse. He asks to be put to death instead.

- Antonio, to show that he is a good Christian, requests that the court allow Shylock to keep half his wealth. Antonio does not want to profit from the situation either and will hold his half in trust for Lorenzo and Jessica.

However, Antonio places two conditions on this offer. Shylock must make a will leaving all he has to Jessica and Lorenzo. Shylock must also become a Christian – for Shylock, this forced conversion is the final humiliation.

- Shylock leaves the court with Gratiano's mocking words ringing in his ears, along with the duke's harsh command: 'Get thee gone, but do it' (line 394). Depending on how the actor handles this scene, audiences are usually moved by Shylock's pitiful exit.

- This is a bleak scene but there are some opportunities for comic relief. For example, Bassanio and Gratiano refer to their wives in court, unaware that their wives are present and can comment on what they hear (lines 279–91).

Useful quotes

> I am sorry for thee — thou art come to answer
> A stony adversary, an inhuman wretch
> Uncapable of pity, void and empty
> From any dram of mercy.
>
> (Duke, lines 3–6)

> I have possessed your grace of what I purpose,
> And by our holy Sabbath have I sworn
> To have the due and forfeit of my bond
>
> (Shylock, lines 35–7)

> If every ducat in six thousand ducats
> Were in six parts, and every part a ducat,
> I would not draw them; I would have my bond!
>
> (Shylock, lines 85–7)

> I am a tainted wether of the flock,
> Meetest for death — the weakest kind of fruit
> Drops earliest to the ground, and so let me.
>
> (Antonio, lines 114–16)

> The quality of mercy is not strained,
> It droppeth as the gentle rain from heaven
> Upon the place beneath; it is twice blest:
> It blesseth him that gives and him that takes.
>
> (Portia, lines 181–4)

> This bond doth give thee here no jot of blood,
> The words expressly are 'a pound of flesh':
> Take then thy bond, take thou thy pound of flesh,
> But in the cutting it, if thou dost shed
> One drop of Christian blood, thy lands and goods
> Are by the laws of Venice confiscate
> Unto the state of Venice.
>
> (Portia, lines 303–9)

> Why this bond is forfeit,
> And lawfully by this the Jew may claim
> A pound of flesh, to be by him cut off
> Nearest the merchant's heart.
>
> (Portia, lines 227–30)

> That thou shalt see the difference of our spirit,
> I pardon thee thy life before thou ask it:
> For half thy wealth, it is Antonio's;
> The other half comes to the general state,
> Which humbleness may drive unto a fine.
>
> (Duke of Venice, lines 365–9)

Questions ?

1 Does the Duke of Venice preside over the trial in a fair and impartial manner? Could Shylock argue that he has not had a fair trial? Give reasons for your answers.

2 Shylock wants the law to be applied in full. Why is that a mistake on his part?

3 Explain Portia's tactics. Why does she appear to support Shylock at first?

4 Two major themes in this scene are hatred and cruelty. Identify two examples of each.

5 There is a pattern to Gratiano's comments in this scene. What is this pattern? Are these comments typical of him throughout the play?

6 Do you think Antonio and his friends would show mercy to Shylock if he were in Antonio's position? Give reasons for your answer.

7 Portia makes a speech about mercy (lines 181–202). Does her conduct of the trial support what she says in that speech?

8 Shylock refuses to have a surgeon present (line 259). What does this tell us about his intentions?

9 The verdict is based on a claim that 'This bond doth give thee here no jot of blood' (line 303). What is your opinion of this interpretation?

10 Is the final judgement on Shylock (lines 345–89) too severe? What does it tell you about the laws of Venice? Note the reference to 'an alien' in line 346.

11 The Duke of Venice and Antonio try to demonstrate that Christians are morally superior to Shylock and the Jewish community. How does their demonstration of Christian virtue strike you?

12 Bassanio finally agrees to give away Portia's ring to please Antonio. What does this episode tell us about Bassanio's loyalty to Portia and about the feelings he has for Antonio?

13 Imagine you were given the task of being Shylock's lawyer during the trial scene. Make a plea to the court in his defence.

14 Shakespeare fails to give Shylock a farewell speech. Compose one for him in which he comments on his sufferings, his losses, his enemies and the trial.

15 Imagine you are Antonio. Write an account of how you felt at different stages of your trial and give your opinion of Shylock's punishment.

Talking point

This scene enacts a most unusual trial. Why is it unusual? Is it a fair trial? Is justice done? How does this court differ from a modern court? What are the advantages of the modern court system? Is justice always done in modern trials? Could our justice system be improved?

ACT 4 † Scene 2

Plot summary

Portia (still disguised as Balthazar) wants to find Shylock and have him sign the deed so that she and Nerissa can get back to Belmont. Gratiano arrives to give Portia the ring she sought from Bassanio. Portia accepts the ring but declines an invitation to dinner. Nerissa (still disguised as Balthazar's clerk) decides that it will be amusing if she can persuade Gratiano to give her the ring he swore to keep forever as well.

His ring I do accept most thankfully;
And so I pray you tell him. Furthermore,
I pray you show my youth old Shylock's house.

PORTIA, Act 4, Scene 2, lines 9–11

Venice. A street.

Enter PORTIA and NERISSA.

PORTIA

Inquire the Jew's house out, give him this deed

And let him sign it — we'll away tonight

And be a day before our husbands home —

This deed will be well welcome to Lorenzo.

Enter GRATIANO.

GRATIANO

Fair sir, you are well o'erta'en: 5

My Lord Bassanio, upon more advice,

Hath sent you here this ring, and doth entreat

Your company at dinner.

PORTIA

                That cannot be.

His ring I do accept most thankfully;

And so I pray you tell him. Furthermore,   10

I pray you show my youth old Shylock's house.

GRATIANO

That will I do.

NERISSA

            Sir, I would speak with you.

[*aside to PORTIA*] I'll see if I can get my husband's ring,

Which I did make him swear to keep for ever.

PORTIA

[*aside to NERISSA*] Thou mayst, I warrant. We shall have old   15
   swearing

That they did give the rings away to men;

But we'll outface them, and outswear them too.

[*aloud*] Away, make haste — thou know'st where I will tarry.

NERISSA

[*to GRATIANO*] Come, good sir, will you show me to this
   house?

Exeunt.

---

1 *Inquire ... out:* find out where Shylock lives
   this deed: the legal document in which Shylock is
   to leave his wealth to Lorenzo and Jessica

2 *away:* go away, leave

4 *well:* very

5 *you ... o'erta'en:* it is a good thing that I caught up
   with you

6 *advice:* thought

7 *entreat:* strongly request

15 *warrant:* bet
   old: plenty of

17 *outface them:* make them back down

18 *tarry:* wait

Key points

This brief scene links the serious business of the trial with the comic business of the rings that will take place in Act 5.

- Portia and Nerissa remain disguised as Balthazar and his clerk, and Gratiano has no idea that they are not who they say they are. This situation can be hard to believe for modern audiences who are accustomed to very realistic forms of drama. In Shakespeare's day, however, it was simply accepted that if a character was in disguise, no one would question or 'see through' that disguise.

- When Portia asks Gratiano, 'I pray you show my youth old Shylock's house' (line 11), she is sending Gratiano and the disguised Nerissa ('my youth') to visit Shylock with the papers that will make Lorenzo and Jessica his heirs. Shylock must sign this deed for Portia to complete her tasks as Balthazar. This act needs to be done quickly so that Portia and Nerissa can get back to Belmont ahead of their husbands.

- Portia remarks, in reference to the legal document: 'This deed will be well welcome to Lorenzo' (line 4). It seems odd that she fails to mention Jessica, without whom Lorenzo would get nothing. This omission may reflect the fact that Jessica's inheritance will be the property of her husband, or it may indicate Portia's tendency to ignore Jessica.

- In deciding that Nerissa will persuade Gratiano to part with the ring she gave him, Nerissa and Portia set the scene for Act 5, in which they will be able to embarrass their husbands when they are reunited at Belmont. They will pretend not to believe the men's explanations and accuse them of giving the rings to other women. In this way Shakespeare uses their disguises (Portia as Balthazar and Nerissa as a legal clerk) to create comic intrigue.

Useful quotes

> *My Lord Bassanio, upon more advice,*
> *Hath sent you here this ring*
>
> (Gratiano, lines 6–7)

> *We shall have old swearing*
> *That they did give the rings away to men;*
> *But we'll outface them, and outswear them too.*
>
> (Portia, lines 15–17)

Questions ❓

1 Why does Portia need Nerissa to find Shylock's house?

2 Imagine you are Shylock's servant and are present at the encounter between Shylock and Nerissa. Write a report of what happens.

3 Why does Portia decline Bassanio's invitation to dinner?

4 Write a short dialogue that takes place over dinner that evening between Gratiano and Bassanio as they look ahead to their return to Belmont.

Talking point

Disguise plays an essential part in this Act. If you were watching a play in the theatre, how might a disguise affect your response to the character and to the actor playing the part? Would it make the play seem less 'real'? Would it make the play more interesting and/or funnier?

ACT 4 ⚔ Key moments

Scene 1

- Shylock is determined to have his pound of Antonio's flesh. Despite various pleas to him to show mercy to Antonio, he insists that the bond be honoured.

- A legal expert called Balthazar arrives in court to represent Doctor Bellario, who is too sick to travel to Venice. Balthazar is Portia disguised as a doctor of laws.

- Portia/Balthazar decrees that while Shylock may take exactly one pound of flesh from Antonio, he may not take even one drop of blood.

- Under Venetian law, Shylock is then punished for his indirect attempt on Antonio's life. He loses half his goods and is forced to become a Christian and to leave all he has to his Christian daughter and son-in-law in his will.

Scene 2

- Portia, still disguised as Balthazar, accepts the ring she gave Bassanio, which is offered as a token of gratitude for saving Antonio's life. It is the ring Bassanio promised never to part with.

- Nerissa, still disguised as a clerk, will try to get her ring from Gratiano while he is showing her to Shylock's home.

ACT 4 ⚔ Speaking and listening

1 Select a student to play the Duke of Venice. He is questioned by members of the class on his conduct during the trial of Antonio. Does he stand over the way in which justice was dispensed? Why did he allow Balthazar to take charge of the trial and act as judge, jury and legal advisor to the court? He might also be asked about his hostile attitude to Shylock, one of the parties to the case, and his sympathetic attitude to Antonio, the other party.

2 Assign the part of Shylock. Select a panel of five students to question Shylock about why he was so determined to have his revenge on Antonio and whether it was always his intention to seek the penalty if Antonio failed to repay the loan on time. The questions put to Shylock might focus on his own comments at various points throughout the play. Select a further group of seven students to act as a jury. Their function is to decide whether Shylock was justified in seeking revenge.

Revision quiz: plot summary

Use the words listed in the panel to fill in the blanks in this summary of Act 4:

alien
Antonio
Balthazar
Bellario
blood
bond
Christian
clerk
confiscated
cut
Duke
fee
flesh
goods
Gratiano
justice
law
money
Nerissa
pound
ring
scales
Shylock
state
Venice

Antonio is to be tried for breaking his _____ with Shylock. He was unable to repay the 3,000 ducats on the agreed date. Shylock hates _____ and is in court to claim the penalty, which is a pound of Antonio's _____. He says it's not about the money, it's about getting _____ for a wrong that has been done to him.

The _____ of Venice has sent for Doctor Bellario of Padua to try the case. Nerissa arrives, disguised as a _____, with a letter from _____. The letter introduces a young legal expert named Balthazar, who has consulted with Bellario on the case and who will judge the matter in court. Shylock sharpens his knife and _____ taunts him.

Portia, posing as _____ and dressed like a doctor of laws, rules that no one has the power to bend the _____ and therefore Shylock may lawfully claim a pound of Antonio's flesh. Antonio prepares to be _____. Shylock has weighing _____, but will not pay for a surgeon to be on standby.

Portia states that Shylock must take exactly one _____ of flesh from Antonio, without shedding one drop of Christian _____. If he fails to do this, he must die and his goods will be _____. She explains that she is sticking to the letter of the law, which is the type of justice _____ wanted.

Shylock is now prepared to take _____ instead, but Portia will not allow it. The laws of _____ state that any _____ who attempts to kill a citizen must give half his _____ to that citizen and the other half to the _____, and it is up to the duke whether he lives or dies. Shylock claims that life will not be worth living without his home and his money.

It is decided that Antonio will keep half of Shylock's wealth in trust, and that Shylock will become a _____ and leave all he has to Jessica and Lorenzo. Shylock leaves the court a broken man.

Portia will not take a _____, but asks Bassanio to give her his _____. He refuses as it is the one he promised Portia never to give away. Antonio persuades him to part with the ring and Portia accepts it. _____ decides to see if she can persuade Gratiano to give her the ring he swore to keep forever.

ACT 5 † Scene 1

Plot summary

It is a moonlit night and Lorenzo and Jessica recall the adventures of famous but unhappy lovers. Stephano informs them that Portia will shortly arrive and then Launcelot brings the news that Bassanio can be expected before morning. They arrange for music to be played outside. Portia and Nerissa return home and request that no one mentions their absence from Belmont.

Bassanio arrives and introduces Antonio to Portia. Nerissa and Gratiano quarrel about his missing ring. Bassanio has to confess that he also gave his ring away. Portia and Nerissa pretend to be angry and announce that they will not sleep with their husbands until they see the rings again. Portia produces a ring and asks Bassanio to swear to keep it safe. He recognises the ring. She claims that she slept with the legal expert who had it. Nerissa does the same. Then they reveal the truth about their roles in the trial.

There is more good news: three of Antonio's ships have returned safely to harbour, and Lorenzo is given the deed Shylock signed leaving his possessions to him and Jessica.

Pardon this fault, and by my soul I swear
I never more will break an oath with thee.

BASSANIO, Act 5, Scene 1, 246–7

Belmont. A grove or green place before Portia's house.

Enter LORENZO and JESSICA.

LORENZO
The moon shines bright. In such a night as this,
When the sweet wind did gently kiss the trees
And they did make no noise, in such a night
Troilus methinks mounted the Trojan walls
And sighed his soul toward the Grecian tents,   5
Where Cressid lay that night.

JESSICA
               In such a night
Did Thisbe fearfully o'ertrip the dew
And saw the lion's shadow ere himself
And ran dismayed away.

LORENZO
             In such a night
Stood Dido with a willow in her hand   10
Upon the wild sea banks and waft her love
To come again to Carthage.

JESSICA
            In such a night
Medea gatherèd the enchanted herbs
That did renew old Aeson.

LORENZO
            In such a night
Did Jessica steal from the wealthy Jew   15
And with an unthrift love did run from Venice
As far as Belmont.

JESSICA
          In such a night
Did young Lorenzo swear he loved her well,
Stealing her soul with many vows of faith
And ne'er a true one.

LORENZO
           In such a night   20
Did pretty Jessica, like a little shrew,
Slander her love, and he forgave it her.

4–6 *Troilus … night:* Lorenzo is recalling an ancient story of unhappy lovers. Troilus, one of the sons of the King of Troy, loved Cressida, who was separated from him when she was taken hostage by the Greeks

7–9 *Did … away:* on Thisbe's way to meet her lover, Pyramus, she saw the lion's shadow and was frightened away

10–12 *Stood … Carthage:* Dido, Queen of Carthage, was abandoned by her wandering lover, Aeneas, and holds a willow as a symbol of forsaken love *waft:* wafted, waved

13–14 *Medea … Aeson:* Medea was a magician who healed Aeson with magic herbs

16 *an unthrift love:* a lover without money

20 *ne'er … one:* not one (of Lorenzo's promises of love) can be believed

21 *shrew:* nagging woman

22 *Slander her love:* speak falsely about her lover

23 *out-night . . . come:* beat you at this storytelling game if we were not interrupted. Jessica and Lorenzo have been competing with each other in telling stories beginning 'In such a night'

24 *hark:* listen
footing: footsteps

31 *holy crosses:* wayside crosses

32 *wedlock hours:* married life

37 *ceremoniously:* with proper ceremony

39 *Sola . . . sola:* Launcelot is imitating the sound of the horn blown by a messenger arriving with news

43 *Leave hollowing:* stop making that noise

JESSICA

I would out-night you, did nobody come:

But hark, I hear the footing of a man.

Enter STEPHANO, a messenger.

LORENZO

25 Who comes so fast in silence of the night?

STEPHANO

A friend!

LORENZO

A friend! What friend? Your name I pray you, friend?

STEPHANO

Stephano is my name, and I bring word

My mistress will before the break of day

30 Be here at Belmont — she doth stray about

By holy crosses, where she kneels and prays

For happy wedlock hours.

LORENZO

                                                            Who comes with her?

STEPHANO

None but a holy hermit and her maid.

I pray you is my master yet returned?

LORENZO

35 He is not, nor we have not heard from him.

But go we in I pray thee, Jessica,

And ceremoniously let us prepare

Some welcome for the mistress of the house.

Enter LAUNCELOT.

LAUNCELOT

Sola, sola! Wo ha, ho! Sola, sola!

LORENZO

40 Who calls?

LAUNCELOT

Sola! Did you see Master Lorenzo? Master Lorenzo, sola, sola!

LORENZO

Leave hollowing, man — here.

LAUNCELOT

Sola! Where, where?

LORENZO

Here.

45

LAUNCELOT

Tell him there's a post come from my master with his horn
full of good news — my master will be here ere morning.

Exit.

LORENZO

Sweet soul, let's in, and there expect their coming.

And yet no matter: why should we go in?

My friend Stephano, signify I pray you

50

Within the house your mistress is at hand,

And bring your music forth into the air.

Exit STEPHANO.

How sweet the moonlight sleeps upon this bank!

Here will we sit and let the sounds of music

Creep in our ears — soft stillness and the night

55

Become the touches of sweet harmony.

Sit, Jessica. Look how the floor of heaven

Is thick inlaid with patens of bright gold.

There's not the smallest orb which thou behold'st

But in his motion like an angel sings,

60

Still quiring to the young-eyed cherubins;

Such harmony is in immortal souls,

But whilst this muddy vesture of decay

Doth grossly close it in, we cannot hear it.

Enter MUSICIANS.

Come, ho, and wake Diana with a hymn!

65

With sweetest touches pierce your mistress' ear,

And draw her home with music.

Music.

JESSICA

I am never merry when I hear sweet music.

LORENZO

The reason is your spirits are attentive:

For do but note a wild and wanton herd

70

46–7	*post … news:* messenger who has just arrived from my master with plenty of good news
47	*ere:* before
48	*let's in:* let us go inside *expect:* wait for
50–51	*signify … hand:* please let everyone inside know that Portia is returning soon
52	*forth:* outside
56	*Become:* suit
57	*floor of heaven:* sky
58	*thick … gold:* richly decorated with small pieces of shining gold *patens:* shallow gold saucers used in Holy Communion services
59–60	*There's … sings:* even the smallest heavenly body moving in the sky is constantly producing beautiful music
61	*Still … cherubins:* always singing to the angels
62–4	*Such … hear it:* our souls, which are immortal like angels, could hear the heavenly music of the stars if they were able to break free of our coarse, decaying bodies
65	*Diana:* Roman goddess of the moon and of chastity
69	*The … attentive:* that is because you respond so well to it
70	*note:* observe *wanton:* playful

71 *unhandled colts:* untrained horses

72 *Fetching mad bounds:* jumping wildly

73 *Which ... blood:* because it is in their nature to behave wildly

74 *perchance:* perhaps

76 *make ... stand:* all stop together

77 *modest:* gentle, quiet

78 *poet:* Roman poet Ovid

79–81 *Did ... nature:* pretended that the glorious music of Orpheus was able to charm all natural things, even trees, since music can change the nature of even the most insensitive things

82–4 *The ... spoils:* anyone who lacks a feeling for music, and who is not moved by its harmony and melody, is fit only to be a traitor, a plotter and a destroyer

85–6 *The ... Erebus:* his instincts and feelings are as dark as the way to hell

87 *Mark:* pay attention to

90 *naughty:* wicked

92 *So ... less:* the brightest light makes others seem dim

93–6 *A substitute ... waters:* a king's deputy shines as brightly as a king until the king himself appears, and then the deputy's glory vanishes as a river does into the sea

98 *without respect:* unless it is compared to something else

100 *Silence ... it:* the surrounding silence makes the music sound sweeter

Or race of youthful and unhandled colts
Fetching mad bounds, bellowing and neighing loud,
Which is the hot condition of their blood —
If they but hear perchance a trumpet sound,
75 Or any air of music touch their ears,
You shall perceive them make a mutual stand,
Their savage eyes turned to a modest gaze
By the sweet power of music. Therefore the poet
Did feign that Orpheus drew trees, stones and floods,
80 Since naught so stockish, hard and full of rage
But music for the time doth change his nature.
The man that hath no music in himself,
Nor is not moved with concord of sweet sounds,
Is fit for treasons, stratagems and spoils;
85 The motions of his spirit are dull as night
And his affections dark as Erebus:
Let no such man be trusted. Mark the music.

Enter PORTIA and NERISSA.

PORTIA
That light we see is burning in my hall:
How far that little candle throws his beams —
90 So shines a good deed in a naughty world.

NERISSA
When the moon shone we did not see the candle.

PORTIA
So doth the greater glory dim the less —
A substitute shines brightly as a king
Until a king be by, and then his state
95 Empties itself, as doth an inland brook
Into the main of waters. Music, hark!

NERISSA
It is your music, madam, of the house.

PORTIA
Nothing is good, I see, without respect —
Methinks it sounds much sweeter than by day.

NERISSA
100 Silence bestows that virtue on it, madam.

PORTIA

The crow doth sing as sweetly as the lark

When neither is attended, and I think

The nightingale, if she should sing by day

When every goose is cackling, would be thought

No better a musician than the wren.　　　　　　105

How many things by season, seasoned are

To their right praise and true perfection!

Peace, how the moon sleeps with Endymion

And would not be awaked.

Music ceases.

LORENZO

　　　　　　　　That is the voice,

Or I am much deceived, of Portia.　　　　　　110

PORTIA

He knows me as the blind man knows the cuckoo —

By the bad voice!

LORENZO

　　　　　　　Dear lady, welcome home.

PORTIA

We have been praying for our husbands' welfare,

Which speed, we hope, the better for our words.

Are they returned?

LORENZO

　　　　　　　Madam, they are not yet;　　　　115

But there is come a messenger before

To signify their coming.

PORTIA

　　　　　　　Go in, Nerissa;

Give order to my servants that they take

No note at all of our being absent hence;

Nor you, Lorenzo; Jessica, nor you.　　　　　120

A tucket sounds.

LORENZO

Your husband is at hand, I hear his trumpet —

We are no tell-tales, madam; fear you not.

102　*attended:* listened to

106–7　*How … perfection:* we admire many things because we see or meet them at the right time

108–9　*how … awaked:* Endymion was a shepherd, with whom the moon-goddess fell in love and so kept him asleep forever. Portia is referring to Lorenzo and Jessica

114　*Which … words:* we hope they have benefited from our prayers

117　*signify:* announce

tucket: trumpet

PORTIA

This night methinks is but the daylight sick;

It looks a little paler — 'tis a day,

125 Such as the day is when the sun is hid.

Enter BASSANIO, ANTONIO, GRATIANO, and their FOLLOWERS.

BASSANIO

We should hold day with the Antipodes,

If you would walk in absence of the sun.

PORTIA

Let me give light, but let me not be light,

For a light wife doth make a heavy husband,

130 And never be Bassanio so for me —

But God sort all: you are welcome home, my lord.

BASSANIO

I thank you, madam. Give welcome to my friend —

This is the man, this is Antonio,

To whom I am so infinitely bound.

PORTIA

135 You should in all sense be much bound to him,

For, as I hear, he was much bound for you.

ANTONIO

No more than I am well acquitted of.

PORTIA

Sir, you are very welcome to our house:

It must appear in other ways than words,

140 Therefore I scant this breathing courtesy.

GRATIANO

[*to NERISSA*] By yonder moon I swear you do me wrong,

In faith, I gave it to the judge's clerk —

Would he were gelt that had it for my part,

Since you do take it, love, so much at heart.

PORTIA

145 A quarrel ho, already! What's the matter?

GRATIANO

About a hoop of gold, a paltry ring

That she did give me, whose posy was

126–7 *We . . . sun:* we'd have the same daytime as they have on the other side of the world, as you make it seem like daylight even when the sun is not shining

128 *be light:* be unfaithful

129 *heavy:* sad, mournful

134 *infinitely bound:* indebted forever

135 *bound to him:* attached to him as a friend

136 *bound:* bound by the bond and by prison chains

137 *No . . . of:* everything he owed me has been repaid to me

140 *scant . . . courtesy:* cut short this verbal welcome

143 *gelt:* gelded, castrated
for my part: I must say

146 *paltry:* cheap

147 *posy:* an inscription inside a ring

148–9	*cutlers' . . . knife:* the verse a knife-maker might inscribe on a knife
149	*'Love . . . not':* do not desert me, and do not give this ring away
150	*What:* why
154–5	*Though . . . it:* if you did not keep your promise for my sake, you should have kept it out of respect for the ardent oaths you swore
157	*wear:* grow
158	*and if:* provided
161	*scrubbèd:* stunted, short
163	*prating:* talkative
165	*to blame:* wrong
166	*slightly:* easily
168	*riveted:* attached, fastened
172–3	*the . . . masters:* all the money in the world
175	*'twere to me:* if I were treated like that

For all the world like cutlers' poetry

Upon a knife, 'Love me, and leave me not.'

NERISSA

150 What talk you of the posy or the value?

You swore to me when I did give it you

That you would wear it till your hour of death

And that it should lie with you in your grave —

Though not for me, yet for your vehement oaths,

155 You should have been respective and have kept it.

Gave it a judge's clerk! No, God's my judge,

The clerk will ne'er wear hair on 's face that had it.

GRATIANO

He will, and if he live to be a man.

NERISSA

Ay, if a woman live to be a man.

GRATIANO

160 Now, by this hand I gave it to a youth,

A kind of boy, a little scrubbèd boy

No higher than thyself, the judge's clerk,

A prating boy that begged it as a fee —

I could not for my heart deny it him.

PORTIA

165 You were to blame, I must be plain with you,

To part so slightly with your wife's first gift,

A thing stuck on with oaths upon your finger,

And so riveted with faith unto your flesh.

I gave my love a ring and made him swear

170 Never to part with it, and here he stands —

I dare be sworn for him he would not leave it

Nor pluck it from his finger for the wealth

That the world masters. Now in faith, Gratiano,

You give your wife too unkind a cause of grief,

175 An 'twere to me, I should be mad at it.

BASSANIO [*aside*]

Why I were best to cut my left hand off

And swear I lost the ring defending it.

GRATIANO

My Lord Bassanio gave his ring away

Unto the judge that begged it, and indeed

Deserved it too; and then the boy, his clerk,   180

That took some pains in writing, he begged mine;

And neither man nor master would take aught

But the two rings.

PORTIA
          What ring gave you, my lord?

Not that, I hope, which you received of me.

BASSANIO

If I could add a lie unto a fault,   185

I would deny it; but you see my finger

Hath not the ring upon it; it is gone.

PORTIA

Even so void is your false heart of truth.

By heaven I will ne'er come in your bed

Until I see the ring.

NERISSA
          Nor I in yours   190

Till I again see mine.

BASSANIO
          Sweet Portia,

If you did know to whom I gave the ring,

If you did know for whom I gave the ring,

And would conceive for what I gave the ring,

And how unwillingly I left the ring,   195

When nought would be accepted but the ring,

You would abate the strength of your displeasure.

PORTIA

If you had known the virtue of the ring,

Or half her worthiness that gave the ring,

Or your own honour to contain the ring,   200

You would not then have parted with the ring.

What man is there so much unreasonable —

If you had pleased to have defended it

With any terms of zeal — wanted the modesty

To urge the thing held as a ceremony?   205

Nerissa teaches me what to believe:

I'll die for't, but some woman had the ring.

182 *aught:* anything

188 *Even ... truth:* I now see how lacking in truth your dishonest heart is

194 *conceive:* understand

196 *nought:* nothing

197 *abate ... displeasure:* stop being so annoyed

198 *virtue:* power, strength (as a love-token)

200 *honour to contain:* duty to keep

202–5 *What ... ceremony?* If you had argued with vigour ('zeal') against giving away the ring, what man would be so lacking in tact or good manners as to press you to give away something you regarded as a sacred token?

BASSANIO

No, by my honour, madam, by my soul

No woman had it, but a civil doctor,

210   Which did refuse three thousand ducats of me

And begged the ring — the which I did deny him

And suffered him to go displeased away;

Even he that did uphold the very life

Of my dear friend. What should I say, sweet lady?

215   I was enforced to send it after him,

I was beset with shame and courtesy,

My honour would not let ingratitude

So much besmear it. Pardon me, good lady,

For, by these blessèd candles of the night,

220   Had you been there I think you would have begged

The ring of me to give the worthy doctor.

PORTIA

Let not that doctor e'er come near my house —

Since he hath got the jewel that I loved,

And that which you did swear to keep for me,

225   I will become as liberal as you:

I'll not deny him anything I have,

No, not my body nor my husband's bed;

Know him I shall, I am well sure of it.

Lie not a night from home; watch me like Argus —

230   If you do not, if I be left alone,

Now by mine honour, which is yet mine own,

I'll have that doctor for my bedfellow.

NERISSA

And I his clerk; therefore be well advised

How you do leave me to mine own protection.

GRATIANO

235   Well do you so; let not me take him then;

For if I do, I'll mar the young clerk's pen.

ANTONIO

I am th'unhappy subject of these quarrels.

PORTIA

Sir, grieve not you; you are welcome notwithstanding.

---

209 *civil doctor:* doctor of civil law (also a mannerly doctor)

213 *uphold:* save

215 *enforced:* obliged

216 *beset with:* overcome by

217–18 *My ... it:* to be so thankless would have stained my honour

219 *blessèd ... night:* stars

222 *e'er:* ever

225 *liberal:* generous

228 *Know him:* sleep with him (a pun as it also means 'recognise him')

229 *from:* away from
    watch ... Argus: keep watching me closely. Argus had a hundred eyes

233 *be well advised:* take good care

234 *mine own protection:* take care of my own honour

235 *take him:* catch him with you

236 *mar:* damage

237 *th'unhappy subject of:* responsible for

238 *grieve not you:* do not be sorry
    notwithstanding: in spite of that

BASSANIO

Portia, forgive me this enforcèd wrong;

And, in the hearing of these many friends,   240

I swear to thee, even by thine own fair eyes,

Wherein I see myself—

PORTIA

                        Mark you but that!

In both my eyes he doubly sees himself;

In each eye, one — swear by your double self,

And there's an oath of credit.

BASSANIO

                      Nay, but hear me.   245

Pardon this fault, and by my soul I swear

I never more will break an oath with thee.

ANTONIO

I once did lend my body for his wealth,

Which, but for him that had your husband's ring,

Had quite miscarried. I dare be bound again,   250

My soul upon the forfeit, that your lord

Will never more break faith advisedly.

PORTIA

Then you shall be his surety. Give him this,

And bid him keep it better than the other.

ANTONIO

Here, Lord Bassanio, swear to keep this ring.   255

BASSANIO

By heaven it is the same I gave the doctor!

PORTIA

I had it of him: pardon me, Bassanio,

For, by this ring, the doctor lay with me.

NERISSA

And pardon me, my gentle Gratiano,

For that same scrubbèd boy, the doctor's clerk,   260

In lieu of this last night did lie with me.

GRATIANO

Why this is like the mending of highways

In summer, where the ways are fair enough!

What, are we cuckolds ere we have deserved it?

239 *this enforcèd wrong:* the wrong I was compelled to do

243 *In . . . himself:* he sees his reflection twice when he looks into my eyes. The suggestion is that Bassanio is two-faced or false

245 *of credit:* one might believe. She means the opposite, of course, since she is speaking sarcastically

248 *wealth:* happiness

250 *Had quite miscarried:* our plans and hopes would have gone entirely astray

252 *advisedly:* deliberately

253 *surety:* guarantee
    this: my ring

258 *lay:* slept

261 *In . . . this:* in exchange for my ring

263 *where . . . enough:* when there is no need to repair them (as they stay in good condition during summer weather). Gratiano means that Portia and Nerissa had no need to take lovers when they already have husbands

264 *cuckolds:* deceived husbands

265 *grossly:* coarsely, rudely
amazed: confused

270 *witness:* testify that

271 *even but now:* only just now

275–6 *argosies . . . suddenly:* large trading ships laden
with cargo have reached harbour

PORTIA

265 Speak not so grossly. You are all amazed.

Here is a letter, read it at your leisure;

It comes from Padua, from Bellario:

There you shall find that Portia was the doctor,

Nerissa there her clerk. Lorenzo here

270 Shall witness I set forth as soon as you,

And even but now returned; I have not yet

Entered my house. Antonio, you are welcome,

And I have better news in store for you

Than you expect: unseal this letter soon,

275 There you shall find three of your argosies

Are richly come to harbour suddenly.

You shall not know by what strange accident

I chancèd on this letter.

ANTONIO

I am dumb!

BASSANIO

Were you the doctor and I knew you not?

GRATIANO

280 Were you the clerk that is to make me cuckold?

NERISSA

Ay, but the clerk that never means to do it,

Unless he live until he be a man.

BASSANIO

Sweet doctor, you shall be my bedfellow —

When I am absent, then lie with my wife.

ANTONIO

285 Sweet lady, you have given me life and living;

For here I read for certain that my ships

Are safely come to road.

285 *life:* by saving my life in the trial
living: by bringing news that I am back in business
and can earn a living again

287 *road:* an anchorage

PORTIA

How now, Lorenzo?

My clerk hath some good comforts too for you.

NERISSA

Ay, and I'll give them him without a fee.

290 There do I give to you and Jessica

From the rich Jew, a special deed of gift,

After his death, of all he dies possessed of.

LORENZO

Fair ladies, you drop manna in the way

Of starvèd people.

293   *manna:* this was the life-saving food the Israelites found in the desert. It was a gift from God

PORTIA

           It is almost morning,

And yet I am sure you are not satisfied   295

Of these events at full. Let us go in,

And charge us there upon inter'gatories,

And we will answer all things faithfully.

295–6   *are . . . full:* do not really understand how all these things have happened

297–8   *charge . . . faithfully:* make us answer like witnesses in a court of law and we will answer fully and truly

GRATIANO

Let it be so — the first inter'gatory

That my Nerissa shall be sworn on is   300

Whether till the next night she had rather stay,

Or go to bed now, being two hours to day.

But were the day come, I should wish it dark

That I were couching with the doctor's clerk.

Well, while I live I'll fear no other thing   305

So sore as keeping safe Nerissa's ring.

Exeunt.

299   *inter'gatory:* question

301   *stay:* wait

304   *couching:* lying in bed

305–6   *while . . . ring:* as long as I live, I will think it is my first duty to guard the ring Nerissa has given me

Key points

Issues left over from earlier scenes are resolved. The three pairs of lovers are reunited at Belmont and, despite some comic confusion over the rings given away by Bassanio and Gratiano, their stories appear to end happily, as does Antonio's.

- The dark material of Act 4 made the play feel like a potential tragedy. However, since *The Merchant of Venice* is a comedy, Shakespeare needed it to end on a happy note that would allow the audience to forget the trial scene and the bitter humiliation of Shylock.

- Shylock, the hated 'alien', has been disgraced and expelled through the trial scene, which presented events in the 'real' world. Now we are left with the main Christian characters in the fairy-tale atmosphere of Belmont.

- Shakespeare uses music and moonlight to banish the bitterness of the previous Act. However, it is worth noting that the lovers of the past whom Lorenzo and Jessica call to mind were all unfortunate.

- The play also takes on a religious tone. It is claimed that Portia stops from time to time on her way home to pray for a happy marriage, kneeling before 'holy crosses' (lines 30–32). She is accompanied by Nerissa and 'a holy hermit' (line 33).

- Lorenzo sounds like a preacher as he celebrates the beauty of the heavens. The imagery of his most famous speech (lines 53–67) is explicitly Christian: the stars are compared to the gold patens used in Holy Communion services; the planets produce heavenly music like angels singing to other angels.

- Belmont seems to have had a civilising effect on Lorenzo. In Act 2, Scene 6 he was a receiver of stolen goods. Now he is a man with deep poetic feeling, celebrating the heavenly choirs of angels, and sensitive to the power of music over men and beasts. It is possible that Lorenzo is not speaking in character, but is being used by Shakespeare to create atmosphere.

- Antonio is given very little to say, yet his role in this scene is interesting and raises a number of questions. What place is there for him in this supposedly happy ending, where love and marriage dominate? Having just escaped with his life, does he remain a sad, depressed figure? Is it too much to expect Antonio to enter into the spirit of these celebrations? After all, can he hope for anything more than a life of loneliness stretching into the future?

- Bassanio's first thought after greeting Portia with flattering words is to ask her to welcome his friend Antonio, the man to whom he is 'so infinitely bound' (line 134). Portia's reply, 'You should in all sense be much bound to him' (line 135), suggests that she hopes their friendship will continue.

- The long-drawn-out episode of the rings (lines 141–284) concludes the action of the play. The argument that Portia and Nerissa have with their husbands is not to be taken seriously. Since this scene is part of a romantic comedy, the audience knows that neither Bassanio nor Gratiano will be punished for parting with the rings. Their wives are merely teasing them.

- It is left to Antonio to bring the episode of the rings to a conclusion when he intervenes to enter into another bond with Bassanio; this time he pledges his soul to guarantee that Bassanio will never again swear a false oath to Portia (lines 248–52).

- Portia's role at the end of the play is to be the bringer of good news for the other main characters. She has unexpected news for Antonio: three of his ships have docked safely and he is a wealthy man again. The future also looks bright for Jessica and Lorenzo: Nerissa informs them that when Shylock dies, all his wealth and property will pass to them.

- The dramatically powerful scenes in the play are those in which Shylock has appeared and been a dominant figure. When he is absent from the stage, there is less tension and therefore less of interest. Act 5, in which he is virtually forgotten except for the money he must leave to Jessica and Lorenzo, reminds us what a vital and fascinating part of the dramatic action he has been, and shows how tame the play becomes without him.

Useful quotes

Sit, Jessica. Look how the floor of heaven
Is thick inlaid with patens of bright gold.
There's not the smallest orb which thou behold'st
But in his motion like an angel sings

(Lorenzo, lines 57–60)

Sweet lady, you have given me life and living;
For here I read for certain that my ships
Are safely come to road.

(Antonio, lines 285–7)

Questions ?

1 Describe the setting at the start of Act 5.

2 The love stories Lorenzo and Jessica recall deal with loss, betrayal and tragedy (lines 1–22). Can you relate these themes to what happens in the play?

3 Candles, music, moonlight. What sort of atmosphere do the returning characters find in Belmont?

4 Describe the welcome that Antonio receives to Belmont.

5 Should Bassanio and Gratiano feel guilty about giving away their rings? Do you find their reasons for doing so convincing?

6 'Fair ladies, you drop manna in the way of starvèd people' (lines 293–4). Does Lorenzo's final comment suggest that he is a fortune-hunter? Give reasons for your answer.

7 What is the purpose of this scene? Does it add to the play as a whole?

8 Do all the characters in the play, including Shylock, deserve what they get?

9 Do you find this scene as interesting as the previous ones, especially those involving Shylock? Give reasons for your answer.

10 Jessica is silent after line 68. Write an account of what she may be thinking.

Talking point

A comedy is supposed to have a happy ending. Do you think this scene serves that purpose? Suppose the play had ended at the close of Act 4, what difference would this have made? Would it have been a better play? Would it still have been a comedy? Why do we like happy endings?

ACT 5 ⚔ Key moments

Scene 1

- Lorenzo and Jessica enjoy a romantic moonlit night in Belmont. They speak about other lovers and about the power of music.

- Portia and Nerissa return just ahead of Bassanio, Gratiano and Antonio. The happy reunion turns into a quarrel over the rings that the husbands gave away, breaking their oaths not to do so.

- Antonio is prepared to guarantee that Bassanio will be faithful to Portia.

- Eventually the truth is revealed: Portia and Nerissa return their rings to their husbands, and a letter from Doctor Bellario explains that Portia was Balthazar and Nerissa was the clerk.

- Antonio discovers that three of his ships have made it back to harbour and he is back in business.

- Lorenzo learns that he and Jessica will inherit Shylock's wealth.

- The couples are reconciled and go indoors to celebrate.

ACT 5 ⚔ Speaking and listening

1 Select a class member to play Antonio. The other students question his recent experiences and his outlook for the future. For example: Is he still sad? Why does he hate Jews? Did Shylock get what he deserved? Why did he insist that Shylock become a Christian? Why, during the course of the trial, did he describe himself as fit only for death? Has he changed his mind about living? How does he feel about the other characters now?

2 Select a class member to play Jessica. The other students question her about her recent experiences and her outlook for the future. For example: Why did she run away from her father? Why did she steal his valuable possessions? Does she feel guilty for what she has done? How does she feel about what has happened to her father since she left him? Is she happy with her choice of husband? Does she enjoy life at Belmont?

Revision quiz: plot summary

Q

Use the words listed in the panel to fill in the blanks in this summary of Act 5:

| atmosphere |
| Bassanio |
| bed |
| bedfellow |
| Bellario |
| Belmont |
| clerk |
| generous |
| happy |
| husband |
| Jessica |
| lawyer |
| Lorenzo |
| marriage |
| moon |
| musicians |
| Nerissa |
| oath |
| penalty |
| Portia |
| ring |
| Shylock |
| three |
| Venice |
| woman |

The last Act brings the play to a _____ ending for all the main characters except _____.

Lorenzo and _____ look up at the bright _____ and compare the night to ancient nights involving unfortunate couples and to the recent night when they ran away from _____.

Stephano interrupts to let them know that _____ has been praying for a happy _____ and will be back before dawn. Then Launcelot announces that _____ will also return before morning.

Lorenzo calls for _____ to play outside as beautiful music will complement the heavenly sky above and create a peaceful and moving _____.

Portia is happy to return to the light and music of _____. She immediately asks whether her _____ has returned from Venice. Relieved to hear that he has not, she gives instructions that no one should mention that she and _____ have been away.

Bassanio and Portia are reunited. Antonio is introduced and welcomed to Belmont. Nerissa and Gratiano squabble over his missing _____. Gratiano swore that he would wear Nerissa's ring until death, but he has given it away to a _____. Nerissa suggests that maybe he gave it to another _____. Portia condemns Gratiano and says she would be very upset if Bassanio gave away her ring. Gratiano then tells her that is exactly what her husband has done.

Bassanio admits the truth, tries to explain why he did it and begs for forgiveness. Portia says that as Bassanio gave the lawyer the ring, she will be just as _____ if she meets him and have him as her _____.

Antonio steps in to guarantee that Bassanio will never break an _____ to Portia again. This time Antonio offers his soul as the _____. Portia hands over a ring that Bassanio must swear to keep. He recognises it, and she says she got it from the _____.

Portia produces a letter from _____ saying that she was the lawyer and Nerissa was her clerk. She gives another letter to Antonio stating that _____ of his trading ships have made it safely to harbour. Nerissa hands over the deed in which Shylock agrees to leave his wealth to _____ and Jessica.

Everyone goes inside to answer more questions, although Gratiano would rather he and Nerissa went to _____.

The Merchant of Venice  Crossword

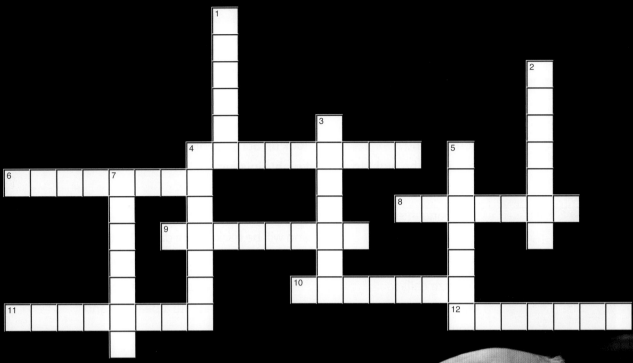

Across

4 Who leaves one master to serve another?

6 Who chooses the lead casket?

8 Who chooses the gold casket?

9 Who is a lawyer living in Padua?

10 Who brings Antonio's letter to Belmont?

11 Who gives his ring away to the clerk?

12 Who is disguised as a lawyer's clerk?

Down

1 Whose suitors must take part in a lottery to win her?

2 Who wants to take a pound of another man's flesh?

3 Who steals her father's valuables?

4 Who elopes with Shylock's daughter?

5 Who chooses the silver casket?

7 Who loses his ships at sea?

Characters

It is hard to know what to make of some of the characters in *The Merchant of Venice*. Are they good or bad, heroes or villains? Shakespeare's text allows for a variety of responses to some of the characters and their roles. They are neither totally virtuous nor totally evil, which has allowed actors to interpret them in very different ways.

Who is the play's main character?

Is it the 'Merchant of Venice' of the title? Who is the 'Merchant of Venice'? Unlike other plays, such as *Hamlet* or *Macbeth*, it is not obvious who the central character of this play is. When the play was published in 1600, its title page read:

> *The most excellent history of the Merchant of Venice. With the extreme cruelty of Shylock the Jew towards the said Merchant, in cutting a just pound of his flesh, and the obtaining of Portia by the choice of three chests.*

This title suggests that Antonio is the 'Merchant of Venice', but that Shylock and the casket lottery are the chief attractions of the play. Antonio is indeed central to the action because his fate is of major concern to most of the other characters.

Based on the amount of lines and the number of speeches each character has and the number of scenes in which each character appears on stage (see table), Portia is the main character.

	Lines	Speeches	Scenes
Portia	22%	117	9
Shylock	13%	79	5
Bassanio	13%	73	6
Gratiano	7%	58	7
Antonio	7%	47	6
Lorenzo	7%	47	7

Although Shylock appears in only five scenes, he has a major influence on what happens to many of the other characters.

Analysing characters

Your opinion of a character will depend on what he or she does and says in the course of the play.

Whenever characters speak directly to the audience in asides or soliloquies, they usually tell the truth. For example, when Shylock says that he hates Antonio in an aside in Act 1, Scene 3, he is showing us his real feelings.

What characters say in dialogue with other characters is more complicated. It may be considered under two headings:

- *Words about themselves:* what characters say about themselves in this play is generally true. When Antonio, in the very first line of the play, says that he does not know why he is so sad, there is no need to doubt him.

- *Words about other characters:* we cannot always take what characters say about each other at face value. For example, some characters use nasty animal images to describe Shylock, but these are simply expressions of prejudice. They tell us more about the flaws of the characters who use them than they do about Shylock. Likewise, characters may be dishonest in their use of praise (or flattery). However, if the person being praised is not on stage at the time, we may assume that the praise is both sincere and deserved.

Sometimes what characters say they believe in is contradicted by what they do. In other words, they do not practise what they preach. For example, Portia suggests that people should be merciful and forgive those who have harmed them, but then she insists that Shylock face the full force of the law, with little mention of mercy.

Shylock

cruel

greedy

selfish

merciless

inhuman

mercenary

frugal

vengeful

vindictive

suspicious

unethical

unfortunate

proud

entrepreneurial

persecuted

Over the years actors have interpreted, and audiences have responded to, the character and role of Shylock in various ways. He is often seen as representing an extreme: either a devilish monster or a tortured scapegoat. In truth, Shylock is a mixture of both.

Shylock is an ambivalent character: he has both good points and bad ones. A sensible account of Shylock must include his evil intentions and his cruelty, but must also admit that he is a victim of the wickedness of others and has strong motives for acting as he does.

Shylock's flaws

The unpleasant, repulsive side of Shylock's character is easily outlined:

- He is greedy and selfish. He makes a profit by exploiting the need of other people for money.

- He is cruel and hard-hearted. He treats Launcelot Gobbo so meanly that he wants to leave Shylock's service. Jessica, his daughter, dislikes him enough to run away from him.

- He is vengeful. Perhaps the most frightening thing about Shylock is his fierce desire for revenge on Antonio. He is determined to have Antonio's life. He shows no mercy to Antonio when he has him in his power.

As a result of his flaws, most of the other characters dislike Shylock. They laugh at his suffering, believing that he is being justly punished for his wickedness. When he leaves the courtroom (and the play) a broken man in Act 4, Scene 1, nobody shows any pity for him.

A pound of flesh

When Antonio and Bassanio come looking for a loan, Shylock seems prepared to ignore the wrongs Antonio has done him in the past: 'I would be friends with you, and have your love, forget the shames that you have stained me with' (Act 1, Scene 3, lines 132–3). Shylock will even let Bassanio have the money he wants interest-free. But then he adds an odd condition: if Antonio cannot repay the loan within three months, Shylock may take a pound of his flesh.

What should we make of Shylock's bargain? Is it a joke? Or is it really a vicious scheme to kill Antonio by legal means? There is some evidence in the play to support this second option. For example, Jessica claims that, even before her elopement, Shylock wanted Antonio's life and said he would rather have Antonio's flesh than 60,000 ducats.

When he makes the deal, however, Shylock cannot possibly know that Antonio will be

unable to pay on the day the money is due. There is nothing in the play to support the idea that he does. Antonio, who must know his situation better than Shylock does, clearly believes his ships will arrive on time.

When the bond is being agreed, all we can say about it for certain is that it is a horrible fantasy on Shylock's part.

Shylock's motives

Shylock's enemies decide that he is no better than a devil or a monster for seeking his pound of flesh. Before we also condemn him, we should try to discover if Shylock has a case.

In fact, Shylock has many motives for behaving as he does towards Antonio:

- Antonio detests Shylock and treats him horribly. He has spat on Shylock, kicked him and called him a dog. He admits that he would do the same again. He encourages Shylock's enemies to hate him more.

- Antonio hates the Jewish race as a whole, of which Shylock is a proud member.

- Antonio deplores the business of moneylending. He has damaged Shylock's trade by lending money without charging interest.

- One of Antonio's friends, Lorenzo, has eloped with Shylock's daughter, Jessica. The couple fled with a huge haul of Shylock's money and valuables, including a ring from his late wife that meant a lot to him. Shylock's biggest loss, however, is Jessica. Without her, his house is no longer a home.

For the above reasons, audience members often feel sympathy for Shylock.

Shylock can rightly blame Antonio and his friends for his losses. And it is little wonder that his grief at these losses drives him to despair. In this black mood, he is ready to take any revenge on his enemies that comes to mind.

In an impressive speech (Act 3, Scene 1, lines 47–60), Shylock makes three strong points that help us to understand fully his motives for trying to take Antonio's life:

- Antonio has disgraced him in public, prevented him from making deals, laughed at his losses, mocked him whenever he made money, showed contempt for the Jewish people, turned friends against him and encouraged enemies to persecute him. Antonio has done all this because Shylock is a Jew.

- Shylock deserves to be treated as a human being, something he is denied by Antonio and his friends. He points out that Jews and Christians share a common humanity and are essentially the same.

- Like everyone else, Jews reflect the society in which they live. Since Venetian society is vengeful, it has taught Shylock this value. He notes that if a Jew harms a Christian, the Christian will resort to revenge. He argues that Jews cannot avoid learning this lesson. As a result, if a Christian wrongs a Jew, the Jew should, as a good citizen of Venice would, look for revenge.

Shylock draws the logical conclusion: 'The villainy you teach me I will execute, and it shall go hard but I will better the instruction' (lines 59–60). In other words, Venetian Christians have taught him that a person who has been wronged should take revenge (the very opposite of Christian teaching: 'forgive us our offences as we forgive those who offend against us'). Shylock will 'improve' on the kind of revenge Christians take on Jews by practising a more horrible form: he will seek a pound of Antonio's flesh.

Playing Shylock

The Merchant of Venice was written to be acted on stage. In the theatre, *The Merchant of Venice* has almost always been Shylock's play. Many of the great actors have played Shylock, seeing it as the play's lead role. He is the life and soul of the play, and is at the centre of attention whenever he is on stage.

It is a tradition that the Shylock actor takes the final curtain call alone. On the face of it, this appears odd. How can a character so often described in the play as a villain, and who threatens the happiness of others, run away with a play in which he features for only one-quarter of the scenes?

To answer this question, it is necessary to look at how some actors have given Shylock life and energy on the stage. There are two extreme, but opposing, interpretations of Shylock. One as a bloodthirsty monster, and the other as a successful businessman:

- Shylock can be played as a devilish villain. The appearance and gestures of the actor can be made to match this idea. For example, his face can show cruelty and wickedness. His hands can be clenched in anger. He can howl like a savage. At times, however, the actor can still convey Shylock's deep resentment at the wrongs he has suffered, commanding some pity from the audience.

- Shylock can be played as a man of great energy, passion and power. The actor can give Shylock an air of dignity and intelligence. His sense of humour and sarcasm can be shown as he speaks such lines as 'Hath a *dog* money? Is it possible a *cur* can lend three thousand ducats?' (Act 1, Scene 3, lines 115–16). The actor can stress Shylock's love of family, his joy in his success and his pride in the Jewish faith and culture. This Shylock is honest and admits to his vices, whereas his enemies can be presented as hypocrites in their virtues. The sympathy of the audience is more often with such a Shylock than with his enemies.

There are many variations on these extreme interpretations. For example, it is possible to focus on the wrongs done to Shylock. When he is played as the victim of suffering and pain, his evil qualities and actions look like a natural response to the cruel way he is treated. In the trial scene, for example, the actor can make him stand firm to the end, remaining dignified while others try to break him. Shylock then becomes someone more to be pitied than condemned.

Costume, hair and make-up choices will also influence how an audience responds to Shylock. If he wears ragged clothes and has a dirty face, he will seem socially inferior to the other characters. If he is well-groomed and refined, the sneers of the Christians will seem absurd.

Some productions make Shylock (and perhaps all the Jewish characters) look exotic or visually different from the Christian characters. Whereas others choose to emphasise their similarities by, for example, dressing Shylock, Antonio, Bassanio, etc. in modern-day business suits.

Thus, there are as many Shylocks as there are actors who play the part.

Some critics claim that Shakespeare wanted to create a monster, but that his humanity got in the way. The result is that Shylock is both grotesque and human. He has hateful qualities, but we cannot blame him for despising those who hate and hurt him.

Summary

- Shylock is an ambivalent character: he has both good points and bad ones.
- He is hated and treated badly because he is a Jew, and because he has become rich by lending money at high rates of interest.
- He hates Antonio because he is a Christian, has treated him badly and is a threat to his business.
- He lends money to Antonio, but makes the penalty for failure to repay the loan on time a pound of Antonio's flesh.
- His daughter elopes and steals from him, and Launcelot leaves his service.
- He is determined to get justice (i.e. a pound of Antonio's flesh) when Antonio cannot repay the money on time.
- He has strong motives for acting as he does.
- He suffers deep loss (e.g. his daughter, his wealth, his religion) and misfortune.
- He leaves the courtroom (and the play) a broken man.
- He dominates the play, even when he is not on stage.

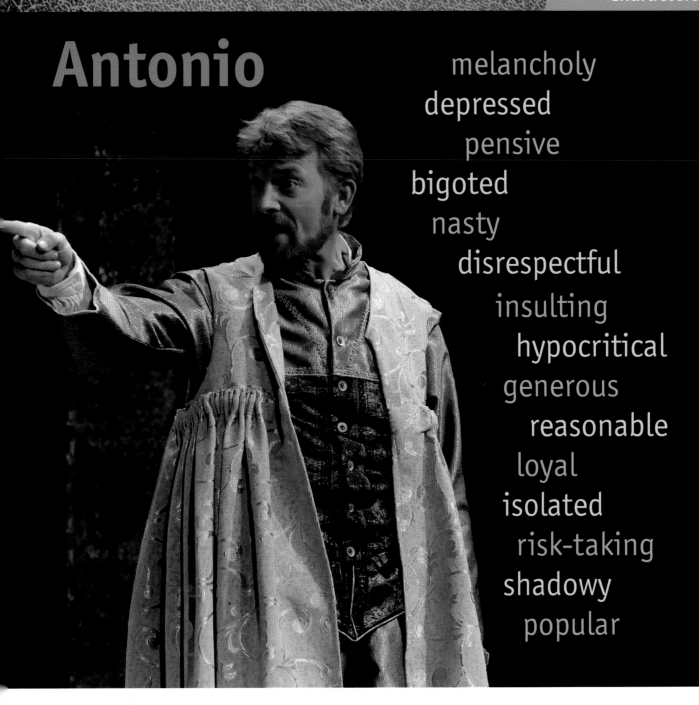

Antonio

melancholy
depressed
pensive
bigoted
nasty
disrespectful
insulting
hypocritical
generous
reasonable
loyal
isolated
risk-taking
shadowy
popular

Antonio is a somewhat mysterious figure. Given that he is the merchant in the title of the play, we might expect his role to be the main one, but this is not the case. In addition, Antonio is given few impressive lines to speak and his character is not clearly defined.

Antonio's depression

In Shakespeare's day people were often described by their temperament or personality. At one extreme were people of a sanguine (cheerful, optimistic) character. At the other were those of a melancholy (sad, pessimistic) nature. Antonio is in the melancholy group.

Melancholy would now be called major or clinical depression, the cause of which is not clear to the sufferer. As Antonio says:

In sooth, I know not why I am so sad.
It wearies me, you say it wearies you;
But how I caught it, found it, or came by it,
What stuff 'tis made of, whereof it is born,
I am to learn

(Act 1, Scene 1, lines 1–5)

Antonio accepts his depression as something that fate has imposed on him. As he sees it, everyone has a part to play in life, and his role is 'a sad one' (Act 1, Scene 1, line 79).

Antonio's love for Bassanio

It has been suggested that Antonio is depressed because he is about to lose his dearest friend, Bassanio. Antonio values Bassanio above all else – 'he only loves the world for him' (Act 2, Scene 8, line 50) – and their close ties are likely to be loosened when Bassanio marries Portia.

The play makes it obvious that Antonio finds it painful to be parted from Bassanio. Salerio reports that Antonio shed tears of sorrow when Bassanio left Venice (Act 2, Scene 8, lines 46–9). Why, then, does he enter into a deal with Shylock that will help Bassanio to marry Portia and live in Belmont?

It could be Antonio's way of letting Bassanio know how deeply he cares for him. It could also be an attempt to bind Bassanio to him. Later, as he prepares to give up his life, Antonio tries to place Bassanio in his debt forever. He asks to be remembered to Portia:

> *Commend me to your honourable wife,*
> *Tell her the process of Antonio's end,*
> *Say how I loved you, speak me fair in death;*
> *And, when the tale is told, bid her be judge*
> *Whether Bassanio had not once a love.*
>
> (Act 4, Scene 1, lines 270–74)

These lines suggest Antonio's desire to maintain some kind of hold over Bassanio, even if it is from beyond the grave.

Antonio's influence over Bassanio is seen again when he insists that Bassanio give Portia's ring to Balthazar. This act can also be seen as an attempt to distance Bassanio from Portia. Antonio places his claim on Bassanio above Portia's:

> *My Lord Bassanio, let him have the ring,*
> *Let his deservings and my love withal*
> *Be valued 'gainst your wife's commandëment.*
>
> (Act 4, Scene 1, lines 446–8)

Antonio's hatred of Shylock

There is a parallel between Antonio's relationship with Bassanio and his relationship with Shylock. Each relationship involves a debt as well as a means of repaying that debt. Antonio's relationship with Shylock, however, is based on hatred and prejudice rather than love.

Antonio despises Shylock because he is a Jew and because he charges interest on the money he lends. He seems to believe that it is acceptable to abuse Shylock, through insults, spitting on him, kicking him, etc. When Shylock turns on him and seeks a cruel revenge, Antonio changes his tune. He tries to plead with him, addressing him as 'good Shylock' (Act 3, Scene 3, line 3).

When Antonio regains the upper hand in their relationship, following Portia's intervention in the trial scene, he is asked to show mercy to Shylock. He does this by releasing Shylock from the requirement to give him half of his goods. In return, however, he demands a high price: Shylock must become a Christian and leave his wealth to Jessica and Lorenzo when he dies.

In forcing Shylock to give up his religion, Antonio often offends modern audiences. Shakespeare's audiences, however, probably saw this as an act of charity. They believed that Antonio was giving Shylock a chance to save his soul, which he would not have had as a Jew.

Antonio's future

Antonio's depressed frame of mind makes him an outsider at the end of the play. He tags along with his three newly married friends and their wives. Although he has just escaped with his life, he is apparently still a sad man. Apart from Shylock, he is the only significant character not to find happiness in love in the play.

There are signs, however, that Antonio's future may not be so bleak. He receives a warm welcome to Belmont from Portia. She recognises that Bassanio owes a lot to Antonio, who has always supported him. He is invited to experience the hospitality, gratitude and friendship that Belmont has to offer. In addition, three of his ships have returned to harbour with their cargoes intact, meaning he is back in business.

Summary

- Antonio is a sad, depressed, melancholy figure.
- He is a successful businessman, liked and respected by the Christian characters in the play.
- He is a generous and unselfish friend to Bassanio, willing to make any sacrifice to demonstrate his love for him.
- He makes a reckless deal with Shylock that almost costs him his life.
- He is an unattractive and cruel enemy to Shylock and those of the Jewish faith.
- When he thinks he has lost everything, he gives up and wants to die.
- He is central to the action: his fate is of major concern to most of the other characters.
- At the end of the play he seems to be a lonely and sombre figure in the background.

Portia

rich
capable
dutiful
intelligent
educated
spirited
generous
resourceful
strong
practical
proactive
controlling
bigoted
hypocritical
ruthless

Portia has many identities. Some of these identities are in conflict with other ones. She presents herself as an innocent young woman, but then plays the part of a clever lawyer. She preaches mercy, but shows no pity as she destroys Shylock. She promotes Christian teachings, but does not always behave in a Christian manner. She is a wealthy, independent, strong-minded woman who puts everything she has under the control of her fortune-hunting husband, but who later re-asserts her ownership of what she has inherited.

Portia the wife

Portia has been attracted to Bassanio for some time: he had visited Belmont when her father was alive. It is only when he gives his reasons for not choosing the gold casket that she knows she loves him. She tells him to ignore her riches, her virtues, her beauty and her social status, saying, 'the full sum of me is … an unlessoned girl, unschooled, unpractisèd' (Act 3, Scene 2, lines 157–9).

After Bassanio has made the correct choice of casket, she addresses him as 'Lord Bassanio' (line 149) and says he is her 'lord', 'governor' and 'king' (line 165). She tells him that she and all she owns now belong to him. Until then she was in full command of her beautiful home at Belmont and all her servants. She gives him her ring – a symbol of her wealth as well as of their marriage.

In spite of her fine words to Bassanio, it gradually becomes clear that Portia has no intention of allowing him to become her master. For example, the ring she gave Bassanio will later be the means by which she tricks him and so confirms her position as the dominant or controlling partner in the marriage.

When she tells Bassanio that everything that once belonged to her now belongs to him, she is merely stating what marriage meant in Shakespeare's time. Then, according to the law, the husband owned all the family property and the wife owned nothing. It is worth noting, however, that when Portia returns to Belmont from Venice, she speaks of the light 'burning in *my* hall' (Act 5, Scene 1, line 88) and tells Nerissa to 'give order to *my* servants that they take no note at all of our being absent hence' (lines 118–19).

Portia the lawyer

Portia claims that she is poorly educated and unable to solve problems. This impression is shown to be false in the trial scene. In the role of Balthazar, a legal expert and a teacher of Christian morality, she shows such skills that the Duke of Venice is astonished.

It might be wondered why Bassanio does not recognise Portia when she appears as Balthazar. The answer to this is simple: once a character assumed a disguise in Shakespeare's theatre, it was accepted that this disguise was impenetrable.

Shakespeare uses Portia to save Antonio from death at the hands of Shylock – he was writing a comedy and if he allowed Antonio to die then the play would have a tragic ending. Portia successfully uses the law to save Antonio's life; however, her role in the trial scene exposes aspects of her character and outlook that are far from pleasant.

In common with other Christians in the play, Portia cannot conceal her contempt for Shylock and for Jews in general. She thinks of Shylock as an 'alien' (line 346), and refuses to speak of him or to him by name. There are many examples of this: 'Which is the merchant here, and which the Jew? … Then must the Jew be merciful … Therefore, Jew … the Jew may claim … The Jew shall have all justice … Why doth the Jew pause? … Thou shalt have nothing but the forfeiture, to be so taken at thy peril, Jew … Tarry, Jew … Art thou contented, Jew?'

Before Portia/Balthazar destroys Shylock's case and humiliates him, she makes a speech on the 'quality' or meaning of mercy (Act 4, Scene 1, lines 181–99). This speech deals with justice and mercy from a Christian point of view. She suggests that Shylock should forgive Antonio and not insist on enforcing their bond.

As Portia knows, Shylock does not consider himself bound by Christian teaching on forgiveness, but instead recognises the Old Testament teaching of an eye for an eye. This is why Shylock dismisses Portia's plea and demands that Antonio should suffer 'the penalty and forfeit of my bond' (line 204).

Portia told Shylock to remember that mercy is not 'strained' (line 181) or forced. Yet she does not object to Antonio's condition that Shylock should be forced to become a Christian as a way of keeping half his goods. Neither does she object to the Duke of Venice's threat that Shylock will face the death penalty if he refuses to become a Christian and to leave all he has to Jessica and Lorenzo in his will.

Portia receives praise for being a learned, upright and wise young judge. However, no experienced, right-minded or fair judge would falsely lead on the plaintiff (Shylock) as she does. Portia knows in advance what her judgement will be, but hesitates to give it. Instead, she tells Shylock that the law gives him the right to deal with Antonio according to the terms of the bond: 'And lawfully by this the Jew may claim a pound of flesh' (lines 228–9).

Portia instructs Antonio to prepare his chest for Shylock's knife, and asks Shylock to have a surgeon on hand to prevent Antonio from bleeding to death. She then allows Antonio to make a speech, and Bassanio to make another one, and once again tells Shylock that he may proceed with cutting off Antonio's flesh, and how he may do so: 'The law allows it, and the court awards it' (line 300).

Portia's approach fills Shylock with a growing feeling of hope, only to shatter this hope unexpectedly. She does this by introducing a convenient interpretation of the law: Shylock may have his pound of flesh, provided he does not shed a single drop of Antonio's blood. She goes further. If he sheds 'one drop of Christian blood', his lands and goods will become the property of the state of Venice (lines 305–9).

When Shylock prepares to leave the court without getting back his loan, Portia orders him to remain, telling him that the law has another hold on him. This is a law she tells him he has just broken:

> *It is enacted in the laws of Venice,*
> *If it be proved against an alien*
> *That by direct or indirect attempts*
> *He seek the life of any citizen,*
> *The party 'gainst the which he doth contrive*
> *Shall seize one half his goods, the other half*
> *Comes to the privy coffer of the state,*
> *And the offender's life lies in the mercy*
> *Of the duke only*
>
> (Act 4, Scene 1, lines 345–53)

Shylock is being told that Antonio may take half his property, and that the Duke of Venice may decide whether he lives or dies. The curious thing about this law is that the duke and the legal experts in Venice seem unaware of its existence until Portia brings it to their attention.

If Portia had mentioned it at the beginning, there would have been no need for further argument. Antonio would have been set free and Shylock made aware of his true position. Instead, Portia needlessly allows both of them to suffer while she displays her legal skills.

Portia the princess

It might be argued that the Portia we see in Act 4, Scene 1 is not the Portia we meet in the rest of the play. In Belmont, she resembles a kind princess in a fairy tale. She is beautiful, rich and clever, and likes to do good deeds. She appears to have a strong friendship with Nerissa, and the other characters all respond well to her.

When Jessica is asked what she thinks of Portia, her approval is unqualified. She admires her:

> *Past all expressing. It is very meet*
> *The Lord Bassanio live an upright life;*
> *For, having such a blessing in his lady,*
> *He finds the joys of heaven here on earth*
>
> (Act 3, Scene 5, lines 63–6)

Jessica is saying that Bassanio will have to live a life of extraordinary goodness to match the standards set by Portia. Bassanio has good reason to agree with Jessica's verdict. After all, Portia's wealth gives Bassanio, a penniless adventurer, a status (as Lord Bassanio) and a way of life he would not otherwise enjoy.

Like a princess in a fairy tale, Portia is admired by princes throughout the world. Her treatment of her suitors, however, reveals the unpleasant side of her character. It shows that she has little time for 'outsiders', meaning people from races or cultures other than her own.

Portia's comments on the Prince of Morocco indicate racial prejudice on her part. The prospect of being married to a Moor does not appeal to her: 'If he have the condition of a saint and the complexion of a devil, I had rather he should shrive me than wive me' (Act 1, Scene 2, lines 114–16). The thought of a black man conjures up an image of a devil in Portia's mind. She would accept such a man as her confessor if he were saintly, but not as her husband.

Summary

- Portia is a wealthy, resourceful and strong-minded woman.
- She is an obedient daughter: despite her concerns about most of the suitors who come to Belmont, she follows the terms of her father's strange will.
- She claims to be a moral character who believes in friendship and good deeds.
- She is unkind to her suitors and engages in racial mockery.
- She loves Bassanio and describes him as her master, but does not show any practical signs of giving up the control she has enjoyed since her father's death.
- She provides suspense and excitement in the trial scene and makes a happy ending possible for Antonio, although this means a miserable ending for Shylock.
- She preaches mercy and forgiveness, but does not show these qualities in her treatment of Shylock.
- She falsely leads on Shylock during the trial; she knows in advance what her judgement will be, but allows first Antonio and then Shylock to suffer.
- She tricks Bassanio during the episode with the rings and takes her time to put him out of his misery.
- She is central to the main events of the play; her intervention in Act 4 has a vital influence on the outcome.

Bassanio

irresponsible
feckless
wasteful
sociable
fun-loving
shallow
superficial
proactive
clever

astute
self-assured
generous
considerate
loyal
lucky

Bassanio is looking for a wealthy wife and wants Antonio to finance his campaign to win Portia. This mission is behind the main events of the play.

Bassanio the suitor

Bassanio compares himself to Jason, a figure from classical mythology who sought and found the Golden Fleece (a symbol of great wealth). Jason was noted for his cleverness. Bassanio is also clever, as shown in his choice of casket.

Portia's late father set up a simple test to find her the right husband. He believed that a suitor who would pick the gold or silver casket would want to marry Portia for money rather than love. The suitor who chooses the lead casket, however, is not fooled by outward appearance and is more likely to love Portia for her own sake rather than for her wealth.

Bassanio knows that appearances are not to be trusted. His experience has taught him that a man living on credit can appear to be rich even though he is in debt. Not wanting to look like a poor fortune-hunter when he is wooing Portia, he borrows money in order to seem like a man of wealth. As he explains to Antonio, he wants to show 'a more swelling port' (i.e. the lifestyle of a gentleman) far above his actual means (Act 1, Scene 1, line 124).

There can be little doubt that Bassanio aims to make his fortune by marrying Portia. She is an attractive solution to his money problems. He thinks of her as a wealthy heiress – 'a lady richly left' (Act 1, Scene 1, line 161) – and a beautiful woman. He knows that he will have to compete with many rivals, but believes that if he could act the part of a wealthy gentleman, he could actually become one:

> *O my Antonio, had I but the means*
> *To hold a rival place with one of them,*
> *I have a mind presages me such thrift*
> *That I should questionless be fortunate*
> (Act 1, Scene 1, lines 173–6)

Bassanio sees that Portia's huge fortune will allow him to live the life of ease that he wants.

Bassanio likes to enjoy life and have fun. His first line in the play is to ask Salerio and Solanio, 'Good signiors both, when shall we laugh?' (Act 1, Scene 1, line 66). It is soon revealed that he has been enjoying the good things in life so much that he is now in debt. His scheme to borrow more money in order to marry Portia and repay all his debts seems shallow and impractical.

Shakespeare gradually prepares the audience to accept Bassanio as a worthy suitor to Portia. For example, Bassanio generously takes Launcelot into his service and orders a fine uniform for him. Portia's elaborate praise of Bassanio and enthusiasm for making him master of her and all she has give him a further degree of dignity and gravity.

Bassanio's choice of the correct casket suggests that he may make a good husband for Portia. Furthermore, when it is confirmed that he has chosen the right casket, he says that the final decision lies with Portia:

> So, thrice-fair lady, stand I even so,
> As doubtful whether what I see be true,
> Until confirmed, signed, ratified by you.
>
> (Act 3, Scene 2, lines 146–8)

Bassanio may have been confident of Portia's answer, but the fact that he does not immediately claim his right to marry her shows his respect for her.

Bassanio the friend

During the play Bassanio changes from being an irresponsible and selfish adventurer into someone with real concern for a friend. The bad news about Antonio's losses and the dangers these expose him to 'steals the colour from Bassanio's cheek' (Act 3, Scene 2, line 242). There is deep feeling in his description of Antonio as:

> The dearest friend to me, the kindest man,
> The best-conditioned and unwearied spirit
> In doing courtesies
>
> (Act 3, Scene 2, lines 290–92)

When Antonio's life is in danger, Bassanio hurries to Venice to be at his side. Although he does this at the insistence of Portia, Bassanio seems genuinely concerned. He knows that he

has caused his friend to find himself in a life-threatening situation, and is happy that he now has the means to attempt to save him.

Bassanio's conduct in the trial scene, however, shows the superficial side of his character. In an effort to cheer up Antonio, he utters some brave words:

> Good cheer, Antonio! What, man, courage yet!
> The Jew shall have my flesh, blood, bones and all,
> Ere thou shalt lose for me one drop of blood.
>
> (Act 4, Scene 1, lines 111–13)

This offer cannot be taken seriously. If Bassanio really means what he is saying here, he might make an attempt to run a dagger through Shylock and save Antonio at the cost of being hanged for murder. Notice that Antonio does not take Bassanio's declaration seriously. Instead, he prepares himself for death.

Bassanio makes a similarly futile comment when he thinks Antonio is on the point of death:

> But life itself, my wife, and all the world
> Are not with me esteemed above thy life.
> I would lose all, ay, sacrifice them all
> Here to this devil, to deliver you.
>
> (Act 4, Scene 1, lines 281–4)

Bassanio the husband

In the business of the rings, the audience is likely to have some sympathy for Bassanio. He is caught between his friend and his wife. He does not want to give Portia's ring to Portia/Balthazar, but is persuaded to do so by Antonio. Then in the closing scene he is made to squirm as Portia and Nerissa extend their practical joke. This is only a temporary setback, however, as Bassanio ends the play a wealthy man with his marriage and friendships intact.

Summary

- Bassanio is a reckless adventurer whose need to borrow money is the catalyst for the play.
- He wants to make his fortune easily by marrying a rich and beautiful heiress.
- He lacks depth and substance, preferring to focus on the fun side of life.
- His choice of casket shows that he is clever and is not fooled by outward appearances.
- He is loved deeply by both Antonio and Portia.
- He does not immediately claim his right to marry Portia, which shows his respect for her.
- He is genuinely concerned for Antonio's plight, but unable to offer an effective solution.
- He supports Antonio during the trial, but does not back up his words with actions.
- He may be caught in something of a power struggle between his friend and his wife.
- He achieves his goal when he marries Portia and becomes a wealthy man.

Launcelot, Lorenzo, Jessica

callous
corrupt
cruel
dishonest
frivolous
immoral
lightweight
selfish
unkind
vulgar

The group of characters involved in Jessica's elopement play a significant part in hounding Shylock into rage and near-madness. The elopement of Jessica, her abandonment of her religion and her theft of her father's property are all deadly blows to Shylock's well-being and peace of mind.

Launcelot

Launcelot strikes twice at Shylock, first by leaving his service and then by helping with Jessica's elopement. It is reasonable to judge any character by the quality of his or her enemies. If we see Shylock in this light, he comes out rather favourably in comparison to Launcelot, who lacks any kind of moral stature or sense of decency.

Launcelot offers two excuses for leaving Shylock and taking up service with Bassanio: the latter will give him a splendid new uniform, and in Bassanio's house he can look forward to coming by eleven widows and nine young women. Later we learn what one of these domestics has suffered from Launcelot's transfer: 'the Moor is with child by you, Launcelot' (Act 3, Scene 5, lines 32–3).

Shylock is not sorry to be rid of him, having found him a huge feeder, a lazy worker and a great sleeper by day. What we see of Launcelot and his activities as an accessory to Jessica's elopement justifies Shylock's low opinion of him, and suggests that Shylock is a good judge of character.

Lorenzo

The behaviour of Lorenzo and his friends in planning the elopement is extremely callous.

Shylock is invited to attend Bassanio's feast only to get him out of the house. Lorenzo is planning to steal away Shylock's daughter (and money), and then, as a piece of cruel fun, bring her disguised as a torch-bearer to the party where her father is a guest. Only a change of wind prevents the enactment of this revolting joke.

Jessica

Jessica, who delivers the worst blow she can strike at her father, is not an appealing character. Her elopement and the theft that accompanies it are of enormous significance to Shylock. In spite of this, she treats the affair lightly and flippantly, and does not seem to care about its consequences for her father.

When she tells Lorenzo that she is 'much ashamed' of her 'exchange' (Act 2, Scene 6, line 35), she is talking about her change of clothes, not her change of religion. In her boys' clothes, she now has an abundance of pockets into which she can stuff a fortune in gold pieces. For this she earns the praise of Gratiano, who describes her as 'a gentle, and no Jew' (line 51). Gratiano, who does not think much, is suggesting that the mark of a gentile (non-Jew) is to be disloyal and dishonest, which is an unintended compliment to Jews.

In light-hearted mood, Jessica spoils everything that Shylock holds sacred, destroys the basis of his life and drives him to the edge of insanity. Her main role in the play is to strengthen her father's motive for revenge.

Shakespeare's early audiences, who tended not to approve of Jews or of those who lived by charging interest on the money they loaned, would have seen Jessica in a more favourable light than modern audiences do. They would have regarded her decision to become a Christian as a sign of virtue. Indeed, the play itself appears to show her as a happier and more fulfilled person after her conversion to Christianity.

Like most of the characters in the play, Jessica is full of contradictions. Christians are expected to obey the Ten Commandments, but in becoming a Christian, Jessica breaks two of these. She fails to honour her father and is ashamed to be his daughter, and above all she commits theft when she steals his money and his jewels.

Jessica and Shylock by Gilbert Stuart Newton (1830)

Shylock and Jessica by Charles Frederick Lowcock (c.1922)

The following diagram illustrates the relationships and interactions between the characters in *The Merchant of Venice*.

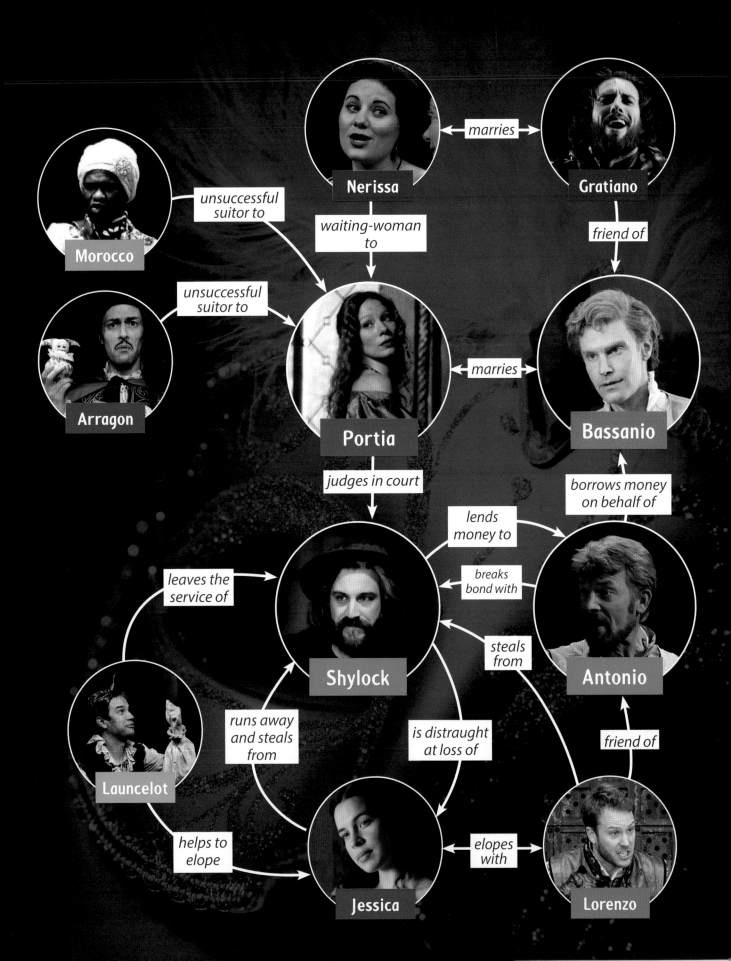

Prejudice and intolerance

Money

Justice, mercy and revenge

Appearance and reality

Love and hate

Prejudice and intolerance

The prejudice and intolerance shown in the play are directed mainly at Shylock, but also by Shylock against those who refuse to tolerate him. To understand why Shylock is treated as he is by the Christian characters, we have to remember that the most important thing about him is that he is a Jew.

Jews were a hated and persecuted minority in much of Christian Europe:

- Their goods were seized and their houses were looted.

- They were accused of evil practices, such as using the blood of Christians in secret ceremonies and eating human flesh. Shylock's bond with Antonio is an echo of these suspicions.

- They were banned from England at the end of the thirteenth century, and there were only a handful remaining there when Shakespeare wrote *The Merchant of Venice*.

- They were said to be possessed by the devil, which explains some of the references to Shylock in the play. For example, as Solanio sees Shylock approach he claims to see the devil 'in the likeness of a Jew' (Act 3, Scene 1, line 18); he then speaks of Shylock and his Jewish friend Tubal: 'a third cannot be matched, unless the devil himself turn Jew' (lines 64–5).

- They were forced to live in special districts in some European cities. Venice was the city that invented the ghetto, or Jewish quarter.

- They were allowed to engage in the business of moneylending, Shylock's occupation. Christians disagreed with the charging of interest, which was considered unnatural. Shylock the Jew charges interest, but Antonio the Christian lends money free of interest to needy people.

In *The Merchant of Venice* Antonio, who is described as a kind and gentle man, treats Shylock with contempt whenever he meets him. He insults him publicly. He does all he can to degrade the Jewish race and Shylock's occupation. There is a strong element of

hypocrisy in this. Venetian Christians make a virtue of not lending money for profit, but, in order to live in luxury and beyond their means, they are prepared to borrow money at interest from Jews they persecute and insult.

Jews are hated by Christian characters in the play simply because they are Jews. They are not regarded as full human beings. Shylock is often referred to as a dog and treated like one. Gratiano's account of Shylock's soul and how he got it is typical:

> ... thy currish spirit
> Governed a wolf, who, hanged for human slaughter,
> Even from the gallows did his fell soul fleet,
> And, whilst thou lay'st in thy unhallowed dam,
> Infused itself in thee; for thy desires
> Are wolvish, bloody, starved and ravenous.
>
> (Act 4, Scene 1, lines 133–8)

Shylock's daughter, Jessica, elopes and makes off with much of his treasure with the help of Christians and for the benefit of one of them, Lorenzo. Solanio and Salerio then poke fun at Shylock's sorrow and loss.

For his part, Shylock has developed a hatred of Christians and their hypocritical behaviour. He expects to be treated unfairly by the Christians of Venice. They have taught him to be intolerant. He has been a good student, and is now motivated to do to them what they have done to him.

The Christians win in the end by forcing Shylock to give up his beloved Jewish faith and convert to Christianity. It is hard for modern audiences to accept that Antonio has any right to insist that Shylock become a Christian. However, Shakespeare's first audiences would have seen

this differently. They were taught to believe that Jews had no chance of getting to heaven. Making Shylock a Christian would mean that his soul could be saved, and was therefore seen as an act of kindness.

The religious prejudices at the heart of the play are part of a general intolerance of anyone who is 'different'. For example, Portia makes jokes about her foreign suitors, and Morocco highlights the issue of racism. It seems that anyone who is not a white, Christian citizen of Venice or Belmont is deemed inferior and tends to inspire fear or suspicion.

Money

Money and other kinds of wealth are mentioned a great deal in the play. Most of the important things that happen depend on money or the lack of it. The lovers discuss their relationships in terms of finance, and the wealth of most characters varies over the course of the play.

There might have been no play at all if Bassanio did not waste money. Then he would not have needed the massive sum that Antonio borrows for him from Shylock. And if Portia was poor, would Bassanio be interested in marrying her? Would Lorenzo elope with Jessica if her father lacked wealth? It is clear that Portia, Jessica, Shylock and Antonio are seen as financial assets, as well as human beings.

Money lies behind each of the main plot lines. For example:

- Shylock is a rich man. The Christians make contact with him only because he has the money they want to borrow. If he did not, they would ignore him, or insult him. Jessica reduces his wealth when she steals from him. His enemies then take control of what is left during the trial scene.

- Antonio is also a rich man. His wealth has helped Bassanio to live in luxury. His credit allows him to borrow from Shylock. Bassanio uses this money to impress Portia, win her love and her money, and continue to live in luxury.

- Portia is a rich woman. Her money attracts Bassanio: he sees that her huge fortune could free him from financial worries forever. When

he mentions her to Antonio, the first thing he thinks of is that she is an heiress, 'richly left' (Act 1, Scene 1, line 161).

- Portia seems to know that the more money she has, the more attractive she will be to Bassanio. She tells him, 'for you I would be trebled twenty times myself, a thousand times more fair, ten thousand times more rich' (Act 3, Scene 2, lines 152–4).

- Jessica says to Lorenzo: 'I will make fast the doors, and gild myself with some more ducats' (Act 2, Scene 6, lines 49–50). The phrase 'gild myself' suggests that she is using gold coins to make herself more beautiful in Lorenzo's eyes.

■ When Lorenzo later learns that he and Jessica will inherit all Shylock's wealth, he is overjoyed: 'you drop manna in the way of starvèd people' (Act 5, Scene 1, lines 293–4).

■ Antonio appears to lose everything, but luckily has much of his wealth restored at the end of the play.

Money is very important in the lives of the characters. Antonio tells his friends that death will spare him from a horrible fate: an old age without money would be worse than death (Act 4, Scene 1, lines 264–9). Shylock has similar feelings when he faces the same fate. There is one exception to this outlook in the case of Shylock. He is the character most attached to his money. However, he draws up a bond hoping to be repaid, not with money, but with a pound of human flesh. He looks for money only when he cannot have his pound of flesh.

Two moneylenders

The play also considers the issue of lending money. In this debate, Shylock and Antonio take opposing points of view:

■ Shylock thinks it is right to charge interest on money. By charging interest, he makes his money create more money.

■ Antonio thinks it is wrong and unnatural that 'barren metal' should breed more wealth through interest (Act 1, Scene 3, line 128).

Both Shylock and Antonio have understandings with their friends when they need to raise money:

■ Shylock tells Antonio and Bassanio that he does not have the 3,000 ducats to hand, but that 'Tubal, a wealthy Hebrew of my tribe, will furnish me' (Act 1, Scene 3, lines 49–52). The idea here is that Tubal will lend Shylock whatever money he needs, free of interest.

■ Antonio wants to help Bassanio, but his money is tied up at sea and he must arrange a loan on the strength of his reputation. He asks Bassanio to 'try what my credit can in Venice do' (line 180) and promises to do the same himself. Antonio hopes that the money can be raised 'of my trust or for my sake' (line 185). In other words, he thinks that someone will lend him the money either because his credit is good or because he is liked.

It appears that neither Antonio nor Bassanio can find any lender among their own (Christian) community willing to lend 3,000 ducats to Antonio. As a result, they turn to a Jewish moneylender, Shylock, who proposes a strange penalty if the loan is not repaid within three months:

> ... let the forfeit
> Be nominated for an equal pound
> Of your fair flesh, to be cut off and taken
> In what part of your body pleaseth me.
>
> (Act 1, Scene 3, lines 142–5)

Shylock makes his living by charging heavy rates of interest on loans. However, in the case of this bond with Antonio, he does not stand to make any money. In addition, the gruesome penalty is said to be merely 'a merry sport' (line 139). This is why Antonio says, 'The Hebrew will turn Christian: he grows kind' (line 172), and Bassanio admits that the terms offered by Shylock are 'fair' (line 173), albeit suspiciously so.

For Shylock, if ever the bond was 'a merry sport', it is no longer that when he loses his daughter, Jessica, and his money and valuables to the Christian Lorenzo. From then on, he sees the bond in a new light. If Antonio fails to pay him back in time, then Antonio's flesh will, as he puts it, 'feed my revenge' (Act 3, Scene 1, lines 43–4).

Shylock insists on enforcing the exact terms of the bond. In doing this, he acts according to the law. When the bond was being drawn up, it was signed in the presence of a lawyer with a solemn religious oath. He confirms this in his statement to the Duke of Venice: 'by our holy Sabbath have I sworn to have the due and forfeit of my bond' (Act 4, Scene 1, lines 36–7). He also confirms it when he tells Portia/Balthazar:

> *An oath, an oath, I have an oath in heaven —*
> *Shall I lay perjury upon my soul?*
> *No, not for Venice.*
>
> (Act 4, Scene 1, lines 225–7)

In Shakespeare's time, moneylending based on the kind of bond drawn up in a lawyer's office by Shylock and Antonio was quite common. Shakespeare, himself a moneylender who sued a number of his debtors when they defaulted on their loans, had personal experience of the law as it is applied in *The Merchant of Venice*.

In the case of such bonds, a date was set on which payment would be due, and there was a penalty (usually about 100 per cent of the amount loaned) if the debtor failed to pay on the due date. The unusual feature of the Shylock–Antonio bond is that Shylock substitutes his 'pound of flesh' penalty for the usual financial penalty.

If Shylock had insisted on the usual penalty, Antonio, having borrowed 3,000 ducats, would have had to pay Shylock 6,000 ducats. This explains why Portia suggests that Antonio should 'pay him six thousand, and deface the bond' (Act 3, Scene 2, line 297), and why Bassanio, carrying large sums of Portia's money, makes a similar offer to Shylock: 'For thy three thousand ducats, here is six' or 'twice the sum' (Act 4, Scene 1, lines 84, 207).

If Shylock accepts these offers he will be making a concession to Antonio, whom he hates. The law is on Shylock's side. Antonio has no defence as he signed the document of his own free will. The only way for Antonio to escape death is for Shylock to show mercy and not to take what he is legally entitled to (i.e. his pound of flesh).

Justice, mercy and revenge

The play is full of talk of justice, mercy and revenge. Shylock wants revenge on Antonio for insulting him in the past. Then he wants revenge on all Christians when his daughter elopes with Lorenzo. He is delighted when Antonio cannot honour his bond because it gives him the excuse to take all the revenge he needs.

Shylock's view

Shylock tells Salerio how he feels about revenge. He believes he speaks for all Jews in Venice when he says, 'And if you wrong us, shall we not revenge?' (Act 3, Scene 1, lines 54–5). He points out: 'If a Jew wrong a Christian, what is his humility? Revenge. If a Christian wrong a Jew, what should his sufferance be by Christian example? Why, revenge' (lines 56–9). In other words, Jews have learned from Christians that if people suffer a wrong they should seek revenge. So when Shylock wants to kill Antonio, he is only doing what Christians have taught him.

In Shylock's mind, revenge and justice are the same thing, since the law gives him the right to take revenge. This is why he is so pleased with himself at the beginning of the trial scene. His daughter has eloped and taken much of his wealth, therefore he is entitled to justice, which will feed his need for revenge.

Shylock does not want to listen when the jailed Antonio begs him for mercy. 'Tell not me of mercy,' he declares (Act 3, Scene 3, line 1). Neither does he accept Portia's plea to show mercy to Antonio in court. He wants strict justice and revenge.

Religion has taught Shylock that revenge is not always wrong. The law of Moses contains the instruction: an eye for an eye, a tooth for a tooth. We cannot expect Shylock to accept

Portia's speech on mercy and forgiveness. She is preaching a Christian teaching that means little or nothing to Shylock, who has been brought up in a different religious tradition.

His enemies' view

Shylock's Christian enemies try to persuade him to forget his plan to take revenge on Antonio. They ask him to show mercy and forgiveness. Portia tells him in court that justice is greatest when it is softened by mercy. She suggests that if we want God to show us mercy for what we have done wrong, we should be merciful to those who wrong us.

When Antonio is saved, an interesting thing happens: Shylock becomes the victim of the law, the court and his Christian enemies. Everybody in the audience must wonder how they will treat the defeated Jew. Will Portia apply her own words on mercy to Shylock? Will she appeal to Antonio to forgive him? Will Shylock's enemies seek their own revenge?

The Christian treatment of Shylock in the trial scene reminds us of Shylock's comment that Christians are better at taking revenge than they are at showing mercy:

- Portia shows very little mercy to Shylock. She treats him as one would treat a dog: 'Down therefore and beg mercy of the duke' (Act 4, Scene 1, line 360).

- Gratiano thinks that Shylock should hang himself, but makes a joke about him not having the money left to buy a rope to do the job (Act 4, Scene 1, lines 361–4).

- The Duke of Venice pardons him his life, but still orders that half his property be given to Antonio and the other half to the state of Venice. Shylock would rather die.

- Antonio pleads successfully with the duke to allow Shylock to keep half his wealth, but then forces Shylock to become a Christian against his will, and tells him what must happen to his money when he dies.

■ Nobody remembers that, under any system of law, the goods stolen by Jessica and Lorenzo should be returned to Shylock, and that the thieves should be punished rather than rewarded.

In a sense, two people are on trial in Act 4, Scene 1: Shylock and Portia. Portia judges Shylock and condemns him to the most extreme punishment, but the audience has to judge Portia. Shylock is condemned by his own words: he demands the law and it punishes him. If we judge Portia by her words on mercy and justice, she is to be condemned as well. She says that victims should forgive those who have done them wrong if they want to receive God's mercy, but forgets this idea when she comes to judge Shylock.

The play shows us justice without mercy, or forgiveness, on every side. Shylock shows no mercy as he demands justice and revenge. There is no mercy for Shylock from a court that is far from fair and impartial. It seems that everyone prefers to seek revenge, albeit to varying extents. They want to make their enemy suffer rather than offer him forgiveness.

Appearance and reality

Outward appearances can be deceiving as they often conceal a different reality underneath. This idea is repeated throughout the play, but is most strongly present in the casket scenes. Bassanio provides the classic statement of the theme: 'So may the outward shows be least themselves — the world is still deceived with ornament' (Act 3, Scene 2, lines 73–4).

The scrolls contained in the caskets repeat the theme:

> All that glisters is not gold;
> Often have you heard that told.
> Many a man his life hath sold
> But my outside to behold.
> (Act 2, Scene 7, lines 65–8)

> There be fools alive, Iwis,
> Silvered o'er, and so was this.
> (Act 2, Scene 9, lines 67–8)

> You that choose not by the view,
> Chance as fair, and choose as true.
> (Act 3, Scene 2, lines 131–2)

The losing suitors, Morocco and Arragon, judge by appearance, even though they claim to know better. Morocco earlier asked not to be judged by his skin colour, and Arragon first criticises 'the fool multitude that choose by show' (Act 2, Scene 9, line 25).

Bassanio is successful in the casket lottery because he is not dazzled by gold and silver, and not put off by the plainest of the three metals: lead.

Most of the characters in the play illustrate this theme of masking or hiding the truth behind a false exterior. For example:

■ Bassanio borrows a large sum of money to put on a good outward show in order to impress Portia. He is in debt but wants to appear wealthy so that she will consider him as a potential husband.

■ Shylock deceives Antonio when they make their bond, but not Bassanio: 'I like not fair terms and a villain's mind' (Act 1, Scene 3, line 173). Bassanio suspects that Shylock's kind offer hides an evil plan. For much of the play, however, Shylock makes no attempt to hide his real purpose, which is to get revenge on Antonio, especially after Jessica's departure from his house.

- In the trial scene, Portia makes a powerful speech about mercy and forgiving one's enemies. However, she shows no mercy in dealing with Shylock. Her words made her appear merciful, but they hid her real desire to punish Shylock.

- The disguises of Portia and Nerissa, one as a male lawyer and the other as this lawyer's male clerk, highlight the theme of appearance and reality. This gender change had a further level of meaning in Shakespeare's day as boy-actors played the female roles in all plays.

So the boys playing Portia and Nerissa then pretended to be females disguised as males. Jessica also dresses as a boy to elope with Lorenzo, who (along with his friends) is in costume for the masque.

- The business of the rings, which takes up much of Act 5, is another example of the theme: despite how things appear on the surface, Bassanio is really faithful to Portia.

An obvious exception is Antonio, who is always what he appears to be: he does not try to deceive.

Love and hate

Some critics narrow the theme of the play to a simple conflict of love and hate. They argue that Shylock stands for the principle of hate, and that his enemies stand for the principle of love.

There is love in the play, between friends and between romantic partners. It would be wrong, however, to suggest that Shylock embodies hate and his enemies represent love. After all, Shylock clearly loved his daughter before she cruelly betrayed him.

It is true that Antonio shows loving kindness to Bassanio, for whom he is prepared to sacrifice his life. It is also true that there is love between Portia and Bassanio, Nerissa and Gratiano, and Jessica and Lorenzo. But against this, it is clear that Bassanio, Antonio, Salerio, Solanio and Gratiano hate Shylock in particular and his Jewish religion in general.

Many words and acts in the play are motivated by hatred. One of Shylock's earliest comments on Antonio is: 'I hate him for he is a Christian' (Act 1, Scene 3, line 36). Later, he says the reason for his court case is: 'a lodged hate, and a certain loathing I bear Antonio' (Act 4, Scene 1, lines 60–61).

Antonio claims that Shylock hates him because he has helped Christians to escape from Shylock's greedy clutches:

> I'll follow him no more with bootless prayers.
> He seeks my life; his reason well I know —
> I oft delivered from his forfeitures
> Many that have at times made moan to me,
> Therefore he hates me.
>
> (Act 3, Scene 3, lines 20–24)

The events of the play show that there are more reasons for Shylock's hatred:

- Antonio hates Jews in general: 'He hates our sacred nation' (Act 1, Scene 3, line 42).

- Antonio has gone out of his way to insult Shylock publicly. He has called him a 'misbeliever' and a 'cut-throat dog' (line 105).

- Antonio has spat on Shylock's robe and beard, and kicked him aside as he would kick a strange dog.

- Worse still, Antonio tells Shylock that he will repeat this behaviour if he gets an opportunity to do so: 'I am as like to call thee so again, to spit on thee again, to spurn thee too' (lines 124–5).

- If Shylock's hatred is built on the hateful way Christians have treated him, it is further inflamed when some of Antonio's friends help Jessica to elope with a Christian and to steal his valuables.

When Shylock argues that Jews should be treated as fellow human beings: 'I am a Jew. Hath not a Jew eyes? Hath not a Jew hands … ' (Act 3, Scene 1, lines 47–60), his plea falls on deaf ears. Immediately afterwards Solanio claims that Shylock and Tubal are fit companions for the devil. In turn, Shylock fails to apply his plea for humane treatment to his own dealings with Antonio. Portia also fails to practise what she preaches about mercy in the trial scene. Despite the apparently happy and loving ending of Act 5, hate would seem to be the more dominant emotion for most of the play.

Genre

*T*HE *MERCHANT OF VENICE* is classified as a comedy and some reasons for this are set out below. It does, however, have several elements that are not comic. It might also be considered to have many of the features of a fairy tale.

Comedy

In the great majority of comedies, the plot concerns a love interest and ends in marriage. A young couple's desire to marry is hindered by some obstacle (e.g. lack of money) that is finally overcome. The ending of the comedy shows the triumph of love, followed by the festive ritual of marriage.

The Merchant of Venice has three love stories: Portia and Bassanio, Jessica and Lorenzo, and Nerissa and Gratiano. For these characters and their friends, the play has the happy ending essential to comedy. The three pairs of lovers end up happily married.

Throughout the play, there are many light-hearted, merry touches. On the night of Jessica's elopement with Lorenzo, there is masquing, feasting and happy music.

There is comedy in Portia's description of her suitors. She has a sharp eye for what she thinks are their ridiculous qualities. For example, she tells Nerissa that the odd young baron from England 'bought his doublet in Italy, his round hose in France, his bonnet in Germany and his behaviour everywhere' (Act 1, Scene 2, lines 66–8).

Two of the characters, Gratiano and Launcelot Gobbo, function as clowns. 'Let me play the fool' (Act 1, Scene 1, line 79) is Gratiano's motto, and he certainly lives up to it.

Launcelot Gobbo is involved in a long comic scene with his father. The comedy here is crude. It depends on Launcelot's misunderstanding of the big words he uses. He finds it amusing to give misleading directions to his almost blind father, and to assume a false identity. This allows him to let Old Gobbo believe for a while that he is dead, and leads to absurd questions: 'I pray you tell me, is my boy, God rest his soul, alive or dead?' (Act 2, Scene 2, lines 63–4).

Salerio and Solanio provide their own cruel, crude comedy, particularly after Jessica has eloped. They mock Shylock's reactions and imitate his mannerisms. These two characters probably find their own 'comedy' more amusing than audiences do. It is in poor taste.

When Antonio's ships appear to be lost at sea, the comedy of the play makes way for a darker mood for a while. With Antonio's life in danger, there is no time for laughter. Once Antonio's life is spared, the threat to the comic spirit has been removed and Shylock's happy enemies can celebrate their triumph.

Act 5 is entirely devoted to comedy, based on a misunderstanding between the husbands and wives over the giving and taking of rings. When this is finally settled, the play ends on a happy note.

Although the play is a comedy, it has many features that are far from comic. There is no comedy in Shylock's savage desire to take Antonio's life, or in Antonio's offensive treatment of Shylock. Neither is there comedy in Jessica's desertion of Shylock, or in the theft of his property by her and Lorenzo. And for one character, Shylock, the play borders on tragedy.

Antonio is not really a comic character either. He is sad and gloomy from beginning to end. During the trial scene he suffers the agony of thinking his death is certain. Portia puts him through this heart-breaking suffering while she pretends he must die at Shylock's hands. Antonio seems a lonely figure at the end of the play, unable to share fully in the happiness of his friends at Belmont.

What happens to Shylock and Antonio makes it difficult to describe *The Merchant of Venice* as a typical comedy. Comedies tend to end in order being restored and harmony being established. They unite as many characters as possible in their final portrayal of society, reconciling or converting isolated or threatening characters.

The comic writer cannot disgrace or expose his victims too much without upsetting the balance of the comedy. Many people would feel that Shylock is exposed and disgraced, as well as cast out from the play. When the leading actor gives a strong performance in the role of Shylock, the play can become the tragedy of the Jew of Venice, with Act 5 as a comic epilogue.

Fairy tale

There is much in the play to suggest the world of the fairy tale. Such elements include the casket challenge, the elopement of Jessica and Lorenzo, and the relationship of Bassanio and Portia.

The casket lottery involves suitors choosing the correct one of three caskets. Three is one of the magic numbers in fairy tales, which often feature groups of three (e.g. three bears, three pigs). In the final casket scene, Shakespeare draws on the awareness among members of his audience of how the fairy-tale convention works: the third suitor is always the successful one.

We do not investigate the psychology of the characters in fairy tales or their motives. Fairy-tale characters act in a simple, symbolic way. There are happy endings for those who are 'good' and unhappy endings for those who are not. If *The Merchant of Venice* were a realistic play based on events and characters belonging to the real world, we would have to think of Bassanio as a shallow, selfish adventurer and Jessica as a cruel, heartless daughter. But in the fairy-tale atmosphere of Belmont, these flaws do not seem to matter.

Shakespeare introduces several improbabilities into his play, which is typical of the fairy tale. For example, Antonio's loss of all his ships, in different parts of the world, in a matter of weeks and at a time when his life depends on the return of at least one, seems unlikely. Equally far-fetched is the idea that Portia could disguise herself as a legal expert, and have all the knowledge and skill of one, and defeat the cunning Shylock by a verbal trick that had not occurred to the wisest leaders in Venice. All this suggests that Shakespeare was not concerned to make his story credible in everyday terms.

Fairy tales compel us to accept improbable, unlikely and fantastic things. In the fairy-tale atmosphere of *The Merchant of Venice*, we believe in the astonishing will that determines the choice of Portia's suitors. We believe that Bassanio will not recognise his own wife in a cap and gown. We believe that Old Gobbo does not recognise his son's voice. We believe in the absurd legal procedure of the Venetian court, in which the plaintiff becomes the defendant. We can even believe in Shylock's pound of flesh.

The legal system of Venice on which the bond and trial scene are based has no parallel in the real world. There is no system of law that permits a man to place his life in danger. In courts in the real world, judges do not address defendants in a sympathetic manner, or criticise plaintiffs.

Nevertheless, no matter how many fairy-tale elements we find in *The Merchant of Venice*, the play as a whole cannot be described as a fairy tale. The main reason for this is Shylock. He is far too real for the world of fairy tales. If Shylock were a character in a fairy tale, he would be a stage villain like the big bad wolf or the wicked stepmother. Shylock is not that kind of character. He is a figure of power and dignity, whose sufferings are bound to engage some sympathy.

Fairy-tale characters tend to be very good or very bad, and reasons are not given as to why they are so. In *The Merchant of Venice*, we are made to understand why Shylock behaves as he does, and it is possible to sympathise with him for the ill-treatment he endures long before the trial scene. Similarly, the 'good' characters in fairy tales do not spit at the bad ones or submit them to verbal abuse.

Turning points in the play

- Bassanio, a spendthrift and fortune-hunter, needs to borrow 3,000 ducats from Antonio if he is to impress the wealthy heiress Portia and persuade her to marry him.

- Antonio cannot raise 3,000 ducats, but offers himself as security to a Jewish moneylender called Shylock, who has long been his enemy.

- Shylock persuades Antonio to enter into a bond: if the debt is not repaid in three months, Antonio will be required to let Shylock have a pound of his flesh in place of the 3,000 ducats.

- Portia's late father has ordered that whoever wants to marry her must guess in which of three caskets (gold, silver, lead) her portrait has been placed. Two of her noble suitors, Morocco and Arragon, fail the test.

- Launcelot Gobbo leaves Shylock's service for Bassanio's. Launcelot also helps Jessica, Shylock's only daughter, to elope with Lorenzo, Antonio's friend, and to take money and jewels from her father's house.

- Jessica's elopement, and her theft of his valuables, hurts and angers Shylock so much that he is determined to take vengeance on Antonio.

- In Belmont, Bassanio gains Portia's love and chooses the right (lead) casket.

- Gratiano wins the love of Nerissa, Portia's waiting-woman.

- News is brought to Bassanio in Belmont that Antonio's ships have been lost at sea, meaning that Antonio cannot repay Shylock other than with his life.

- Portia, disguised as Balthazar, a young male lawyer, appears in court to defend Antonio. She is assisted by Nerissa, dressed as a male clerk.

- Portia satisfies the court that the law, and the bond, do not allow Shylock to take his pound of flesh if in the process he spills a drop of blood. Furthermore, Shylock is guilty of seeking the life of Antonio, a Venetian citizen.

- Shylock is allowed to keep half his goods on condition that he turns Christian. Antonio gets the other half, but promises to keep it in trust for Lorenzo and Jessica. The humiliated Shylock leaves the court a broken man, having accepted the verdict arrived at. He also leaves the play for the last time.

- The three married couples (Portia and Bassanio, Jessica and Lorenzo, Nerissa and Gratiano), together with Antonio, are reunited at Belmont.

- Antonio learns that some of his ships have been saved: this allows for a happy ending for Shylock's enemies. We are not told how Shylock fares after he has fulfilled the conditions imposed on him.

Exam tips

Read all the questions carefully. Make sure you understand what is being asked in each question. Then choose the one that you are best prepared to answer.

Make sure you deal equally with all the elements in the question.

You must support your answer with suitable reference to the play. In order to do this you must be thoroughly familiar with the details of the plot, as well as with the characters and their actions.

Your answers will benefit from brief, relevant quotations from the play. There is no need for lengthy quotations. Short quotations can make a point just as well, and leave more space for making further points.

From the beginning to the end of your answer, it is important to stay with the exact terms of the question you are dealing with. Remember that marks are awarded for making relevant points clearly and economically.

Know in advance how much time you will give to each question, and stick to this plan. Giving too much time to one question will mean that you have too little time for other questions.

Through your study of the play you will have formed opinions on the play's characters, plot and themes. Examiners would like to know *your* opinions on these topics. This is why you should *think* about them in advance.

Your opinions should be based on facts presented in the play. For example, when you are judging characters, observe what they do and what they say, and also what other characters think and say about them.

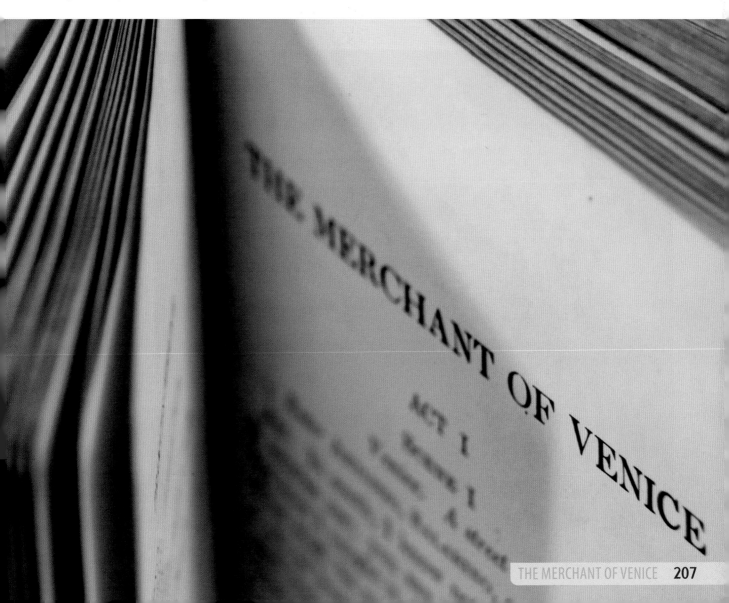

Revising

When revising you should aim to gain a good knowledge of:

- the **plot** of the play and the scenes in which something interesting, exciting, important, strange, unpleasant or pleasant happens

- the **characters** in the play and how they relate to each other

- significant **themes** or ideas in the play, for example prejudice, money, love, justice.

You should cover the following four kinds of exam questions.

1 Questions about the plot of the play or about single scenes

To answer these, you need to know what happens in the play in general and in each individual scene. When you are looking at an individual scene, answer these questions:

- Is it exciting? Does it involve conflict, or suspense?

- Is it sad or happy?

- Does it include strange or surprising elements?

- What impact has it had on you?

- What does it tell you about the characters who feature in it?

- Does it feature a turning point in the play?

2 Questions about the characters

When you are examining the characters, answer these questions:

- Looking at each character in turn, do you like or dislike the character? Why?
- Choosing a character you dislike, what happens to him or her?
- Choosing a character you like, what happens to him or her?
- Choosing two connected characters, what is the nature of the relationship between them?
- Choosing two contrasting characters, what are the differences between them?
- Is there tension or conflict between any characters?
- Does any character rebel against another, or hate another? Why?
- Which character do you find most interesting? Why?
- Does any character experience good luck or bad luck? How?
- Which characters deserve the title hero, heroine or villain? Why?
- Which character would you like to play in a stage or film version of the play? Why?

3 Questions about themes

Think about ideas or subjects that keep on turning up in the course of the play. For *The Merchant of Venice*, you will be conscious of such themes as:

fate	prejudice	intolerance	money
justice	mercy	revenge	love	marriage
hatred	feuds	deception	cruelty

When studying a theme, answer these questions:

- How is this theme introduced?
- How is this theme developed?
- Is this theme associated with particular places or characters?
- What interests you about this theme?
- Is this theme relevant to your own life and/or to today's world?
- What impression of this theme does the play leave you with?
- In what ways could this theme be highlighted in a stage/screen production of the play?

4 General questions

Other questions that you should think about include:

- What is the world depicted in the play like?
- What impact or effect did the play have on you?
- Did you like or dislike the play? Why?
- Would you recommend the play to students of your own age? Why or why not?

Past papers

It is worth looking at past exam papers in order to familiarise yourself with the types of questions asked. The following are some examples.

Ordinary Level Paper, 2015

Name a play or film you have studied in which there is an important friendship between two characters.

(a) Name the two characters who have an important friendship.

(b) Which of the two characters did you prefer? Give a reason for your answer.

(c) Describe a moment in the play or film when you see how important their friendship is.

Ordinary Level Paper, 2014

Name a play or film you have studied where a character did something that surprised the audience.

(a) What did the character do that was surprising?

(b) Why was this behaviour surprising?

(c) Did this surprising behaviour make the character more likeable or less likeable? Give a reason for your answer.

Ordinary Level Paper, 2012

Name a play or film you have studied that had some suspense or mystery in it.

(a) Describe the suspense or mystery.

(b) Did this suspense or mystery add to the play or film? Explain why / why not.

(c) How did the play or film end?

(d) Do you think this was a good ending? Give reasons for your answer.

Higher Level Paper 2, 2015

Answer one of these questions:

1 Choose a character from a play you have studied who experiences a significant problem or difficulty.

  (a) Identify the problem or difficulty your chosen character experiences and describe a moment in the play when that problem or difficulty is particularly apparent.

  (b) Imagine you are an actor playing the part of your chosen character. Outline two things you would do, when performing the moment described above, to represent the character's predicament to an audience. Give reasons for your suggestions, supporting them with reference to the moment you described in part (a) of this question.

      OR

2 The way in which a play is staged can help an audience to understand an important theme in that play.

    (a) Identify one important theme in a play you have studied and outline the importance of that theme in your chosen play.

    (b) Imagine you are directing this play. You wish to highlight the theme you have identified in part (a) of this question. Choose a moment in the play when this theme is particularly evident. Explain how you would use any two dramatic techniques, in staging your chosen moment, to help an audience to understand the theme.

Higher Level Paper 2, 2014

Answer one of these questions:

1 (a) Explain how two characters from a play you have studied are different from each other in their attitudes and in the ways that they behave. Support your answer with reference to your chosen play.

    (b) In your view how does the playwright's use of contrasting characters help to make the play more interesting? Support your answer with reference to your chosen play.

        OR

2 Choose a moment from a play you have studied that is, in your view, a dramatic turning point in that play.

    (a) Describe what happens at this moment and explain why you consider it to be a dramatic turning point. Support your answer with reference to your chosen play.

    (b) In your view how does the moment you have chosen help you to understand either an important theme in the play or an important character in the play? Explain your answer with reference to your chosen play.

Higher Level Paper 2, 2013

1 Choose a character from a play you have studied.

    (a) What was your first impression of your chosen character? Support your answer with reference to the play.

    (b) To what extent does your impression of your chosen character change as the play progresses? Explain your answer with reference to your chosen play.

        OR

2 Choose a scene from a play you have studied that has a strong mood or atmosphere.

    (a) Describe what takes place in your chosen scene and identify the mood or atmosphere created. Support your answer with reference to the play.

    (b) Imagine you are directing your chosen scene on stage. Explain some of the decisions that you would make in order to create the mood or atmosphere successfully. Support your answer with reference to the play.

Sample questions and answers

Suitable for Ordinary Level

Name a play you have studied. Choose two characters from the play, one a winner and the other a loser.

(a) Explain why you think one of your chosen characters is a winner and why the other is a loser, referring to the text in support of your answer.

(b) Do you think your chosen characters deserve what finally happens to them?

The play I have studied is *The Merchant of Venice*. The two characters I have chosen are Bassanio and Shylock. Bassanio is a winner and Shylock is a loser.

(a) I see Bassanio as a winner for a number of reasons. The first is that Bassanio starts out in the play as a man who already owes money and is about to take on an even more serious debt, but ends up as the husband of an extremely rich heiress who loves him very much.

My second reason for seeing Bassanio as a winner is that he is able to persuade his friend Antonio to arrange for him to have a huge sum of money on loan so that he may impress the beautiful heiress and marry her.

My third reason for seeing him as a winner is that he possesses one talent that enables winners to get what they want. This talent is his attractive, persuasive personality, which he uses to advantage in winning 'sweet Portia'.

I see Shylock as a loser mainly because he begins the play as an extremely successful merchant and moneylender, but ends up

a broken man. As such, his career path follows the opposite direction to Bassanio's.

Shylock's life is centred on acquiring wealth and on keeping his daughter and only child close to him at home. His failure to retain the wealth he has acquired, and to keep Jessica results from flaws in his character. As far as Jessica is concerned, he is a loser as a father, failing to provide her with a happy home.

Shylock is also a loser when he breaks the law in an absurd contract involving a threat to Antonio's life. As a result he places his own life at the mercy of the court, and loses control over half his wealth.

Having already lost his daughter to a Christian, Shylock then suffers what he regards as a much more serious loss: that of his Jewish identity and his Jewish religion, when Antonio insists that he convert to Christianity.

(b) I do not think that Bassanio or Shylock fully deserve what happens to them.

The events of the play in which Bassanio is involved suggest to me that he is a lucky character rather than a deserving one. His career in the play is not notable for good deeds done in the service of others, although he expects Antonio to humiliate himself on his behalf by resorting to Shylock, a man he detests, to borrow the money Bassanio needs to impress Portia. Bassanio is also lucky in that the very rich woman he wants to marry has already taken a liking to him, and subtly helps him to choose the right casket and so win the right to marry her. In other words, he achieves his main objective in life without having to take much trouble in the process. Of course, since Portia finds him an ideal husband and would not choose any other, she must feel that he richly deserves her and the delightful way of life marriage to her will bring. She cannot be expected to see him as the fortune-hunter he appears to be at the beginning of the play.

It may also be claimed that although Bassanio does act selfishly, he does no harm to anybody else and makes Portia happy. To that extent, he may be said to deserve what happens to him.

When it comes to Shylock, it is more difficult to decide whether he deserves what happens to him. There is no doubt that he deserves some form of punishment, since he is determined to take the life of Antonio. On the other hand, his intended victim has signed a bond permitting him to do this.

It might also be argued that Shylock is not in a normal frame of mind when he demands his pound of flesh from Antonio. This is because he has recently lost his daughter and some valuables to the Christian Lorenzo, who has behaved like a thief in the night. Shylock has reason to associate Lorenzo with Antonio, which gives him a personal motive, as well as a legal basis, for what he tries to do to Antonio.

The important question is whether Shylock deserves what happens to him as a result of Portia's decisions on his case in the court. She exposes him to a death sentence until the Duke of Venice decides to spare him. She also uses the law to reduce his wealth severely. Then Antonio intervenes to insist that Shylock becomes a Christian, a heavy penalty for a man who, as we see from the play, is a believing Jew devoted to his religion.

Shylock's treatment in the trial scene is far from what one might expect from any court of justice in the civilised world. The self-appointed judge in the case, Portia disguised as Balthazar, a mysterious legal expert, allows spectators to mock and abuse Shylock. Gratiano, for example, twice suggests that instead of showing mercy, the duke should give Shylock permission to hang himself. Portia acts more like a lawyer for Antonio than a neutral judge.

To sum up, I feel that the Venetian legal system is guilty of overkill in Shylock's case by reducing him to a pathetic wreck and depriving him of his dignity. I cannot agree that he deserves this fate.

Name a play or film you have studied where there is an important friendship between two characters.

   (a) Name the two characters who have an important friendship.

   (b) Which of the two characters did you prefer? Give a reason for your answer.

   (c) Describe a moment in the play or film when you see how important their friendship is.

The play I have studied where there is an important friendship between two characters is *The Merchant of Venice*.

(a) The two characters who have an important friendship in *The Merchant of Venice* are Antonio and Bassanio.

(b) Of these two characters, I prefer Antonio. When he and Bassanio came face to face early in the play, Bassanio struck me as the kind of man who likes to live a life of luxury without caring very much where the money to support this kind of life comes from. He admits to Antonio that he has been living beyond his means to support the lifestyle of a gentleman. The result is that he is now in debt, and at the worst possible time. He has designs on marrying a very rich, very beautiful heiress, Portia, who appears to like him. He does not want to approach her unless he can appear as a man of means. To do this he urgently needs a lot of money. He knows that Antonio is the kind of friend who will do all he can to help him. This is why he approaches Antonio for a loan of 3,000 ducats. This money will help him to pay off his debts and to keep up the appearance of a gentleman to impress Portia.

I cannot think much of an individual who is content to live a life of excess, as Bassanio is, at the expense of others. Another aspect of Bassanio's attitude to other people also troubles me. He appears to see marriage to Portia as a good financial investment, since such a marriage will make him financially secure for life. This attitude makes him appear very much like a fortune-hunter.

I believe that the above considerations justify my preference for Antonio, who is willing to help Bassanio out of friendship rather than for reasons of personal gain. Indeed, Antonio's generosity to Bassanio creates a terrible problem for himself. He is so unselfish, compared with Bassanio, that he is willing to endure death at the hands of Shylock. Antonio wants no reward for making it possible for Bassanio to prosper: all he wants is to say farewell to Bassanio before he dies and this will be a sufficient reward, as he points out in his letter to Bassanio.

As I see it, the main contrast between Antonio and Bassanio in terms of their friendship is that between the unselfish giver (Antonio) and the self-centred taker (Bassanio). When it comes to choosing between these two, I have no hesitation in preferring the unselfish, self-sacrificing giver.

(c) The importance of the friendship between Antonio and Bassanio, however one-sided this may be, is seen when Antonio is on the point of death during the trial scene. Bassanio, who has achieved his ambition and won the love of Portia, realises that his success has been due to the fact that his 'dearest friend' Antonio has placed himself at the mercy of his enemy Shylock in order to raise the money Bassanio needed. It is Bassanio's turn to repay Antonio's generosity with his own act of friendship to the man he calls 'the dearest friend to me, the kindest man'. Both Bassanio and Portia think that if Shylock is offered enough money, he will spare Antonio's life. This money, enough to pay the debt twenty times over, is provided by Portia, not by Bassanio. Portia takes the initiative in sending Bassanio with this money to the court.

Although Bassanio does nothing directly to save Antonio's life, his friendship with Antonio is the indirect cause of saving it. Portia takes on the role of judge in order to undermine Shylock's case. She does this because Bassanio is indebted to Antonio, and because Antonio is Bassanio's loyal friend. She cannot allow it to be said that Bassanio has been the cause of the death of his best friend.

Antonio's friendship with Bassanio provided the money that enabled Bassanio's marriage to Portia, while the same friendship has influenced Portia's scheme to save Antonio's life.

Suitable for Higher Level

Choose a character from a play you have studied who experiences a significant problem or difficulty.

(a) Identify the problem or difficulty your chosen character experiences and describe a moment in the play when that problem is particularly apparent.

(b) Is the problem experienced by your chosen character dealt with? If so, how is it dealt with? If not, what happens to your chosen character as a result?

The play I have studied is *The Merchant of Venice*. The character I have chosen is Antonio.

(a) Antonio's problem arises as a result of his agreeing to lend 3,000 ducats to his best friend, Bassanio. Antonio does not have this sum of money to hand. This means that Bassanio uses Antonio's credit to borrow the 3,000 ducats from Shylock, a Jewish moneylender. Shylock agrees to give Bassanio this money on loan on one condition. This condition is that Antonio must sign a bond agreeing to pay Shylock back the 3,000 ducats within three months. If he fails to pay back the loan on time, Antonio will face a terrible penalty: Shylock will have the right to take a pound of Antonio's flesh.

When he agrees to Shylock's rather bizarre terms, Antonio is confident that he will be able to pay back the loan on time. He has six ships at sea trading in valuable merchandise. He expects that these will soon return to Venice having earned more than enough profit to enable him to pay back Shylock. He is certain that he will be able to repay the 3,000 ducats to Shylock a month before the due date.

A major problem emerges for Antonio when news gradually comes that his ships are in trouble. Eventually it appears that all his ships have been lost at sea. When the time for repaying Shylock comes and goes, and Antonio cannot pay, Shylock takes him to court to demand his pound of flesh. This will bring about Antonio's death if the court allows it.

The moment in the play when Antonio's problem is particularly apparent arrives in the course of his trial. The court allows Portia, disguised as a legal expert called Balthazar, to act as the judge of the case. She announces that the law supports Shylock and permits him to take one pound of Antonio's flesh. The reason for this is that Antonio agreed to the bond's conditions of his own free will. Portia advises Antonio to bare his chest. This is the moment in the play when Antonio's problem becomes fully apparent and he faces death.

(b) As soon as Antonio's problem comes to a head, it begins to be dealt with, by the same judge (Portia/Balthazar) who seemed to be about to allow him to be killed. Before Shylock can proceed to take his pound of

flesh, Portia orders him to stop. She warns him that in taking his pound of flesh, he must take exactly one pound (weighing scales are on hand) and he is not allowed to take one drop of Antonio's blood. If Shylock sheds even the tiniest fraction of a drop of Antonio's blood, he will be sentenced to death and all his goods will be confiscated. This pronouncement marks the end of Shylock's project to bring about Antonio's death. It is impossible for him to proceed. What was a life-threatening problem for Antonio has now become a benefit. Portia finds Shylock guilty of planning to kill Antonio, and allows Antonio to seize one-half of all the goods the 'alien' Shylock has.

Antonio, happy to have escaped with his life, does not want to profit from Shylock's misfortune. Instead he pleads with the court to allow him to keep half of Shylock's goods in trust for Shylock's daughter, Jessica, and her husband, Lorenzo. He also insists that Shylock must convert to Christianity and make a will leaving his remaining money and possessions to Jessica and Lorenzo.

Having survived this life-threatening episode, Antonio travels to Belmont, where he is warmly welcomed and receives the good news that three of his ships have survived. He is alive, with friends, and back in business.

Often plays combine both serious and light-hearted elements.

(a) Did you find the play that you studied to be mainly serious or mainly light-hearted? Explain your answer with reference to the play.

(b) Which element in the play had the greater impact on you, the serious element or the light-hearted element? Clearly explain your choice with reference to the play you have studied.

The play I have studied is *The Merchant of Venice*.

(a) Although *The Merchant of Venice* is classified as a comedy, and has light-hearted elements, I find it to be mainly serious. In fact I see it as a tragi-comedy. My reason for thinking this is that for the most interesting character in the play, Shylock, the play ends in near-tragedy. For the other main characters, with the possible exception of Antonio, the play ends happily, which is why it is called a comedy. The serious note is sounded in the very first line, when Antonio cannot account for the fact that he feels sad. He carries a melancholy feeling throughout the entire play. Even at the end, when most of the other characters are rejoicing, Antonio remains aloof.

Antonio's bond with Shylock casts a grim shadow over the play. The bond places Antonio in Shylock's power unless he can redeem it within three months. Antonio is depending on his ships returning safely and on time to harbour. When the news arrives that these ships have run into difficulties, Antonio's death at Shylock's hands seems likely. Shylock is determined to proceed with the grim business of cutting off a pound of flesh near Antonio's heart. There can be no light-hearted elements in the play while this threat persists. The arrest and detention of Antonio in a Venetian jail is another grim element.

Some of the minor characters seem to think that the elopement of Jessica and the theft of some of Shylock's property by her and Lorenzo are comic events. Salerio and Solanio, who are privy to the elopement and the theft, deplore Shylock's attempt to recover his property, calling him 'the villain Jew' and 'the dog Jew' for doing this, and mocking him for being deeply upset at the loss of his daughter and his valuables. I cannot find any comedy in this episode.

There is no light-hearted element in Shylock's moving complaint about the way he is treated by Christians, mainly because he is a Jew. There is no comedy either in his heartrending comment on, for him, the most precious item stolen from his house by Jessica and Lorenzo and given away by them in exchange for a monkey: a valuable ring given to him by his late wife before their marriage.

Much of what passes for comedy in the play is absurd rather than entertaining, especially the scenes involving Gratiano, Launcelot Gobbo and Old Gobbo. Launcelot is a clown, but I do not think that modern audiences would find him funny.

Gratiano, although not described as a clown, often behaves like one. Shakespeare gives him a long speech early in the play that begins 'Let me play the fool', something he does for most of the play. He is undisciplined, coarse and loud-mouthed.

Shylock's influence is profoundly serious. A few of the minor characters try to make him a figure of fun, but he is never that.

He suffers deeply and is often a pathetic figure, as well as a cruel, vengeful one before and during the trial scene. The issues he raises are all serious ones, and the threat he poses to Antonio in particular cannot be lightly dismissed.

(b) The serious element in the play had a much greater impact on me than the light-hearted element had. In particular, I was affected by the scenes in which Shylock appears and imposes his powerful personality.

The light-hearted, comic element consists largely of clownish behaviour and foolish comments made by silly characters who embarrassed rather than amused me. I also found it difficult to be entertained by the confusion about the rings in Act 5. This happy, light-hearted ending, in my opinion, cannot be expected to have anything like the impact of the powerful, disturbing drama of the trial scene in Act 4.

I was moved by the way in which Shylock conveys the difficulties faced by a Jewish merchant operating in a trading

city dominated by Christian merchants who hate and despise Jews as a group and Judaism as a religion. For example, Shylock reveals that as he is transacting his business in the trading quarter of Venice, Antonio has called him a 'cut-throat dog' and spat upon his Jewish garments and upon his beard. Antonio does not deny this, and indicates that he is likely to repeat the abuse.

I was disturbed by the appalling treatment of Shylock by his daughter, Jessica, who elopes with Lorenzo. They steal a substantial amount of Shylock's wealth. The 'light-hearted' element that surrounds this episode is in such bad taste that the only impact it had on me was to induce a feeling of revulsion at the spectacle of the victim being mocked and derided by associates of those who cheerfully deprived him of his property.

The most serious episode in the play, the trial scene, had the greatest impact on me. It is a scene in which issues of life and death are involved, with the lives of both Antonio and Shylock seemingly hanging in the balance.

The trial also raises serious questions about the administration of law and the dispensing of justice. It features a self-appointed judge who has been doing legal research in order to help Antonio, one of the parties in the case, and who insults and demeans the other party, Shylock, as well as allowing hostile spectators to do the same. The same judge knowingly misleads Shylock into thinking he has a good case, and then tells him that, if he proceeds, he faces serious losses of property and even death.

The same scene introduces a racist theme into the court proceedings. Shylock's Jewish race and religion are treated with contempt by the entire court, including the judge, who regards the word 'Jew' as a term of abuse.

In summary, I found the serious matter in the play moving and thought-provoking and can definitely say that it had a much greater impact on me than did the light-hearted matter.

Ordinary Level questions to try:

1 Pick a scene you best remember from a play you have read.

   (a) What happened in the scene?

   (b) Write about how any one character behaved.

   (c) How do you remember this scene?

2 Think about a play you have studied in which there are two very different characters.

   (a) Describe the differences between these characters.

   (b) How did their differences affect the outcome of the play?

   (c) Which of the two characters did you prefer? Explain why.

3 Pick a very dramatic moment from a play you have studied.

   (a) What exactly happened?

   (b) Which characters were involved?

   (c) Why did you find it dramatic?

4 Think about a play you have studied. Pick a scene where something happens to make one of the characters happy or sad.

   (a) What exactly happened?

   (b) Which characters were involved in the scene?

   (c) What made the character happy or sad?

5 Think about a play you have studied. Use ONE of the following headings to write about the play:

   ▪ Why I found the play enjoyable.

   ▪ Why I did not enjoy the play.

Higher Level questions to try:

1 Consider a character from a play you have studied. Choose a significant time of *either* good luck *or* bad luck that this character experiences.

   (a) Briefly describe this experience of good luck *or* bad luck.

   (b) Discuss how the character deals with it in the play.

2 Plays teach us lessons about life. Choose any play you have studied and explain how it has made you aware of any ONE of the following:

   Love *or* Prejudice *or* Conflict *or* Harmony.

3 Name a play you have studied and state what you think is its main idea and/or message. Explain how this main idea and/or message is communicated in the play.

4 You have been asked to recommend a play for people your age who are studying drama. Would you recommend the play you have studied for this examination? Give reasons based on close reference to your chosen text.

5 The opening scenes of a play often convey information that is important to the audience. What important information is conveyed in the opening scenes of the play you have studied? In your opinion, how successful is the playwright in capturing the attention of the audience in the opening scenes of the play? Support your answer with reference to your studied play.

Photo credits

Alamy Stock Photos: *The Merchant of Venice,* Phoenix Theatre © Alastair Muir – page 4: Dustin Hoffman as Shylock; William Shakespeare's *The Merchant of Venice*, directed by Michael Radford Film Company, Sony Pictures © AF archive / Alamy Stock Photo – page 4: Al Pacino as Shylock; pages 48, 83, 191: Zuleikha Robinson as Jessica; pages 111, 123: Heather Goldenhersh as Nerissa and Lynn Collins as Portia; page 180: Jeremy Irons as Antonio and Joseph Fiennes as Bassanio; page 181: Jeremy Irons as Antonio; pages 182, 191: Lynn Collins as Portia; page 186: Joseph Fiennes as Bassanio; page 196: Al Pacino as Shylock, Jeremy Irons as Antonio and Joseph Fiennes as Bassanio; Globe Theatre © Vibrant Pictures – pages 38, 83: Stefan Adegbola as Launcelot Gobbo; page 176: Phoebe Pryce as Jessica and Jonathan Pryce as Shylock; page 193: Jonathan Pryce as Shylock and Dominic Mafham as Antonio; page 13: Jeremy Irons, *Merchant of Venice* (2004) © Moviestore Collection Ltd

Atlanta Shakespeare Company, photographs by Jeff Watkins/ASC, pages 37, 133, 154, 161, 170, 188; pages 79, 191: Arragon; pages 85, 123: Shylock; pages 92, 123: Bassanio et al.

Cincinnati Shakespeare Company, pages 27, 175, 179, 191, 208; Used with permission

Shakespeare's Globe Picture Library, 2015 *Merchant of Venice*, Manual Harlan – pages 51, 83, 191: Lorenzo, Salerio and Solanio; pages 66, 83: Morocco and Portia; pages 71, 83: Solanio; pages 117, 123: Jessica; pages 148, 152: Portia

Shutterstock: page 1: Stratford-upon-Avon, Claudio Divizia; page 2: Visitors at The Shakespeare's Globe, 29 May 2011, Kamira; pages 13, 20, 30, 36, 46, 50, 54, 58, 64, 69, 74, 81, 90, 104, 109, 115, 121, 144, 150, 167: Lighting candle against classical Venetian mask, cosma; page 32: Piles of gold coins on a black background, Elena Blokhina; page 83: Carnival mask in spotlight on black background, Natalia Van Doninck; page 123: Sailing ship, Alvov; page 152: Weighing scales, R. Gino Santa Maria; page 170: Moon among thousands of stars in deep space, AstroStar; page 192: Yellow Star of David sewn onto clothing, Timothy R. Nichols; page 194: Chest full of money, treasure chest with gold coins, Olesja Yaremchuk; page 197: Statue of Justice, Sebra; page 199: Man with Love and Hate tattoos on his hands, Stocksnapper; page 207: *Merchant of Venice* Shakespearian Classic, Bruce Rolff

TopFoto: page 4: Patrick Stewart as Shylock, Royal Shakespeare Company, Nigel Norrington, ArenaPAL; pages 34, 83, 191: Chris Jarman as Morocco, RSC, Colin Willoughby/ArenaPAL

Utah Shakespeare Festival, 2010 production of *The Merchant of Venice*, photographs by Karl Hugh © USF – pages 5, 64, 141, 144, 168, 206: scenes from the production; page iv: Michael A. Harding (left) as Salerio and Tony Amendola as Shylock; pages 22, 32, 205: Gary Neal Johnson as Antonio and Tony Amendola as Shylock; pages 6, 32, 214: Gary Neal Johnson as Antonio and Grant Goodman as Bassanio; pages 15, 20, 21, 32, 137, 185, 202, 204, 206, 217: Chelsea Steverson as Nerissa and Emily Trask as Portia; page 30: Grant Goodman (left) as Bassanio, Tony Amendola as Shylock and Gary Neal Johnson as Antonio; pages 46, 202: Aaron Galligan-Stierle as Launcelot Gobbo; page 49: Monica Lopez as Jessica; pages 55, 83: Monica Lopez as Jessica and Tony Amendola as Shylock; page 59: Tony Amendola (left) as Shylock, Monica Lopez as Jessica and Aaron Galligan-Stierle as Launcelot Gobbo; pages 60, 83, 199, 218: Michael Cotey (left) as Lucentio, Ryan Imhoff as Gratiano and Jason Michael Spelbring as Stephano; page 65: Jason Michael Spelbring as Stephano; pages 75, 107, 123, 145, 172, 174, 200, 217: Tony Amendola as Shylock; pages 76, 83: Emily Trask as Portia and Dave Barrus as Prince of Arragon; page 81: Daniel Molina (left) as Arragon's attendant, Dave Barrus as Prince of Arragon, Emily Trask as Portia and Chelsea Steverson as Nerissa; pages 82, 201: Dave Barrus as Prince of Arragon; pages 91, 203: Michael A. Harding (left) as Salerio, Tony Amendola as Shylock and John Oswald as Solanio; pages 99, 105, 106, 183, 202: Ryan Imhoff as Gratiano, Chelsea Steverson as Nerissa, Grant Goodman as Bassanio and Emily Trask as Portia; page 116: Chelsea Steverson (left) as Nerissa, Emily Trask as Portia and Will Mobley as Balthazar; page 121: Daniel Molina as Lorenzo; pages 125, 152: Max Robinson as Duke of Venice; page 146: Tony Amendola as Shylock and Ryan Imhoff (left) as Gratiano; page 147: Jason Michael Spelbring (left) as Stephano, Max Robinson as Duke of Venice, Tony Amendola as Shylock, Ryan Imhoff as Gratiano and Jesse Easely as Citizen of Venice; pages 150, 191, 199: Chelsea Steverson as Nerissa; page 151: Chelsea Steverson (left) as Nerissa, Ryan Imhoff as Gratiano and Emily Trask as Portia; page 169: Daniel Molina as Lorenzo and Monica Lopez as Jessica; page 173: Emily Trask (left) as Portia, Chelsea Steverson as Nerissa, Tony Amendola as Shylock, Ryan Imhoff as Gratiano, Grant Goodman as Bassanio and Gary Neal Johnson as Antonio; pages 184, 212: Emily Trask as Portia and Tony Amendola as Shylock; pages 187, 203, 212: Emily Trask as Portia and Grant Goodman as Bassanio; page 189: Aaron Galligan-Stierle as Launcelot Gobbo and John Oswald as Solanio; Ryan Imhoff (left) as Gratiano, Michael Cotey as Lucentio, Jason Michael Spelbring as Stephano, and Daniel Molina as Lorenzo; page 191: Ryan Imhoff as Gratiano, Grant Goodman as Bassanio, Aaron Galligan-Stierle as Launcelot; page 200: Max Robinson as Duke of Venice and Tony Amendola as Shylock; Jesse Easley (left) as Citizen of Venice, John Oswald as Solanio, Gary Neal Johnson as Antonio and Tony Amendola as Shylock; page 205: Jesse Easley (left) as Prince of Morocco, Robert Ramirez as Morocco's attendant, Emily Trask as Portia and Chelsea Steverson as Nerissa; Emily Trask as Portia and Dave Barrus as Prince of Arragon; Max Robinson as Tubal and Tony Amendola as Shylock